The Changing
Primary School

CONTEMPORARY ANALYSIS IN EDUCATION SERIES
General Editor: Philip Taylor

Contemporary Analysis in Education Series

The Changing Primary School

Edited by
Roy Lowe
University of Birmingham

 The Falmer Press

(A member of the Taylor & Francis Group)
London, New York and Philadelphia

UK   The Falmer Press, Falmer House, Barcombe, Lewes, East Sussex, BN8 5DL

USA   The Falmer Press, Taylor & Francis Inc., 242 Cherry Street, Philadelphia, PA 19106-1906

First published 1987

Library of Congress Cataloging-in-Publication Data

The Changing primary school.

   (Contemporary analysis in education series ; 16)
   Includes index.
   1. Education, Elementary—England—History—20th century. I. Lowe, Roy. II. Series.
LA633.C46 1987   372.942   87–15602
ISBN 1–85000–188–X
ISBN 1–85000–189–8 (pbk.)

Jacket design by Leonard Williams

Typeset in 11/13 Garamond by
Imago Publishing Ltd, Thame, Oxon

Printed and bound in Great Britain by
Redwood Burn Limited, Trowbridge, Wiltshire

Contents

Contents

General Editor's Preface

In a world ever more instant, history takes an increasingly important role, that of telling it how it was as recently as yesterday. Among other things, history reveals the choices that were made and why they were made. In the light of history nothing was inevitable and very little foretold.

This book tells the recent history of primary education. It chronicles the past rhetoric; how it influenced judgments about primary education; its worth and its perceived shortcomings. It recounts the changes in the education of the young; how they came about and the grounds of their justification. In doing this, we come to see present primary education in the widest perspective of history. It is the authority of this book not only that it is well informed but that each of its contributors writes with directness and lucidity. Much credit too must go to its editor, Roy Lowe, for bringing together the themes of this book which together enables us to understand more than we did why primary education is as it is.

Finally, this is a book not only for the historian but also for the student of primary education whether experienced or beginning teacher, college student or student on an advanced course. For each of them primary education will be seen in all its fullness.

Philip Taylor
Birmingham 1987

Introduction

This book sets out to examine some of the key issues confronting primary schools at the present time, and to place them in the context of the recent history of primary education. It is written in the belief that we cannot fully understand present problems unless we have at least some awareness of how they developed historically, and the context we have chosen for this analysis is the development of primary education in England since the Second World war.

It begins with a brief account of the ways in which the schools have responded to the social changes of the post-war period and the suggestion that some, at least, of the characteristics of primary schools today are inherited from an earlier elementary school tradition. We go on to examine, from several points of view, the 'progressivism' of the post-war years which culminated in the 1967 Plowden Report. We consider the implications of this progressivism for school design; we see how it was implemented in one pioneering local authority, Leicestershire; and we analyze the origins and nature of the open plan movement and the variety of meanings it took on in professional debate. The Plowden Report itself is the subject of a retrospective analysis, and the ways in which teacher training courses responded to the changing demands that were being made upon primary school teachers are also reviewed.

A reconsideration of the 'Black Paper' movement focuses particularly upon its intellectual origins and its significance for modern English society. This is the first of several contributions which deal with the rise of the populist critique of primary schooling during the 1970s, and which was linked to governmental attempts to establish closer control over the management and curricula of the primary sector. The HMI survey of 1978 and the Taylor Report are the central foci of this analysis. We look at their origins, and their practical implications for classroom teachers. Finally, we turn to three important issues of concern to primary school teachers at the present time: 'multiculturalism', curriculum design and content, and gender stereotyping.

Whilst we would not claim that this work constitutes a definitive history of primary education in England since the Second World War, we hope that the insights gained from locating contemporary problems in their historical context will be of value and interest to teachers, students and parents, as well as to all those involved in the planning and study of the primary sector.

Roy Lowe
University of Birmingham
June, 1987

Primary Education Since the Second World War

Roy Lowe

The 1944 Education Act decreed that, henceforth, in England and Wales, education should be organized into three 'progressive stages' which were to be known respectively as 'primary', 'secondary' and 'further' education. It was made the duty of local education authorities to ensure an adequate provision of buildings, staff and facilities for primary education to be available to all young people between the ages of five and eleven years. This was the beginning, in legal terms at any rate, of the primary sector of English education, which has survived with modifications down to the present time. Its survival is all the more remarkable when one pauses to reflect on the social changes of the post-war period which modified profoundly popular expectations and perceptions of formal schooling. In this chapter an attempt will be made to offer a brief review of the more important of these changes and to assess their implications for primary schooling in England.

Changing Social Contexts

One of the most important determinants of primary schooling since the war has been demography. Changes in the birth rate have impinged directly on the primary sector. While it has been increasingly easy to identify the number of women of child bearing age in England and Wales, it has proved far more difficult to make accurate predictions of the birth rate, even for a very short period ahead. The result is that the relatively swift changes in the numbers of live births have caused particularly severe problems for those involved in planning the provision of primary schooling. In 1941 the number of live births dipped below 700,000, but within two years

1

it was increasing spectacularly, to reach the post-war peak of 1,025,000 in 1947. Another trough was followed by a steady climb back to the figure of 1,015,000 in 1964, and it was not until 1970 that the level fell below 900,000 again. Through the 1970s the birth rate continued to fall, to a new low point in 1977 very close to the 1941 figure. Since then it has rallied, but has not approached the higher levels of the late 1960s.

The direct effect of these changes has been rapidly fluctuating school populations; the figures for pupils of primary school age in the maintained sector in England are as follows:[1]

    1947: 3,422,000
    1951: 3,730,000
    1955: 4,305,000
    1960: 3,925,000
    1965: 4,002,000
    1970: 4,716,000
    1973: 4,831,000
    1977: 4,406,000
    1980: 3,970,000
    1985: 3,542,000

In recent years a succession of DES *Reports on Education* have focused upon the changing numbers of pupils and have attempted to gauge the implications for teacher supply and provision of buildings with an uncertainty bordering upon despair. One prediction in 1976 forecast, accurately, 'a switch of well over a million pupils between primary and secondary schools' during the period 1986 to 1991.[2] By May, 1982, the DES was forecasting that the primary school population would reach a low-point of 3.3 million in 1985, rising by 1996 to a figure somewhere between 3.4 million and 4.5 million.[3] Within a year these estimates had been revised upwards, to a low variant of 4.0 million in 1996 and a high variant of 5.2 million.[4]

This demographic factor is possibly the single most potent element in determining the experience of schooling for children in post-war England. It has influenced decisions at national and local level on teacher supply and the provision of new buildings; it has impinged directly on the largely female labour force in the primary schools, influencing the length of stay of teachers in schools and the numbers of teachers leaving the profession. Within schools, the changing population has been a key determinant of decisions on the deployment of staff and on class size. The influence of demography has percolated throughout the primary sector.

Another important factor influencing the schools has been the post-war suburbanization, linked closely to the onset of affluence which enabled, first, a swift growth in the number of owner occupiers, mostly housed in new suburbs and, subsequently, during the sixties and early seventies, the creation of large overspill housing estates for the resettlement of inner-ring and middle-ring council tenants. This development forced the building of a large number of new primary schools and led to some redefinition of the role of the primary school teacher. The new suburbs signalled the demise of the extended family, to be replaced by smaller 'nuclear' family units. Linked (perhaps inevitably) to an increase in the incidence of divorce and of single parent families, these trends involved primary school teachers in new and more exacting pastoral roles. More positively, suburbanization meant the appearance in schools of children who were more widely travelled than their parents' generation, with heightened expectations in terms of leisure, holiday-making and careers. This too reverberated upon the ethos of the primary schools.

If the growth of the new suburbs meant the onset of a more mobile society, dependant as never before upon the motor car and a variety of rapid transport system, it also led to heightened social contrasts, at first between suburbs but, increasingly during the seventies and eighties, between the north and south of the country. It was impossible that the primary schools could fail to reflect these contrasts. The vast majority of new primary schools built immediately after the Second World War were located in the new overspill suburbs, so that a contrast in building stock was at once apparent, with the old Victorian Board schools still serving as primary schools in the inner city areas, while more modern and airy premises were the norm in many of the younger suburbs. More directly from the teachers' point of view, differences in pupils' social backgrounds, levels of achievement and aspirations became more clearly designated between schools and between catchment area in the new suburban world of post-war England. Suburbanization meant, too, that it became more common for the teachers to commute to their place of employment and this development involved some redefinition of role as the village teacher gave way, once and for all, to a modern professional whose lifestyle was that of the new middle class suburbs.

The phenomenon of increased mobility was an international as well as a national trend and many economically developed societies experienced the appearance of new ethnic minority groups, respond-

ing to the post-war labour shortage. England had long experience of
immigration: Irish labour to cut canals, build railways and people
the cotton mills; Jewish refugees from Eastern Europe into the
industrial cities; Belgians during the First World War and German
Jews during the inter-war years. All were, relatively quickly, integrated into English society and the English school system. The
response of educators was assimilatory, and the schools played an
important role as catalysts of this integration. In contrast the post-
war immigration appeared to many contemporaries to present unprecedented problems, in part because of its scale, and in part
because the fact that many of the new arrivals were non-whites gave
some elements in the press the chance to depict a social crisis. Until
the mid-1960s government and local education authorities attempted
assimilation against a background of housing policies which were to
lead, by the 1980s, to whole suburbs being predominantly peopled
by first and second generation Asians and Afro-Caribbeans. The
recent attempts of some primary schools to respond to the challenges this situation created are described in a later chapter.

Another important development during the post-war era has
been an increasingly widespread awareness of the importance of
gender as an educational issue. Much of the sociological research of
the fifties and sixties obscured gender issues by focusing upon
social class (or in North America upon race) as key determinants of
educational opportunity. But the appearance of women's liberation
groups led to an increasing official readiness to acknowledge this
issue. The Plowden Report had little if anything to say on the
question of gender differences. But, a few years later the publication
by the DES in 1975 of *Curricular Differences Between the Sexes*
derived from enquiries by Her Majesty's Inspectorate (HMI) into
the extent to which girls were disadvantaged within schools,
through the fostering of an awareness of sexual differentiation, or
through limitation of access to courses or institutions. In the same
year the Sex Discrimination Act confirmed the rights of women in
the workplace and so impinged directly upon the work of the
primary schools. By the end of the decade, the growth of women's
studies enabled Olive Banks to write, in a survey of the contemporary scene

> The concern of feminists to show that what appears to be
> natural, i.e. femininity, is in fact an artificial construct, that
> women are made and not born, gives a special emphasis to

education, which is seen as having a major role to play in the construction of femininity.[5]

Gender had emerged as an important issue for educators, and Nanette Whitbread's contribution to this volume deals with this problem in the context of primary schooling.

One final characteristic of the period since the Second World War is the increasing susceptibility of the schools to external controls, and this relates to the increasing bureaucratization of the educational system. Peter Gosden has shown the extent to which the 1944 Act was underpinned by an intention to control the education system more efficiently

> disparity of provision was no longer acceptable ... far more emphasis needed to be placed on national policy and on national levels of provision. Greater centralization was essential if there were to be purposeful national planning.[6]

Successive modifications to the administrative structure have marked the stages in the increasing power of external authorities. The incorporation of the Ministry into the DES in 1964 and the inception of the Schools Council in the same year both strengthened the central authority. Similarly, the reorganization of local government in April 1974 meant the creation of larger and more powerful metropolitan education authorities. The introduction of the block grant system in the early 1960s and of rate capping in the 1980s were financial modifications both of which enhanced the power of central government to exercise direct control over the educational system. So, the 1978 HMI survey, which is the central focus of the chapter by Jayne Woodhouse, and the involvement of parents in school governorship, dealt with by Mike Arkinstall, are increments in a very long-term and deep-seated historical process.

The Elementary School Inheritance

Although there were several significant factors in the quickly changing post-war situation which forced those in the primary schools to rethink their roles and their social function, it would be wrong to forget the deep conservatism of educational institutions, which led the primary sector to take on many of the characteristics of the elementary school system from which it was descended. Many of those characteristics have persisted, albeit in a diluted form, down to the present time.

The greatest period of expansion for the elementary sector was the nineteenth century, and it was during the second half of this century, in particular, that its key characteristics were confirmed. Initially, the main providers of this form of education were the religious denominations, with the Anglican church being by far the most active. In mid-century, the Anglican National Society and the nonconformist British and Foreign School Society provided in total more than 90 per cent of the places available in voluntary schools. The 1870 Education Act enabled the building of the first state schools, the Board schools, alongside those of the churches, and when, in 1902, the church schools were enabled to claim support from the local rates on equal terms with the state schools, the continuation of this dual system by which both kinds of school coexisted was made possible. This situation was further confirmed by the 1944 Act and has not subsequently been seriously challenged. Some recent statistics of school provision released by the DES show the extent to which the primary sector in particular is still influenced by this nineteenth century inheritance.

Providers of Schools: 1984

	Primary Schools	Grammar Schools	Comprehensive Schools
Local Authority	12,447	116	2,654
Church of England	4,855	5	133
Roman Catholic Church	1,892	2	389

By the close of the nineteenth century several other characteristics of the elementary sector which were to persist in the post-1944 primary schools had become apparent. In contrast to the secondary schools of the day, the elementary schools were staffed predominantly by women, and the pupil-teacher system ensured that many of these were drawn from working-class origins. This, too, was in marked contrast to the grammar schools. Formal training for work as an elementary school teacher was provided by the denominational training colleges and through pupil-teacher centres. The day-training departments, which began to appear in the university colleges towards the end of the nineteenth century were almost exclusively concerned with the preparation of graduates for work in the secondary schools. These different routes into teaching ensured the distinctiveness of these two sectors of education: the sense of separateness which persists today between the primary and secondary schools is in part the residue of this inheritance. It is reflected also in contrasting patterns of recruitment to schools of different kinds.

Staffing of Schools in England, 1983

	Nursery	Primary	Secondary
Men	10	40,000	131,000
Women	1,600	133,000	109,000

If it is borne in mind, when considering these figures, that about a half of all male teachers, but only one third of female teachers are graduates, then it will be seen that the staff of primary schools are typically female and non-graduate. These characteristics are traditional, and clearly owe something to the nineteenth century origins of the present system. Since that period, too, the post of Head Teacher has been far more accessible to males than to females. At first glance, the statistic that in 1984 in England and Wales there were 12,140 male and 9881 female Head Teachers in primary schools is hardly remarkable. It takes on far more significance when set against the observation that, in the same year, there were at scale one level 3582 males and 46,292 females employed in maintained primary schools. Similarly, the contrasts in staffing ratios between schools of different types, as the figures below suggest, reflect a pattern which was established at a time when the elementary schools constituted a separate sector of the educational provision:

Staffing Ratios in Maintained Schools in England and Wales (1984)

Primary	Secondary Grammar	Secondary Comprehensive	Secondary Modern
22.1	15.9	16.0	17.0

The figures presented in this section are the numerical evidence of a deeper historical phenomenon which has to do with status hierarchies, and which continues to pervade the English educational system. The elementary schools of the nineteenth century were schools for the working classes, and their relatively parsimonious funding, which was reflected in less well-qualified teachers and in larger classes, stemmed from this fact. During the twentieth century, as the elementary schools became increasingly recognized as part of an articulated educational system, the popular prestige which attached to the grammar schools and to the public schools was never fully afforded to schools for younger children. So, their post-war position within an established status hierarchy of schools was largely predetermined: the fact that women comprise the majority of the teaching force has served only to confirm the lack of esteem in which primary schools were held.

Developments in Primary Schooling since 1945

How then did the primary schools respond in practice to these conflicting pressures of a swiftly changing social context and a deeply conservative educational inheritance? It became clear very quickly after the war to those involved in the primary schools that the longed for social reconstruction could only be of the most limited kind in the prevailing economic climate of stringency. The forties and fifties were an era when the prevailing ideologies of education were 'progressive' in their general slant. The pre-war Hadow reports had emphasized the need for a child-centred approach to schooling, and a welter of post-war books and articles from educationalists confirmed this view. These ideas seemed to be of particular significance for the new primary schools. As Philip Taylor has commented:

> After the Second World War, 'free activity', 'the play way' and readiness were to become bywords in primary education culminating in the root metaphor of the 1952 *Handbook of Suggestions*: 'First the blade and then the ear, then the full corn shall appear'. Primary education came to be conceived as cultivation.[7]

But the extent of this progressivism was severely curtailed in practice in the face of almost overwhelming practical problems. The upturn in the number of births meant that the immediate issues were those of providing enough places in primary schools and of providing enough teachers. Design initiatives involving prefabrication were pioneered by several local authorities, most notably Hertfordshire, and in 1949 a Development Group was set up within the Architects Branch of the Ministry of Education to offer advice and support to the local authorities. But schools had to compete with a swiftly developing programme of private house building for resources, and similarly the full employment of the post-war era made it difficult to attract teachers in sufficient numbers. The emergency training scheme did result in an extra 34,000 teachers by 1951 and the foundation of thirty-four new LEA training colleges. But the very brief and frenetic training offered to these recruits made it difficult for them to absorb fully the practical implications of the new progressivism. The National Advisory Council for the training and Supply of Teachers was obliged to lobby for over a decade before it won the extension of all initial training courses to three years.

A further problem was the 11+ examination which quickly began to impinge on the curriculum of a growing number of primary schools as local authorities established tripartite and bipartite systems of secondary schooling in the wake of the 1944 Act. By the end of the decade streaming was becoming increasingly common as primary schools endeavoured to identify their likely 11+ 'successes' at as early an age as possible. Further, it soon became clear too that the new airy schools which were winning acclaim in the architectural press were those being provided for the new lower-middle-class suburbs peopled in the main by first generation owner occupiers. Schools were to reflect a growing contrast between old and new suburbs.

So, when Labour left power in 1951, there were still nearly a million children in unreorganized 'all age' schools, and overcrowding remained a major problem in many primary schools. There were still nearly 2000 classes which contained fifty or more pupils. It was clear, too, that the heightened social aspirations of post-war Britain meant in reality that particular pressure was placed on the education system to provide for more older pupils. The raising of the school leaving age in 1947, the tendency for more pupils to stay on at school, together with the steady upturn in demand for higher education, all meant that the primary sector faced powerful opposition in the struggle for resources. The reality was that progressivism became fashionable within an economic context of austerity.

Despite this, the 1950s witnessed a steadily increasing commitment to 'child centred' education in the primary sector. As Peter Cunningham and Don Jones show in later contributions to this book, local authority advisers and, in some areas, HMIs were influential in cajoling and coercing classroom teachers to reconsider their methods. In Leicestershire Dorothea Fleming and L.G.W. Stanley were particularly influential local advisers, both appointed by Stuart Mason; in Oxfordshire, the HMI Robin Tanner was the catalyst of a classroom revolution which placed a premium on self-expression through art, on a greater liberty of movement for children in school and on a far more heuristic approach to the study of nature. Although these counties were exceptional, there is no doubt that their primary schools encapsulated the mood of the fifties. In 1957 one Ministry publication summarized developments with the observation that:

> we see a school no longer as a mere machine for giving
> lessons, but as a social unit concerned with the all-round
> development of boys and girls.[8]

Two years later, the Ministry's Handbook on *Primary Education*
confirmed that:

> primary education today is deeply concerned with children
> as children.[9]

The first Building Bulletin was issued by the Ministry of
Education in 1949, and it dealt with the subject of *New Primary
Schools*. It anticipated a movement away from the currently popular
'finger plan' designs towards arrangements which enabled freer
movement around the building. During the 1950s such schools
began to appear. At the new Amersham Primary School (1958),
classrooms were retained, but grouped in fours to allow easy circulation without the use of corridors. At Finmere in Oxfordshire
(1959) and at the Rolleston Infants' School, Glen Parva in Leicestershire (1960) more thorough going open plan designs were adopted.
The formation in 1957 of a consortium of local authorities (CLASP)
to cooperate on questions of school building led to some standardization, but also made it possible for more new schools to be
influenced by these developments. By 1970 there were seven such
consortia at work involving most English county authorities. During the 1960s a growing number of schools experimented with
resource areas, with the integrated day or with family grouping. It
seems, though, that they were never more than an influential minority. One survey in 1962 indicated that only 4 per cent of primary
schools had rejected streaming as an internal device, and there was
continuing concern at the political level during the late fifties and
early sixties about the extent to which primary schools continued to
resort to streaming under the influence of the 11+ examination.

What little research there was suggested that these developments had a beneficial effect upon pupil progress. S. Wiseman's
(1964) *Education and the Environment* drew on an extensive research project carried out in the North of England to demonstrate
substantial improvements in standards of educational attainment
among pupils during the 1950s.

Once again during the 1960s a major problem confronting the
primary schools was demographic in origin as the numbers in
schools continued to rise, while the primary sector, with its largely
female teaching cohort, was particularly susceptible to premature

retirement, often taken after only a few years of teaching. In February 1961 the Ministry announced a campaign to attract women teachers back into the profession in an attempt to meet this problem. In the years immediately following the publication of the Robbins Report (1963) a rapid expansion of teacher training was part of a general sudden enhancement of access opportunities, as planners worked to implement the recommendation which was central to Robbins, namely that places in higher education should be available to all those who were able and qualified to benefit from them. In this process the character of teacher training changed drastically. New appointments to the staff of the training colleges enabled a far greater emphasis upon the educational disciplines, and the introduction of BEd degrees in the late-60s mostly validated in the first instance through university institutes of education, enabled unprecedented numbers of primary school teachers to gain graduate status. The precise impact of these developments upon the professional self-image of teachers, or, more pertinently, on classroom practice, is difficult to judge, but they certainly help to explain why the early 1970s were the period when progressive ideologies of one sort or another were being most vigorously canvassed in primary schools.

In 1964 two important developments took place which were to have effects upon the primary sector. The Curriculum Study Group which had been at work for two years was transmuted into the Schools Council which went on to produce a succession of research reports and projects. These materials not only widened the horizons of those classroom teachers who were able to gain access to them, but, equally significantly, added to the general air of professional expertise which successive governments were keen to attach to schooling and school teachers during the 1960s. Secondly, and of more direct consequence, the Education Act of 1964 responded to the growing complexity of the plans for comprehensivization which were coming in from LEAs by allowing the establishment of middle schools. Within a few years a number of LEAs had abandoned transfer at 11+ and so brought to an end the uniformity of the primary sector only a few years after the closure of the last of the all-age schools (it should be remembered that transfer from preparatory to public schools — the private sector — has remained at 13+ throughout the post-war era, so there was at no time complete uniformity of practice across the country). The general movement at local level towards comprehensive reorganization during the 1960s led not only to the appearance of middle schools, but released many primary schools from the tyranny of the 11+ examination. This, too, was a factor which enabled the more widespread adoption of child centred approaches.

The sixties saw also the emergence of educational policies of 'positive discrimination'. Prefigured by the sociological and psychological researchers of the late-50s and early 60s, and hinted at in the 1963 Newsom report, *Half our Future,* a commitment to the identification and compensation of under-privileged children was the clear and unambiguous central recommendation of the Plowden Report. It was an emphasis which promoted primary schooling to the centre of the political debate on education. At the hustings in 1970 both Margaret Thatcher and Ted Short promised that priority would be given to primary education, with smaller classes, better buildings and more nursery provision being key objectives. Sadly, when A.H. Halsey produced his first report on the working of the educational priority areas, he compiled a catalogue of unrealized aspirations, pointing out that rapid population movements in the inner city, high rates of absenteeism and a quick turnover of school staff were almost insuperable obstacles. He concluded that:

> poor children fall even further behind as they progress through school ... When we analysed the test scores of children in the EPA schools by age we found that on average they deteriorated over the course of the primary school career.[10]

The first *Black Paper* was published in 1969, the fifth and last in 1977. They signalled the rise of a New Right in English politics which had the education question clearly on its agenda. Key items in the programme were an assault on educational standards (which were thought to be falling), demands for greater accountability from the teaching profession and for a return to 'traditional' teaching methods focused at primary level on a 'core curriculum', and the establishment of more direct governmental control over the education system. Powerful elements in the media have underpinned this campaign which persists into the late-1980s, and which, significantly, is international in scope, being paralleled in North America.

The outcome during the 1970s was an increasing distance between what was actually going on in primary schools, as revealed by a succession of reports and enquiries, and what was commonly believed to be the case as presented in the popular press. In 1972 HMI reported favourably on the work being done in a sample of over fifty open plan schools, although a further survey three years later showed that only one primary pupil in ten was being taught in an open plan classroom. In 1975, too, the Bullock Report, *A Language for Life* did not provide the widely-anticipated evidence to support press claims that standards of literacy were falling in the primary schools, although this report was non-commital on the value of the integrated day and of vertical grouping of children. During this period the willingness of many primary school teachers to experiment with the briefly fashionable initial teaching alphabet was further evidence of the commitment of teachers to sustain and improve upon standards of attainment. It seems, then, that while there is no clear evidence that standards declined in primary schools during the 1970s, there is also very little evidence of a 'classroom revolution' taking place. Perhaps the best evidence on this question was provided by the ORACLE project undertaken at the University of Leicester between 1975 and 1980. Brian Simon, summarizing this research, concluded that:

> teaching was found to be largely didactic in character. The promotion of enquiry or discovery learning appeared almost non-existent ... Further, as regards the content of education, a major exmphasis on 'the basics' was also found ... There was little evidence of any fundamental shift, either in the content of education or in the procedures of teaching and learning.[11]

All this was in contrast to the increasingly interventionist stance of successive governments and to the growing hostility of large sections of the press towards teachers and the process of schooling. The publication in December 1972 of a White Paper *Education: a framework for expansion* signalled the increasingly readiness of government to intervene on educational issues. Two years later the Assessment of Performance Unit was set up, and in 1976 three events confirmed the demand for the accountability of primary school teachers. First, the Auld Report on the William Tyndale School gave the press, and critics of progressive schooling a field day. Secondly, the Bennett Report was popularly interpreted as confirming that primary school children benefited more from 'traditional' teaching methods that were well-structured and teacher dominated, rather than from discovery methods. Finally, James Callaghan's Ruskin speech initiated a public debate which placed the schools under even closer scrutiny.

The most immediate developments were to do with the management of schools. The Taylor Report (1977) resulted in a White

Paper in December 1978 on the composition of school governing bodies, and in legislation in 1980. Mike Arkinstall, writing elsewhere in this volume, sees this as no less than 'a structural shift in primary school management'. A cynic might observe that in practice what has been established is a device by which funding and resources are switched disproportionately to those schools in middle-class areas whose parents are most effective in making their voices heard and in exploiting these new committee structures: it cannot be disputed, though, that these developments have brought parents into the domain of primary schooling as never before.

Into the 1980s pressure from the DES to exercise more direct control over the content of schooling at primary level has continued, although, as Jayne Woodhouse explains in her contribution to this book, this has been set against a background of HMI reports and recommendations which have been far more understanding of the difficulties confronting teachers: the HMI *View of the Curriculum* (1980) and *The Curriculum from 5 to 16* (1985), another HMI publication, are two such surveys.

Nonetheless, governmental pressure has been unremitting. In 1980 *A Framework for the School Curriculum* suggested appropriate time allocations for 'core' subjects at primary level and initiated a nationwide review of the content of primary school curricula. This task was, in many cases, conducted through the new governing bodies and resulted in many areas in primary school teachers reporting on their curricula to elected parent governors. The attempt to bridle the powers of local authorities was sustained through the early 1980s by the introduction of rate capping, which curtailed sharply the funds available to support maintained primary schools, and through the publication of HMI reports from 1983 onwards, a procedure which substituted an appeal to public opinion for a dialogue between the representatives of national and local government. The demand for an improvement of standards in *Better Schools* (1985) is the most recent initiative in the same vein. Similarly, the establishment of the Council for the Accreditation of Teacher Education marks an attempt to secure more direct control of the content of teacher education courses.

It is ironic, but perhaps not surprising, that a major problem confronting the primary schools at this time, that of the supply of an adequate number of teachers, stems from the fact that the recent upturn in population has taken place at a time when popular perceptions of teaching are at their lowest ebb. While the DES has acted with alacrity during the 1980s to make the necessary adjustments to target figures for teacher training courses, it is quite unable to reverse the long-term effects of a decade of assaults from the popular press and of a protracted industrial dispute which has itself resulted in intervention by the Secretary of State. With a significant number of teachers leaving the profession at the present time, it appears that the results of this recent history will be with us well into the 1990s.

It will be seen then that the changes which have taken place in primary education have been profound, but they are not those which might have been foreseen at the outset. Through the fifties and sixties a progressive ideology was dominant, and, as some contributors to this book show very clearly, it had a major impact in some schools. Equally, it seems that these were never more than a significant minority, and one conclusion which emerges is that many primary school teachers may have deployed a rhetoric of progressivism but remained in practice, behind the classroom door, fairly conservative in methodology. The key changes which have taken place in the schools, in internal organization, curriculum and methodology, as well as in relation to parents and administrators, represent a set of responses to quickly changing social conditions. The challenges which confront primary schools today are only fully comprehensible in the light of their recent history. It is the relationship between that history and present problems which is explored in the chapters which follow.

Notes

1. The figures in this chapter are drawn from the *Statistics of Education* published annually by the Ministry of Education and, more recently, the DES.
2. DES (1976), *The Future School Population* Report on Education No. 85.
3. DES (1982), *Pupils and School Leavers: Future Numbers* Report on Education No. 97.
4. DES (1983), *Teacher Numbers: Looking Ahead to 1995* Report on Education No. 98.
5. BANKS, O. (1980), Women and Education, *British Journal of Sociology of Education*, 1, 1, pp. 129–134.
6. GOSDEN, P. (1983), *The Education System Since 1944*, Oxford, Robertson.

7. TAYLOR, P.H. (1986), *Expertise and the Primary School Teacher*, Windsor, NFER-Nelson.
8. MINISTRY OF EDUCATION (1957), *The Story of Post-war School Building*, London, HMSO.
9. MINISTRY OF EDUCATION (1959), *Primary Education*, London, HMSO.
10. HALSEY, A.H. (1972), *Educational Priority*, London, HMSO.
11. SIMON, B. (1981), The primary school revolution: Myth or reality?, in SIMON, B. and WILLCOCKS, J. *Research and Practice in the Primary Classroom*, London, Routledge and Kegan Paul.

The Post War Revolution in Primary School Design

Malcolm Seaborne

The years following the Second World War were immensely important for the development of primary school design and of primary
education generally. There had been a virtual suspension of school
building for a period of seven years between 1939 and 1946, and
over 5000 schools were damaged by air-raids. The return of service-
men and women from the war, and the generally optimistic social
atmosphere of the post-war years, contributed to a rise in the birth
rate in the middle and late 1940s and another even more rapid rise in
the period between 1956 and 1964. The building of new housing
estates and of the New Towns also led to major demands for new
schools. Indeed, the post-war years may be compared only with the
period following the 1870 Education Act for the attention given to
new school buildings and to the kind of education taking place in
them.

Now is a good time to assess the results of the post-war boom
in primary school building. The change in the social climate in the
late 1980s compared with the late 1940s could hardly be more
complete. More specifically, the peak in the number of births in
1964, which in turn led to a growth in the number of children in
maintained primary schools in England and Wales to nearly five
million between 1971 and 1976, was followed by a rapid decline
which resulted in a very marked reduction in the number of new
primary schools being built. The demand for new primary school
teachers similarly went into decline and, although advantage was
taken of the new situation to improve the pupil-teacher ratio in the
schools, there can be no doubt that, considered along with the
growth of unemployment and the many social problems associated
with it, the morale of school staffs has been under great strain.
There are, however, indications that the birth rate is now beginning

to increase once more and, while the number of pupils in secondary schools will continue to decline until the early 1990s, the number in primary schools is expected to rise again from 1986 onwards. For this reason government policy at present is to keep the number of new secondary teachers at a relatively low level but to increase the number of new primary teachers as rapidly as possible.

As we now enter a new phase of primary school expansion it is well worth considering the results of the earlier expansion in primary school building and to note what of value is likely to be carried forward as a result of the experience gained during the rapid changes of the fifties and sixties.[1] The story of the post-war developments in school building has been told by a number of participants from those heady days, as well as being detailed in a series of government reports and surveys. Since the new demand was first felt in the primary sphere and, arguably, because it was thought that new teaching strategies could more readily be applied in the earlier years of schooling, a good deal of the literature on the subject of school design refers particularly to the primary stage. Other reasons for this may also be suggested. In the first place, it has always been taken for granted that children aged under eleven should have access to schools near to their homes and, if possible, within walking distance of them. Although there were certainly some very large Victorian elementary schools, and others built for large numbers of children in the pre-war period, these have always constituted a minority. It has also been common practice, particularly in urban areas, for the infant (five to seven year old) children to be organized separately from the juniors (seven to eleven). Thus relatively small primary schools were typical of pre-war practice and continued to be so even when the birth rate accelerated after the war. This made it easier for architects and administrators to plan new buildings to satisfy the perceived needs of each locality, and the technical problems involved in using new building materials and methods of construction were also more manageable when considered in relation to schools of limited size. It may even be suggested that, because of the experience gained in retaining a human scale in building the post-war primary schools, much of value was learnt before tackling the design problems of the new secondary schools, where great care was taken (admittedly with variable success) to break up even the largest comprehensive schools into smaller units.

Let us consider for a moment the problems faced by local education authorities up and down the country in satisfying the need for a major expansion in the number of primary school places immediately after the war. Too much is sometimes made of the desire of administrators and architects to introduce 'progressive' forms of primary teaching, while the central government officials whose task it was to oversee the major building programmes may even, it has been suggested, have been seeking to employ buildings as vehicles for propaganda.[2] A more commonly expressed view is that some of the educational ideas embodied in new school buildings were prompted more by the need for cheapness than anything else.[3] An objective review of the situation will, I hope, show that neither of these viewpoints is justified by the facts.

The main preoccupation of the 1950s and 1960s was to keep pace with the expansion of the school population and to follow what were usually called 'basic need' or 'roofs over heads' policies. Given the unprecedented demand and the shortage of building materials and skilled labour — or rather, the many other competing demands on limited resources for building the welfare state of the post-war years — the adoption of prefabricated methods of construction was probably inevitable. The word 'prefabrication' still has pejorative overtones, yet in some form or another (for example, in the making of windows to a standard pattern in Palladian mansions) it has been a feature of major buildings for many centuries.[4] The Wood Report of 1944 had recommended that schools should be planned in 8ft. 3in. bays, which simplified planning but had the disadvantage of encouraging plans with long wings of classrooms (the so-called 'finger plans' which had begun to appear in the 1930s). The real break-through came with the adoption of grid patterns which, by using units of smaller dimensions, made for much greater flexibility of design. Another major advantage of using factory-made standard components in school buildings was that it reduced the time needed for construction on the site by eliminating many of the wet techniques of traditional building methods. It was the Hertfordshire Authority which demonstrated that prefabricated components could produce varied plan forms and a humane environment for teaching. By reducing the time and, to some extent, the money spent on providing the basic structure, much more attention could be paid to such matters as colour and light inside the buildings and making use of the potentialities of the sites, for example in providing trees, ponds and so on. The Hertfordshire schools, and many others built elsewhere by similar methods and with a similar emphasis on the aesthetic quality of the buildings, were justly acclaimed by experts and laymen alike. This was a real break with the traditional institutional image of the pre-war elementary school. The scale was more human, the light and colour refreshing and the presence of trees and gardens a delight to everyone using the school.

The development of post-war primary school building was further pioneered by another local authority, Nottinghamshire (whose Architects' Department, incidentally, recruited several members of the Hertfordshire team). Nottinghamshire was faced not only with the problem of a rapidly increasing school population, but also with long-standing difficulties associated with mining subsidence in many parts of the county. It was found that light and flexible structures built on the grid pattern responded to earth movements much more effectively than was the case with the previous practice of building schools on reinforced concrete rafts. Although this was certainly a major point in favour of the new building methods, the main advantage foreseen was that of standardizing components and rationalizing the procedures for their supply. This soon led to cooperative schemes with other LEAs with similar problems and to the formation of the first of the building consortia, known as CLASP (Consortium of Local Authorities Special Programme) in 1957. The voluntary association of a number of local authorities — soon to be imitated by other groups of LEAs — was, at the time, a remarkable triumph over the traditionally independent planning by individual authorities. Much stress was laid on the fact that schools built by authorities which used prefabricated components and rationalized their programmes to gain the benefit of bulk purchasing, were cheaper to build than schools of traditional construction. The economic argument was, however, never fully demonstrated. It was certainly the case that money saved on the basic components was well spent on providing better quality internal finishes and furniture and on improving the school sites. As time went by, however, cost controls tended to eliminate some of these spin-off effects and no clear results emerged from a number of enquiries into the subsequent maintenance costs of the lighter forms of construction. The balance sheet is still in favour of the new methods if account is taken of the aesthetic and educational benefits which were undoubtedly gained by those authorities who were guided by administrators and architects committed to this approach and sensitive to the benefits made possible by adopting it.

There was a further important result arising from the new approach to the planning of primary schools. At a time when many other social services were competing for resources, a fresh look was taken at the fundamental purposes of school buildings. They were being built for teaching children and yet a high proportion of the floor area in traditional schools was taken up by non-teaching accommodation and particularly by circulation space, that is, corridors and passageways. This was an additional reason for abandoning the finger plans of the pre-war pattern, which were themselves a reflection of the over-emphasis given in the inter-war period to hygienic conditions and to the need to differentiate between pupils of differing abilities.[5] More compact lay-outs now began to be introduced, with the widespread reduction of corridors which, it was argued, were used relatively rarely in schools where the children usually spent much of the day with the same teacher. The dual use of rooms also became more common with, for example, dining in the entrance foyer or in the assembly hall. Although there were some schools where this principle of reducing circulation space was taken too far (particularly in the early years of a new school building when the number of children was often increasing annually) this development was seen as a sensible one by most teachers and parents.

It is not possible in a short chapter to illustrate the development of post-war plans in detail.[6] The general move towards more compact planning may however be illustrated by considering two schools built twenty years apart, which will bring out some of the major changes which took place. The first is the plan of Whitby County Primary School in Yorkshire built in 1949 to accommodate seven classes of children aged from five to eleven (see Figure 1). It will be seen that each classroom (apart from the reception class) was of identical design, with forty children accommodated in rows of dual desks in each room.[7] Much space was taken up by corridors, and the area for practical work was totally divorced from the classrooms. In contrast, we illustrate an infant school for six classes built at Stapleford in Nottinghamshire in 1968 (see Figure 2). Each class, numbered one to six on the plan, had its own 'home base', with sufficient room for the children to sit on the carpeted floor to listen to the teacher telling a story or talking to them as one group. Most of the school time, however, was spent in varied activities in specially-equipped spaces nearby, as shown on the left-hand side of the plan. (The three classes on the right-hand side of the plan were similarly organized.) Although it would be possible with such a plan for each teacher to spend virtually the whole time with the same class, this plan was designed to work with two groups of three teachers cooperating to make the best use of the resources available, and the school was in fact successfully organized in that way.

The Ministry of Education (later the Department of Education

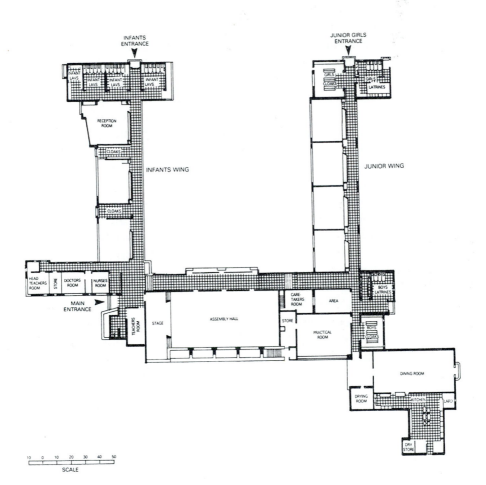

Figure 1. Whitby County Primary School, based on plan in Education, 30 September, 1949.

and Science) did all it could to encourage the developments undertaken by authorities like Hertfordshire, and a revolutionary change was made in 1949 when a Development Group was set up in the Architects' Branch of the Ministry to promote similar changes throughout England and Wales. Significantly, several of the Hertfordshire architectural staff became members of the new Group.

They were supported by able administrators and a number of experienced HM Inspectors, so forming a 'tripod' of administrative, educational and technical staff, who actively worked with local authorities on new school lay-outs and publicized the results of their work in a whole series of building bulletins and other publica-

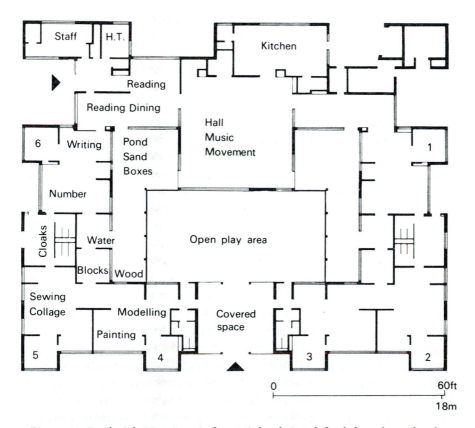

Figure 2. Frederick Harrison Infants' School, Stapleford, based on plan by Nottinghamshire County Architect, 1968.

23

tions, which brought developments in English school architecture not only to national but international attention.

No doubt it was the impact made by the initiative taken by certain LEAs and, more particularly, by the DES which has more recently led to accusations of using school buildings as means of propaganda. It has, for example, been suggested that the Development Group showed a 'selective and discriminating preference for progressive educational practice' and the question has been raised that 'if architectural practice is brought to the aid of promoting and popularizing particular strains of educational theory, quite who decides what is and what is not good primary school practice?'.[8] Such questions may seem to have been given further point by the discussions arising from the introduction of the so-called open plan schools. It can certainly be shown that the desire on economic grounds to reduce circulation space led to the introduction of more compact plans and it is sometimes argued that the provision of large open areas is the cheapest way of providing a given area for teaching purposes. This, however, is a considerable over-simplification. The need to make the fullest possible use of space must be a paramount consideration in discussing any building paid for out of public funds. The obvious difficulty comes in defining the phrase 'fullest possible use'. There will always need to be some space for non-teaching purposes (for example, storage, cloakrooms, etc.) and even the areas designated for teaching may be used for a whole variety of educational purposes. Certainly there is no necessary connection between progressive teaching methods or open planning and the reduction of teaching space (usually, in fact, quite the opposite). Moreover, the technical problems involved in building so-called 'schools without walls' are very considerable, as is the cost of overcoming them.[9] One of the leading DES architects, who had previously worked in Hertfordshire, has stated concerning the schools of the immediate post-war period that 'there was no intention that these schools should reflect changes in educational organization, but they were more than severely practical. They were also an aesthetic statement which in their sense of space, colour and light made a real break with the past'.[10] It is true that members of the Development Group claimed to base their designs on the need to make good teaching possible and that 'good teaching' was often defined by members of the Inspectorate sympathetic to certain approaches to teaching. It is, however, hard to see how else the Group could have proceeded or by what other means new thinking could have been stimulated. The DES made no claim to exclusive insights and the emphasis was consistently on providing a variety of teaching spaces where activities within the main norms of primary school practice as it then existed could be carried on. Many of the complaints made about over-tight planning have come since rising inflation caused the abandonment of the cost place system in 1974: this was an economic rather than an educational change of climate.[11]

Whatever the attitude of the Development Group, it should be borne in mind that the schools were actually built and owned by the LEAs, whose councillors and officers had the responsibility for providing satisfactory buildings and whose teachers were responsible for making them work efficiently. Certainly it can be shown that some teachers disliked some of the lay-outs adopted, or did not use the spaces provided in the manner for which they were designed. Equally it can be shown that many new school buildings were greatly appreciated by the teachers and children and that an increasing number of teachers welcomed the opportunity to try out some of the new teaching strategies which the design of the buildings facilitated. The result in practice has been a great variety of approaches to the teaching of young children, but with a continuing insistence on traditional values such as considerate behaviour, competence in reading and mathematics, and so on. It is worth noting that a major longitudinal study of junior school children in inner London has recently demonstrated that, in spite of differences of race, sex and social background, the school attended is still the most significant factor in influencing the educational progress of young children. This study also showed that among the characteristics of effective junior schools are not only such vital matters as continuity of teaching and the avoidance of over-large classes, but also the need for a good physical environment.[12] As for the attitude of the Inspectorate on matters of school design, a group of them who examined a selection of open plan schools in 1972 were cautious in their conclusions and stressed the need for full discussion between the teachers if cooperative teaching methods were to be adopted.[13] Similarly, a major Schools Council project on open plan schools published in 1980 took the view that only 10 per cent of all primary schools in England and Wales were of open plan design and that even in units of identical lay-out there was very little similarity in the organization of the teaching. The authors of the survey concluded that 'there is no one factor which could be said to influence how the building is used, but a complicated interaction of several different factors. In different designs one or other of these will be stronger, and these could be architecturally or educationally dictated, depending on what the architect conceived and what the teachers perceived'.[14] A similarly pragmatic attitude towards school design was adopted by the chief HMI for junior and middle schools in replying to questions by the House of Commons Select Committee on Education in 1984. He criticized the 'aeroplane hangar' type of design of some open plan schools, which in his view had the serious disadvantage that it magnified noise and interference. He pointed out, however, that 'the best open plan designs were those suited to a definite theory of primary education and allowed a lot of flexibility in types of teaching space', and added that 'there was no profit in returning to the single-class teacher in a box'.[15]

How then may one summarize the achievements in primary school design in the post-war period and how far is one justified in calling them revolutionary? First, there is no doubt of the achievement in quantitative terms, that is, in providing for the primary school population which was accelerating at an unprecedented rate. Secondly, the changes which took place both at central and local government level were revolutionary in leading to the adoption of many new administrative and building techniques and contributing to what has sometimes been called the post-war revolution in the building industry, which was needed to meet the demands of the new welfare state not only in education but in building houses, hospitals and so on. The greatest achievements, however, were qualitative ones. The institutional image of the pre-war elementary schools was broken down and the scale of primary schools became domestic in character, rather than testifying merely to civic pride or to the dominant position held by the adult community. The view that primary education should be more 'child-centred' was given a valid manifestation in the many new schools built for younger children. It is true that cost controls operated against sprawling lay-outs and led to the adoption of more compact plans but this is not to say that the traditional class-teaching method of organization could no longer be maintained in the newly-designed schools. It has always been agreed that class teaching, as distinct from the teaching of individuals or groups, is an essential part of any teaching strategy. Teacher-pupil interaction is a matter of considerable complexity and almost infinite variety. Thus attempts to force particular teaching strategies on schools were not generally made and, when they were, they were usually unsuccessful. The methodology of learning is still not fully understood and the good teacher is constantly varying his or her approach. Thus the perfect school design does not exist, but we should be grateful that the post-war period produced architects and teachers who were prepared to increase the range of options available. That was the change which was truly revolutionary and which is still working itself out in everyday practice in the schools.

It is therefore not without reason that the new primary schools have been called 'the main success of post-war British architecture'.[16] In some cases there were distinct aesthetic gains in terms of siting, the use of colour, space and so on, but the quality which characterized many more was the sense of the fitness of the buildings for their purpose. Fortunately, there was a considerable degree of consensus about their purpose. The concern of parents for the education of their children and the growing contact between teachers and the parents particularly of younger children, underpinned the domestic character of the organization of the schools. Above all, as noted earlier, the tradition had always been for primary schools to be relatively small. Although mass-produced components were increasingly used in the construction of the buildings and although the lay-outs became more compact, there was no attempt at high-rise building or social engineering on the scale of some of the new housing estates, whose tower blocks have in too many cases turned out to be a disaster. Individual families might not have been able to influence the design of some municipal housing but, united with other families and with the teachers of their local schools, they were able to influence, if only indirectly, the design of the new primary schools.

Regretfully, we cannot end this review of primary school building on the same relatively optimistic note. Despite the major expansion of school building programmes after the war, a survey carried out in 1976 showed that 53 per cent of all primary schools in England and Wales were built before 1946. Nearly a half of these had been built before 1903 and had not been remodelled to modern standards and a quarter had grossly inadequate sites. In spite of the decline in school rolls, a fifth of the primary schools operating in 1976 were more than 10 per cent overcrowded; in addition, many of the defects mentioned above were concentrated in schools situated in areas of special social need.[17] The authors of the survey proposed that capital resources should be set aside to allow for the renewal of existing stock, particularly in the areas of greatest need, but financial constraints have led to the shelving of most of these proposals. Even more serious has been the effect of continuing financial constraints on revenue expenditure, which has led to the neglect of maintenance work in many areas. In the report made by HMIs on the effects of local authority expenditure policies in 1985, the state of repair in schools was judged less than satisfactory or poor in sixty-two LEAs, and in thirty-five of these the level of expenditure on maintenance was actually decreasing. In primary schools, poor accommodation was judged to be restricting one-sixth of lessons where the work was considered satisfactory, while nearly three-tenths of lessons where the work was unsatisfactory were similarly affected.[18]

Lack of finance for buildings is also a key issue in considering the future of the smaller rural primary schools which are, in general, expensive to maintain but greatly appreciated by their local communities. Primary education in the countryside , at any rate in terms of buildings, reached its widest extent in the late Victorian period. Few villages, even in remote areas like the Fens, were without their own school buildings and anyone who explores the countryside today will find many examples of village schools now converted to other uses or standing derelict. Reliable figures for the closure of rural primary schools since the war are not available, but it is known, for example, that there were 115 closures in the Highland region of Scotland in the period between 1960 and 1980, and 180 in Gwynedd, Dyfed and Powys during a similar twenty-year period.[19] New strategies for 'cluster schools' and 'area community schools' are being developed but government policy continues to stress the need to dispose of surplus school places, ostensibly so that the sale of the buildings and the saving on maintenance costs can contribute to renewing the building stock in other areas of social need. In one respect at least the falling primary school rolls of the seventies and eighties have had a more useful side-effect, in that in many areas it has been possible to convert surplus primary school places to nursery classes. Nevertheless, the provision of nursery education is very patchy and many more nursery school places are being provided by the private sector on a fee-paying basis, compared with public provision.

What lessons may be said to have been learnt as a result of the rapid post-war expansion of primary school building, followed by an even more rapid decline, and what points of permanent value may be carried forward as we move into a new period of expansion in primary education? The essential attitude of the educationalist on the subject of school architecture was well summed up by the chief education officer for Norfolk during the controversy which arose over the building of a school of novel design at Hunstanton in the 1950s: 'Nothing', he wrote, 'can change the fundamental conviction that the educational function of a school must take precedence over any theory of aesthetics'.[20] That, however, is not to say that aesthetic considerations are unimportant or that the best schools cannot give satisfaction both from the educational and architectural points of view. We owe a continuing debt to those who designed and built some of our post-war primary schools for considering afresh the impact of light and colour within the buildings and of the surroundings in which the schools were set. The greatest contribution of the post-war period, however, was the importance attached to designing for the essential educational purposes for which the schools were needed. The best designs took as their starting point a study of the activities of the teachers and children and were not wedded to any particular theory of teaching or of architecture. The widespread assumption that open plan schools are places where informal or open teaching is the norm is not borne out in actual practice. The traditional 'one teacher, one class' system has largely been maintained and there is even some evidence that open designs can actually create a more rigid organization.[21] This merely confirms the fact that architecture can certainly affect the physical environment but not necessarily the activities that take place within it.

Yet these arguments should not be used to condemn the continuing search for forms of building best suited to educational purposes, nor should the disadvantages as well as the advantages of the concept of 'one teacher, one class' be ignored. The best primary schools are those where the teachers work together as a team, not necessarily in formalized activities, but through a constant interchange of ideas and knowledge about the children and their background. There will also increasingly be occasions when children are taught by teachers other than those responsible for their particular class and when the activities taking place can better be carried on outside the individual classroom. The idea of the 'classroom box' has already disappeared in many schools, since the class teacher has a variety of teaching spaces at his or her disposal. The notion that the formal teaching of a class of children in one group should be the only method of teaching is no more than an uninformed attempt to turn the clock back to the last century. The views of those responsible for planning new primary schools in the post-war period are still largely valid. These may be summed up in the words of Eric Pearson:

> Architects should be designing for an ever increasing variety of interconnected activities, readily available to groups of children and their teachers for the exploration of the problems they set themselves.[22]

Perhaps the main aspect of school planning in the post-war period which should be retained and expanded now is the example set by the Development Group of the DES and by some LEAs of consulting practising teachers when preparing briefs for new schools. Planning should result from an analysis of the activities of groups of varying size for varying periods of time, that is, it should grow out of the need to accommodate particular people for particular purposes. In spite of the post-war expansion, however, a study undertaken by the School of Advanced Urban Studies at Bristol University in 1978 showed that only a minority of LEAs was proceeding in this way. Many were still using predetermined schedules of accommodation or standard plans as their starting point.[23] It is vital to remember that good design requires the collaboration of administrators, educationalists and architects operating as equal partners. 'Educationalists' should include practising teachers, and more should be done to involve elected members and parents in discussing the assumptions on which the designs of new schools are based. In addition, after the school has been built, there should be a briefing of those who will use the building and an appraisal of the success of the building in actual use. All this may seem to be a counsel of perfection, but, bearing in mind the considerable investment of human and material capital in any new building, it really is a necessity. Only in this way can we build on the achievements and correct the mistakes of the revolution in school design which characterized the post-war period.[24]

Notes

1. Major studies include: MINISTRY OF EDUCATION (1957) *The Story of Post-War School Building*, London, HMSO; SEABORNE, M. and LOWE, R. (1977), *The English School: its architecture and organization, Vol. II, 1870–1970*, London, Routledge and Kegan Paul; and MACLURE, S. (1984), *Educational Development and School Building: aspects of public policy 1945–73*, London, Longman.
2. COOPER, I. (1981), 'The politics of education and architectural design: The instructive example of British primary education', in *British Educational Research Journal*, 7, 2, pp. 125–34.
3. As, for example, in MANNING, P. (1967), *The Primary School: An Environment for Education*, Pilkington Research Unit, University of Liverpool, Department of Building Science, p. 15.
4. For a wide-ranging and interesting account see WHITE, R.B. (1965), *Prefabrication: A History of its Development in Great Britain*, National Building Studies Special Report, London, HMSO.

5. See further SEABORNE, M. (1971), *Primary School Design,* London, Routledge and Kegan Paul, chapters 4 and 5.
6. For a fuller sequence of plans and illustrations see Seaborne and Lowe and particularly Maclure (note 1 above) which has many plans chosen by David and Mary Medd.
7. For a discussion of the influence of seating arrangements on children's learning see WHELDALL, K. *et al* (1981) 'Rows versus tables: an example of the use of behavioural ecology in two classes of eleven-year old children', in *Educational Psychology,* 1, 2, pp. 171–184.
8. COOPER, I. (1981), *op. cit.,* p. 134.
9. See, for example, the report of the SCOTTISH COUNCIL FOR RESEARCH IN EDUCATION (1984), *An Open Question* reported in *Education,* 16 March, p. 219.
10. MEDD, D. (1984), in 'School architecture', a digest in *Education,* 21 December, p. ii.
11. Such constraints particularly affected junior and middle schools. See WALLACE, G. (1980), 'The constraints of Architecture on aims and organization in five Middle Schools' in HARGREAVES, A. and TICKLE, L. (Eds.) *Middle Schools: Origins, Ideology and Practice,* London, Harper and Row, pp. 122–138.
12. ILEA RESEARCH AND STATISTICS BRANCH (1986), *The Junior School Project,* reported in *The Times Educational Supplement,* 18 April, p. 5.
13. DES (1972), *Open Plan Primary Schools,* London, HMSO, p. 18.
14. BENNETT, N. *et al* (1980), *Open Plan Schools,* London, NFER, p. 183.
15. *Education,* (1984), 29 June, pp. 521–2.
16. MacEWAN, M. (1974), *Crisis in Architecture,* London, RIBA, p. 16.
17. DES (1977), *A Study of School Building,* London, HMSO, pp. 7–9.
18. DES (1986), *Report by Her Majesty's Inspectors on the Effects of Local Authority Expenditure Policies on Education Provision in England — 1985,* London, HMSO, pp. 30–33.
19. Quoted in 'Rural schools', a digest in *Education,* (1983), 14 October, p. i.
20. Quoted in *Education,* (1954), 29 October p. 658.
21. See, for example, MUSGROVE, F. (1971), *Patterns of Power and Authority in English Education,* London, Routledge and Kegan Paul, pp. 58–9, and EVANS, K. (1978), 'The physical form of the school', in *British Journal of Educational Studies,* 27, 1, p. 39.
22. PEARSON, E. (1972), *Trends in School Design,* London, Macmillan, p. 15.
23. Reported in DES (1979), *The Briefing Process in School Design,* Architects and Building Group Occasional Paper 5, London, HMSO.
24. Since this chapter was written, the following major study has appeared and is highly recommended: SAINT, A. (1987), *Towards a Social Architecture: The Role of School Building in Post-War England,* London, Yale University Press.

Planning for Progressivism: The Changing Primary School in the Leicestershire Authority During the Mason Era, 1947–71

Donald K. Jones

One could be forgiven for believing that the progressive movement in the English primary school, that is the movement toward a child-centred education, began and developed in the period after the Second World War, reaching a climax with the Plowden Report in 1967.[1] Admittedly there was tremendous interest in autonomous learning, in what became known as 'the integrated day' in this period, encouraged, in particular, by the gradual elimination of the 11+ examination during the 1960s, as local education authorities moved toward comprehensive education. Compared, however, with its predecessor of the 1930s, the Report of the Consultative Committee to the Board of Education on *Infant and Nursery Schools* (Hadow Report, 1933),[2] the Plowden Report does a disservice to the reader by failing to provide an historical introduction to its findings; an omission avoided by Dr R.F. Young in 1933, whose introduction to the Hadow Report of that year provides a most scholarly account of the evolution of the infant and nursery school. His introduction to the 1931 Hadow Report performs a similar service on behalf of the primary school, reminding one that progressive practice has a long history.

Before focusing upon the post-war developments in infant and primary education in Leicestershire, it is worth remembering that the infant school, even when it was in its embryonic form of an infant department in a large board school, was often the seed-bed of more adventurous practices, which were to infiltrate the education of older age groups as time went on. As will be seen, in the

Leicestershire of Stewart Mason, Director of Education there for a quarter of a century between 1947 and 1971, this kind of permeation was fostered as a deliberate policy. However, it must be borne in mind that for nearly two centuries the British Isles have provided a sympathetic environment for the kinds of educational methods which are particularly appropriate for young children, the work of Robert Owen at New Lanark, Samuel Wilderspin in London, David Stow in Glasgow, and Charles and Elizabeth Mayo at the Home and Colonial Infant School Society being the best known early examples.

Moreover, notwithstanding the system of payment by results which dominated the elementary schools from the 1860s until the 1890s, the Committee of the Privy Council on Education encouraged the training colleges to train young people specifically for the teaching of very young children.[3] The London School Board, meanwhile, in the aftermath of Forster's Elementary Education Act of 1870, always a pioneer in new ventures, appointed Miss Caroline Bishop for the purpose of spreading the Froebelian 'kindergarten' gospel at the bottom end of the London board schools, and already, by 1873, the Reverend J.H. Rigg could congratulate himself on the fact that compared with Germany and America, where the infant school was not part of the educational system, in England it was very much a part, and 'one of our chief advantages'.[4] Similarly, in 1874, E.R. Robson, architect to the London School Board, remarked that only in England was the infant school regarded 'as part — a very important part — of the national educational system'.[5] In that year the Froebel Society was founded, to be followed fourteen years later by the founding of the National Froebel Union as an examining body for the London School Board.[6] The Inspectorate, particularly the women's branch, meanwhile emphasized the need for teachers to understand the true nature of the kindergarten practice by allowing it to permeate the whole school day, not merely confining it to a particular time in the morning or the afternoon.[7]

The inter-war period saw further progress in the work of the New Education Fellowship, which acted as a forum for progressive ideas from both sides of the Atlantic, many of which were absorbed into the received wisdom of the already-mentioned Hadow Reports of 1931 and 1933,[8] while the infant school, catering for pupils of the 5–7 age group, immune to the influence of the 11+ selection examination which, to some extent, hampered the junior school, could develop its own ethos,[9] a fact made clear in the Hadow Report of 1933 when, in celebrated phraseology, it described the infant school as an 'instructive environment' in which the curriculum was to be thought of in terms of 'activity and experience rather than knowledge to be acquired and facts to be stored'.[10] Moreover, the fact that 70 per cent of 5–7 year olds were in separate infant schools by 1933, some of which were grouped vertically, a common practice today, promoted their peculiar progressive ethos, emphasising a combination of individualized learning, group work and creative activity.[11]

In the quarter of a century after World War Two these practices were able to permeate the junior schools and, latterly, even the secondary schools, as will be seen with regard to Leicestershire. When Stewart Mason took up his directorship in 1947, he had already been influenced by the work of the New Education Fellowship, of which he became a member when a schoolmaster at Harrow, where he taught between 1931 and 1937.[12] It was as a trainee HMI in Cambridgeshire, however, that he began to formulate his own ideas about the kind of school organization which he considered most appropriate for the very young. Advised by Fox, his district HMI, to spend his first year getting to know the Cambridgeshire schools, he alighted upon one particular village school at Quy where the children were encouraged to draw and paint on large sheets of sugar paper, using the stimulus of the village environment to remarkable effect. Mason, using this school as a growth point, began to hold discussion groups of teachers after school hours, which were all the more effective, he believed, because as a non-report writing HMI, albeit temporarily, he held no threat over the teachers. He was merely a stimulator and adviser, a status which was to hold considerable significance for the future, for herein lay the model for the Leicestershire advisory service, which he began to develop directly he succeeded Sir William Brockington as director of Education in 1947, having spent the war as a Civil Servant in the Admiralty.

Stewart Mason's objective was to create a climate of change and innovation by means of advice, as distinct from inspection, and to this day Leicestershire advisers only enter schools with the agreement of the headteacher, a practice deriving from Mason's conviction that inspection is threatening, whereas advice is not. The advice when proffered by an individual blessed with a certain dynamism could, nevertheless, be disturbing, which is no doubt what Mason wished it to be.

Characteristically, for one who throughout his career in education was thoroughly enamoured of both the infant school and its diminutive clientele, Mason appointed, almost immediately he took up his directorship, an adviser for infant education in the person of Dorothea Fleming. Froebelian trained, and a great protagonist of the English Nursery School Association, she had previously been a lecturer at Goldsmith's College and, although the circumstances of her appointment are obscured in the mists of time, there is evidence that Mason knew of her prior to her appointment and persuaded her to come to Leicestershire. He clearly hoped that she would make a considerable impact on the village schools of the county, some of which, housed in buildings dating back to the last century, were nothing if not primitive, their teaching methods and sanitation, in several cases, harmonizing with their architectural style.

She did not disappoint him. A lady of formidable determination, she swept into the schools with immense vigour, leaving devastation in her wake. Nevertheless, younger teachers embraced her as a liberating influence, as Vicky Stanley, a retired teacher who vividly remembered her impact, related:

> I am thinking of when I was at Albert Road (Hinckley), we used to have classes of over fifty in such tight rows that nobody could leave the room until somebody stood up. Then Miss Fleming came, and caused a great deal of consternation among many heads. She was the catalyst. She would come sweeping into the classroom saying, 'Do away with discipline, do away with formality, get freedom, and let the children play, to start with.'[13]

Blissfully impractical, she inspired teachers with ideas, and with the belief that nothing was impossible, which, according to Vicky Stanley, is what advisers should do. An iconoclast, moreover, she had little respect for protocol, considering that uncooperative headmasters were there to be ignored and even criticized behind their backs to their members of staff.

She was equally derisive about Parliamentary legislation, as Alec Stanley, Headmaster of Albert Road Junior School in Hinckley, and in many ways sympathetic to her ideas, explained:

> I crossed swords with her over the question of morning assembly. I knew that the 1944 Education Act said that the day must begin with a corporate act of worship. She said, 'Rubbish'. That was her actual expression. She had no diplomacy at all.[14]

Clearly, she was prone to raising the hackles of any headteacher, few of whom could sympathize with her favourite exhortation to 'throw the furniture out of the window', and if she had stayed too long in the county her strategy would have been counter-productive, but after ten years she moved on. Nevertheless, as an educational storm-trooper, she achieved objectives which others were able to consolidate, and as Philip Sherwood, a retired head-master of two Leicestershire primary schools, remembered, she established a platform upon which her two immediate successors Vivian Gibbon, infant adviser, and L.G.W. Sealey, primary adviser, could build.[15] As another retired infant school head, Elizabeth Irons, recalled, 'She set Leicestershire alight with freedom.'[16]

Clearly her task was not easy, but Stewart Mason made it clear where his sympathies lay by addressing teachers at conferences and workshops which she held for practising teachers, and by sitting on the appointing boards for the headships of the schools which he recognized as growth points for innovation. Moreover, without ever directly telling teachers what they ought to do, he nevertheless made it perfectly clear what he considered to be good practice by promoting particular people to headships and by holding regular meetings of primary school heads.

Isobel Irons, who had started her teaching career in Leicester-shire in 1932, but had been obliged to retire temporarily on getting married a few years later, noticed the difference in the educational climate when she returned in 1947:

> I came back into the new and exciting atmosphere created by Miss Fleming. I came back into what, in that brief spell fourteen years before, I had considered to be true education. The main noticeable change was the freedom of movement that the children had in their classrooms. Previously they came in, sat down, and didn't move, and the teacher was a person apart from the children. You had to make children write with their right hands, whereas by 1947 you left them alone. I am sure that to have trained the kids of the thirties in the way that we did later on would have been better. To let children use paint in the way they want to instead of telling them to 'all bring a leaf', and allowing a few kids to move into a quiet corner and pick up a book, compared with them all having to go at the same speed: these are great improvements.[17]

Above all she appreciated Stewart Mason's willingness not only to spend time with headteachers in order to discuss new ideas, but also to visit schools when asked:

> It was very encouraging to know that Mr Mason was interested in what we were doing. He would call us to meetings for discussions about the future trends in education, but he was interested mainly in what you yourself hoped to achieve. For example, I got fed up with children marching in to assembly, and decided to let them come in and sit with whom they liked, while a teacher played soft music on the piano. The children took part, made up their own prayers appropriate to a particular theme, and made up their own little prayer books. I told Stewart Mason about this, and he came along and sat on the floor with the children and talked to them. I thought he was excellent. He was never too busy to listen.[18]

By such means did Stewart Mason ensure that his message was heeded. Already, however, as R.J.W. Selleck has indicated, the training colleges were encouraging progressive methods[19], which meant that Mason did not have to rely solely on the advisory service for bringing about change. There were people coming out of college either just before or just after the war who had been strongly influenced by their training.

One such person was the late Marjorie Kay, Stewart Mason's third adviser for infant education in succession to Vivian Gibbon. As a student shortly before the war at Bishop Otter Training College at Chichester, she had beem profoundly influenced by her training and, moreover, had been fully conscious of the fact that she was being taught by people who were pioneering new methods; people such as Dorothy Gardener, who was well known in progressive circles at the time, and Sylvia Grey, both of whom moved on to the London Institute of Education, the former eventually succeeding Susan Isaacs as Head of the Department of Child Development.

The main emphasis of the college training was strongly on the individual, 'They were quite explicit about it: you should not be teaching the whole class, you should focus on the individual child', a message which, as will be seen, was not lost on Stewart Mason.[20] The college, moreover, was well connected with progressive schools in London, one of which was in the 'East End, where the Headmistress, Edna Boyce, went to the trouble to persuade the fathers of the impoverished children to hand over money at the beginning of the week so that she could provide the children with milk and something to eat at lunchtime. In Marjorie Kay's opinion 'She was creating a social revolution just as much as the MacMillans did.' the students not only visited such schools, but also took the children on holiday under Dorothy Gardener's guidance, to Sevenoaks in Kent, in the summer vacation, catching in the process a glimpse of the deprived conditions in which they lived. All of which was remarkably good experience, and Marjorie Kay considered herself to have been very fortunate as a student to have rubbed shoulders with people who were operating at the forefront of all the new practices and ideas of the time.

As already noted, Stewart Mason was extremely interested in these 'new practices', and contrived to let it be known that Leicestershire welcomed them, so that, having taught for a few years and then been turned down for a headship in Northamptonshire for waxing over-enthusiastically about the concept of 'readiness' and the emphasis on the individual child, Marjorie Kay eagerly responded to an advertisement for an infants school headship in neighbouring Leicestershire, which invited applications from 'young and imaginative teachers' a stipulation which was quite unusual in the late forties. Unsuccessful initially, she was invited at the interview to apply for another headship (a common Leicestershire practice) at the colliery village of Whitwick, and this time she was successful. Here, along with other changes, she 'de-militarized' morning assembly, just as Isobel Irons had done, Dorothea Fleming paid a visit and departed in ecstasy, and thus she became one of Fleming's 'golden girls'. Consequently, when Vivian Gibbon, Fleming's successor, left in the mid-sixties, Marjorie Kay was her obvious successor.

London, however, was not the only place in the late thirties and early forties where new ideas were being put into practice. Mary Brown,[21] later to become the co-author of *The Integrated Day in the Primary School*, distinctly remembers, when a student at Edgehill Training College, Ormskirk, paying visits to highly innovative schools in Liverpool and South Lancashire in the mid-forties, and later being profoundly influenced in a school in Nottingham by the work of Alice Yardley. Although not immediately impressed by the seeming lack of structure in the organization of such schools, she was later to become an exponent of such methods. The important point, however, is that her college experience had opened her eyes to them.

By the end of the fifties, the encouragement of a less formal structure to the school day was beginning to show results, and in some schools there was a gradual move towards the 'integrated day'. As Rosemary Armington remembered, when she started teaching in the late forties in Leicestershire, the day would begin in a number of schools with a 'choosing time' in the morning, when children were allowed to experiment with materials. This extended period would then be followed by a maths or a reading period. Gradually, however, the maths and reading periods were incorporated into the 'choosing' period, and what became known as the 'integrated day' began to develop, so that by the end of the fifties, half a dozen schools, Stewart Mason's growth-points, which were known to be more progressive than others, were already operating the fully integrated system.[22]

At Whitwick, however, Marjorie Kay had to go rather more slowly. At Bishop Otter College the students had been encouraged to begin the day with a period called 'free activity'. It had acquired a bad name, she recalled, and became synonymous with 'chaos', so that when she became head at Whitwick she changed the name to 'creative activity'.[23]

It was not always the head who converted her staff to less formal approaches, however. Sometimes the school was the instrument of conversion. For example, when Rosemary Armington became headmistress of Westfield Infants School in Hinckley, she was happier with rather more structure than less in the school organization. Under its former Head the school had gained a reputation for being one of the most progressive schools in the county, Isobel Nourrish having been one of Mason's leading figures in the implementation of the 'integrated day'. It was the school, and the deputy head, Edna Jones, in particular, Rosemary Armington admitted, who 'did more to enable me to understand what young children are capable of than anybody else'.[24]

By that time, 1960, Vivian Gibbon, Mason's second infant adviser, had taken over from Dorothea Fleming, consolidating the ground that she had made, and bringing much welcome practical advice on how these changes could be made in an orderly manner. Alec Stanley, whose experience of progressive methods had begun in 1932, when with his Headmaster's encouragement he implemented Helen Parkhurst's Dalton Plan at Hinckley Senior Boys' School, recalled that gradually, although Dorothea Fleming's initial impact was to create confusion in the minds of some teachers, freedom became more controllable when a framework was set within which children could exercise a range of choice.[25]

Leicestershire headteachers, meanwhile, were accorded a remarkable degree of autonomy, and it was quite normal for them to
exchange schools periodically for brief periods, not only to bring
fresh ideas to assistant teachers, but also to themselves. In spite of
the encouragement of new ideas, however, many schools remained
untouched by them, and when Marjorie Kay joined the advisory
service in 1966 she was surprised to find how much still remained to
be done. Nevertheless, in the primary school a quiet revolution was
being effected.

As already noted, the teacher training colleges, or some of them
at least, were a fruitful source of new ideas. So also were their less
lauded off-shoots, the Emergency Training Colleges, which were
responsible in the immediate post-war years, for bringing people
into teaching from a remarkable variety of backgrounds, and in some
cases imparting a wealth of skill and experience into the classroom.
As one of their alumni and future Leicestershire headmaster, Philip
Sherwood, remembered, the kind of training that they offered could
be remarkably stimulating, and could certainly lead those who
wished to follow toward exciting methods of teaching:

> The Emergency Training Colleges were staffed by good
> practising teachers, and they gave a twelve-month course in
> classroom survival and in interesting children in what they
> were doing. They were people who had made the grade in
> schools and were passing on their ideas. I think my ideas on
> education have been framed very much by Emergency
> Training. There were some quite cranky characters among
> them. Wicksteed, the Wicksteed Park (Kettering) chap was
> one of the maths lecturers, and he would take us down the
> Bedford Ouse in an old Royal Engineers' pontoon with a
> motor stuck on the back. That was how you were intro-
> duced to topics. When we went to the college we were given
> three weeks to choose a topic from a list, work on it
> together, then present it before we had a lecture on educa-
> tion of any sort. The topic down the Ouse was so popular
> that it went on every weekend long after it had finished —
> people were going off down there in November. That was
> the approach to practical outdoor work — with the emph-
> asis on doing and activity.[26]

Few authorities, however, can have benefited more from this source
of ingenuity than did Leicestershire, mainly as a result of Stewart

Mason's inspired appointment of L.G.W. Sealey as Adviser for Primary Education in 1957.

Sealey had been an engineering officer in the Royal Navy during the war. On demobilization he worked briefly in industry, and then went into teaching, by way of the emergency training system, in primary schools. Encouraged by his Headmaster, also a former naval officer, he began to innovate by bringing all kinds of materials into the classroom. He was then appointed headmaster of Thringstone Primary School, a two-form entry school near Coalville. A remarkably dynamic and talented man, he not only developed materials for teaching mathematics, but possessed a fund of ideas for developing language and was also no mean artist.

One day he was working in his school when he found Stewart Mason standing behind him. The Director had come to tell him that he was about to advertise for an adviser in primary education, and that if Sealey applied he would certainly be considered.[27] When the day of the interview arrived, having recruited some NUT members to the interviewing panel, presumably to make the proceedings appear to be democratic, Mason found himself violently in opposition to the teacher representatives who, understandably enough, wanted to see the post go to a primary head of a large school with many years' service. Mason characteristically dug in his heels, and eventually got his way. The primary heads in several schools, however, threatened to refuse to allow Sealey to enter their schools, because not only did they think his experience inadequate but, worse still, he was only emergency trained and therefore, in their opinion, as Mason put it, 'below the salt'.[28]

In spite of these threats, and Mason's offer to let him withdraw, Sealey took on the job and within a year had overcome most of the prejudice against him. The main thrust of his work, according to his successor, W.E. Browse, was to look for ways of involving children in the learning process as much as possible, providing motivation to replace the spur of the 11+ examination. In language, therefore, children would make up their own novels, anything between five and a hundred pages in length, edit each other's work, and illustrate and bind them, ready to be placed on a bookshelf. Similarly, in art and craft, when weaving was being done the whole process from raw wool to dyed cloth was followed.[29] He was, moreover, an early pioneer in the introduction of practical activities into science and mathematics teaching, which amounted to far more than measuring and observing, for he developed the use of the balance and the spike abacus and, in 1957, produced a series of work cards which were later published as a set of books, the very beginning of the School Mathematics Project. He also collaborated very successfully with Vivian Gibbon on a series of books on infant mathematics. He was, in fact, an educational entrepreneur in every sense of the word.[30]

His great strength, however, was his power of persuasion, for not only did he bring vast quantities of materials into the classroom, but he had the ability to persuade his client that the material he was bringing was the very thing that the latter needed. The advent of Sealey in fact marked the beginning of what, for several Leicestershire primary heads, was an incredibly fascinating and stimulating period in their careers. In retrospect, W.E. Browse, now adviser in primary education in the authority, remembers the excitement generated in the county in the late fifties and early sixties when, if as he did, one was teaching in one of a group of particularly adventurous schools, there was a feeling abroad of being at the centre of exciting educational developments. At this time, he argues, genuine innovation was being brought about by teachers who were highly skilled, thoroughly understood what they were doing and, in an orderly manner, could exploit new ideas with confidence. Their schools became cells of innovation where assistant staff could develop and then, as heads or deputy heads, take their ideas into other schools.[31] It was, moreover, about these schools that the Americans became enthusiastic, adding yet a further interesting episode to this fascinating period of education in Leicestershire.

Appropriately it was L.G.W. Sealey, whose work toward improving the teaching of mathematics in junior schools, aroused this interest. At a party in 1957 he met Dr Z.P. Dienes, a lecturer of Hungarian origin, in mathematics at Leicester University, who had developed a set of materials to help children understand the place value element in the arithmetical process. Sealey immediately recognized this as the perfect adjunct to his own ideas. Starting with two schools in 1958, the numbers using the materials had risen to twelve a year later, and Sealey began to put on courses for teachers at which Dienes demonstrated the use of his materials. In 1961, however, Dienes went as visiting professor to Harvard for six months, and there met J.S. Bruner, well known as the author of *Towards a Theory of Instruction*, and also for his curriculum project, 'Man, a course of study', which is still used in some Leicestershire schools. Of more significance for Leicestershire, however, was the fact that he also met W.P. Hull, who had taught for many years at the Shady Hill School in Cambridge, Massachusetts, a well-known institution in the National Association of Independent Schools, with a reputation for progressive teaching.

Hull, like Dienes, was interested in developing logic blocks in mathematics teaching, which were later produced by the Elementary Science Study, a government-funded agency in Massachusetts, while Dienes, on returning to England, developed his own logic blocks, which were later produced commercially in this country. The important point, however, is that Dienes encouraged Hull to visit Leicestershire, where he would find schools which, encouraged by a go-ahead director, would positively welcome the kinds of materials on which they had both been working.

The result was that in 1961 Bill Hull duly arrived in the county in order to visit classrooms which were using Dienes' multi-base and algebraic materials, his itinerary having been planned by L.G.W. Sealey. So began a most remarkable interchange of ideas and visits, involving many hours of transatlantic travel between Leicestershire and North America, and the phenomenon of battalions of teachers, not only from Leicestershire but also from the West Riding and Oxfordshire, spending their summer holidays working on educational workshops in the schools of North America.

What impressed Hull more than anything, however, was not so much the fact that the materials were being used, but that such experimentation was being permitted in the public sector for, it must be remembered, it has invariably been the independent sector in the United States which has had the freedom to experiment. His reactions, therefore, provide some fascinating insights into what was going on in the schools from an American viewpoint. His remarks and observations were recorded in a paper which he wrote in 1962, entitled 'A visit to the Leicestershire Schools', and circulated to sympathizers of progressive education, 'the undergound grape-vine' as it is known in the United States, on his return.

One part of his account[33] describes a class making a collage of a street scene. Although there were over thirty children 'there was little confusion', he remarked. The teachers had a special interest in that kind of work, and were proud of the fact that every child had had a chance to make a contribution. He saw handwriting patterns in the style of Marion Richardson, listened to music played on the recorder, and observed a science experiment carried out according to instructions on work-cards devised by the teacher. He also noted the mathematics work-cards which a teacher had developed, critics of the teaching profession please note, during the summer vacation.

Perhaps the most fascinating insight reflecting the work of

Dienes and Sealey, whose *Creative Use of Mathematics in Junior Schools* had been published by this time, is provided by a passage, clearly illustrating the collaborative learning that the materials, which Hull describes, permitted. Children made up problems of their own which they worked out with their blocks, arranging their materials on pieces of cardboard marked off for units, longs, flats and blocks. Some children worked in pairs, but there were also groups of three or four, owing to shortage of materials and limitations of space. The children wrote their problems in their notebooks on squared paper, while the teacher went from group to group checking each problem and keepimg a record of what each child had accomplished in the back of each notebook.

Hull noted that the children were obviously familiar with this routine and got on with their work comfortably and without confusion. His description of a third year junior school class, moreover, provides an insight into the effect that Sealey had already wrought in receptive schools, noting the balance-beams, strips and squares, triangles, trapezia and pegboards, all of which were in use, as children explored the mysteries of multiplication and approached quadratic equations, the source for which, Hull noted, was Z.P. Dienes' *Building up Mathematics*.[34] He also remarked on the presence of other visitors in the classroom in addition to himself, which adds weight to the assertion by one retired headmaster that Leicestershire was a much visited authority even before the Americans found it,[35] and the fact that headmasters spent far more time in the classroom than their American equivalents. In fact, he recognized the support and involvement of headteachers as crucial to the success of these innovative ventures, being particularly impressed by one headteacher who had taken over the mathematics teaching of a group of children in order to allow their teacher time to gain confidence in the use of the new materials.

More than anything else, however, as already noted, he was impressed by, and also unprepared for, the experience of seeing large numbers of children using the materials, not in independent schools, as he had already in America, but in state schools. Two-thirds of the two hundred or so schools in the county, he affirmed, were using some of Dienes' materials, a remarkable achievement, the main impetus for which had come from Dienes and Sealey and, he might have added, indirectly from a Director of Education who positively welcomed new ideas.

There is neither need nor space to elaborate any further on what was going on in the Leicestershire infant and junior schools.

The visible transformation was remarkable. People came to see them not only from the United States but also from both sides of the Iron Curtain. It was in America, however, that the greatest impact was made.

Hull returned to England in 1964, bringing with him a colleague, David Armington, intrigued by what Hull had described as a 'mind-blowing experience', and on their return to the USA they spread the news that they had seen progressive education in action in state schools. It was not always perfectly executed, and some of the teachers were not sure whether they were happy with the new methods. Nevertheless, the quietness of the classrooms, and the children's unforced industry combined with their freedom to move and talk with each other, commanded their unreserved admiration, and convinced them both that there was something to be learned from the Leicestershire experience. On their return to America Hull wrote another paper entitled *Leicestershire Re-visited* which, although initially unpublished, later appeared, in 1971, in C.H. Rathbone's *Open Education: the informal classroom*.[36]

Its immediate impact, however, was upon the sympathizers with progressive education in the United States. These two papers, together with Joseph Featherstone's three articles collectively entitled 'The Primary School Revolution in Britain' and published in August and September 1967 in *The New Republic*,[37] created something of an explosion in American interest in England. Not only did it lead to the setting up of summer vacation workshops on which Leicestershire teachers and their colleagues from the West Riding and Oxfordshire worked, but it also led to the recruitment of L.G.W. Sealey as director of the Regional Educational Laboratory Programme in the United States. When the Follow Through programme, which succeeded the Headstart compensatory education programme in 1968, set up a series of models of school organization which local school districts could opt for, Sealey, prompted by Hull, managed to persuade the Educational Development Centre (EDC), the American educational powerhouse based at Newton, Massachusetts, to sponsor one based on what the US office of Education called 'the English Infant School Model', a name which was eventually changed to 'Open Education' by the EDC staff.[38] With David Armington as its director and Rosemary Williams (soon to become Mrs Armington), whose school, Hinckley Westfield Infants School, was one of two featured in Featherstone's articles, as a key adviser, the Open Education model inevitably bore the stamp of Leicestershire.

All this activity reached a crescendo first at the time that Stewart Mason retired in 1971. By that time the influence of the primary school in Leicestershire had intruded into the secondary sphere, sometimes by means of promoting primary school heads to headships of secondary schools, and by the deliberate design of school buildings.

Mason struck up a highly productive partnership with the County Architect, Tom Collins, with the result that Leicestershire shared in the post-war architectural revolution in primary school design. Always looking to do something exciting, Mason and Collins alighted in 1960, in their vision of the future, on the design of Rolleston Infants School, Glen Parva, where corridors were completely eliminated, the over-riding concept being not the individual class, but the 'family of classes', each with its own cloakroom, lavatories and small work space. Rolleston, he wrote in *In Our Experience,* is 'a school not of nine classes, but of three families of classes'. Moreover, it was the first infant school in Leicestershire in which a library was deliberately provided.[39]

The infant school, Mason emphasized in *In Our Experience*, has been the incubator of so many of the progressive practices that have infiltrated other parts of the school system 'What we can see and feel is good for elevens can, with modifications', he urged, 'scarcely be bad for twelves and thirteens.'[40] Eventually, in response to the Ministry's reduced cost limits per place, Mason and Collins, not without controversy, arrived at the open-plan school, yet it was not this model but the family of classrooms grouped around a resource area, the latter being a revolutionized library of anything up to 950 square feet, which was to be the medium through which the primary school influenced the Leicestershire secondary schools. The prototype of this idea appeared in 1966 at Bushloe High School, Wigston, in the form of a first-year unit of four classrooms grouped around a resource area, reaching its complete form in Oadby Manor High School two years later which, in the opinion of E.D. Smith, Collins' deputy, represented the culmination of twenty years' collaboration between Mason and Collins.[41] With its four groups of four classrooms, each complete with their own common workspace, toilets, cloakrooms and entrance, grouped around a large central resource area, the school was in reality an amalgam of three primary schools. As Caroline Nicholson pointed out in the *Weekend Telegraph* of 9 December 1966, it was a 'school without classes', most of the light coming from the roof, and consequently allowing an incredibly high degree of concentration of teaching and activity space.

Finally, this concept of concentrated teaching space in close proximity to a vast resource area was repeated in the early 1970s in the designs of the community colleges at Countesthorpe and Wreake Valley, thereby extending the influence of the primary school throughout the secondary age range.[42]

Stewart Mason retired at the end of a career, the latter part of which coincided with a remarkable period of educational expansion and progressivism in this country. Already, however, with the publication in 1969 of the first of the Black Papers,[43] the reaction against what was considered to be the deleterious effect of the progressive primary school on the national ethos had set in. This was followed in the mid-seventies by the 'back to basics' movement, signalled by Prime Minister James Callaghan's Ruskin College speech in 1976. Since then, Brian Simon, from the diametrically-opposed end of the political spectrum to the Black Paper writers, has attacked the whole concept of 'readiness' and emphasis on the individual, which governs the organization of the modern primary school, as divisive and inimical to the successful implementation of a form of education which is truly comprehensive.[44] Meanwhile, the research findings of the ORACLE project at Leicester University have cast doubt upon whether, from a pedagogical point of veiw at least, any revolution at all has taken place in the primary school.[45]

Such criticisms and qualifications carry much weight. Stewart Mason, however, looking in retrospect over a lifetime in education, was in no doubt about the progress that had been achieved. In an undated talk to teachers given in the mid-sixties entitled 'The changing face of the primary school', he described the scene twenty-five years previously when, as an HMI in Cambridgeshire he had gazed at the serried ranks of children seated at ironframed desks built for two, four, and sometimes eight children, and more often than not screwed to the floor. As he explained, in such a situation the teacher was the chief, perhaps the only centre of interest, and the whole class at any one moment was doing the same thing. Now, he argued, the teacher's role had changed to that of facilitator and adviser. By far the most significant change, however, was the place occupied by the library in the primary school. 'Children today move freely in and out of the classroom, bringing reference books from the library, the whole trend being to get the children to discover for themselves ... more attention being given to the differing pace and interests of each child.'[46] The individual was supreme.

As for the difficulties created in the comprehensive secondary school by such practices, as alleged by Brian Simon, Mason would have been unrepentant. After all, in his view the secondary school was merely an extension of that most marvellous of all educational creations, the infant school. If secondary schools could only be organized like infant schools, as he deliberately planned them to be in Leicestershire, the problem would never arise. Diversity was a virtue to be catered for by the extended primary school.

Notes

1. The full title of the report, compiled by the CENTRAL ADVISORY COUNCIL FOR EDUCATION, is *Children and their Primary Schools.* It was published by Her Majesty's Stationery Office in 1967 and is considered to mark the high point of progressivism in education in England and Wales.
2. See the report of the CONSULTATIVE COMMITTEE TO THE BOARD OF EDUCATION, *Infant and Nursery Schools* (Hadow Report 1933), pp. 1–46.
3. *Ibid.*
4. Quoted, *ibid*, p. 22.
5. Quoted, *ibid*, pp. 22–23.
6. *Ibid.*
7. BOARD EDUCATION, (1905), *Reports on Children Under Five Years of Age*, London, HMSO.
8. For an account of inter-war developments in primary education see SELLECK, R.J.W. (1972), *English Primary Education and the Progressives*, London, Routledge and Kegan Paul.
9. These developments are fully explored by WHITBREAD, N. (1972), in *The Evolution of the Nursery-Infant School 1800–1970*, London, Routledge and Kegan Paul.
10. CONSULTATIVE COMMITTEE OF THE BOARD OF EDUCATION, (1933), *Hadow Report*, London, HMSO.
11. WHITBREAD, *op. cit.*
12. The information on Stewart Carlton Mason, CBE, Director of Education for Leicestershire 1947–71, was supplied by Mr Mason in a series of recorded conversations with the writer between 1981 and his death in 1983. They are referred to below as 'Conversation with SCM'.
13. Information received in a recorded conversation with Alec and Vicky Stanley, respectively a retired headmaster and retired assistant teacher in junior and infant schools, 11 July 1983.
14. *Ibid.*
15. Recorded conversation with Philip Sherwood, formerly Headmaster of Burbage Junior School, Leicestershire, 12 November 1981.
16. Conversation with Isobel Irons, formerly headmistress of Blaby Infants School.
17. *Ibid.*
18. *Ibid.*
19. SELLECK, *op. cit.*

20. Recorded conversation with the late Marjorie Kay, formerly adviser for infant education in Leicestershire, 7 March 1982.
21. Information received in conversation from Mary Brown, Headmistress of Sherrard Primary School, Melton Mowbray, 5 February 1982.
22. Recorded conversation with David and Rosemary Armington (née Williams), 21 April 1981. Rosemary Armington was formerly Head-mistress of Westfield Infants School, Hinckley.
23. Conversation with MARJORIE KAY, *loc. cit.*
24. Conversation with ROSEMARY and DAVID ARMINGTON, *loc. cit.*
25. For the impact of the Dalton Plan in England see SELLECK, *op. cit.*
26. Conversation with PHILIP N. SHERWOOD, *loc. cit.*
27. Information received by letter from L.G.W. Sealey, 8 September 1983.
28. Conversation with S.C.M.
29. Information received in conversation with W.E. BROWSE, Adviser for Primary Education, Leicestershire Education Authority, 3 July 1983.
30. Information received in conversation with J.S.FRIIS, Adviser for Mathematics, Leicestershire Education Authority, 18 August 1986.
31. Conversation with W.E. BROWSE, *loc. cit.*
32. *Ibid.*
33. The following account is taken from W.P. Hull's unpublished paper, (1961) 'A visit to the Leicestershire Schools', a copy of which is in the author's possession.
34. *Ibid.*
35. SHERWOOD, P.N. *loc. cit.*
36. HULL, W.P. (1971) 'Leicestershire revisited', in RATHBONE, C.H. (Ed.), *Open Education: the informal classroom*, New York Scholarly Book Service.
37. Joseph Featherstone's three papers were published in *The New Republic* of August 10, September 2 and September 9, 1967, under the titles 'Schools for Children', 'How Children Learn' and 'Teaching children to think'.
38. Information contained in a transcript of a recorded conversation between Rosemary Armington, David Armington, Sara Hull, W.P. Hull and Edward Yeomans who was formerly Academic Director of the National Association of Independent Schools.
39. MASON, S.C. (Ed.) (1970), *In Our Experience*, London.
40. *Ibid*, pp. 5–6.
41. Recorded conversation with E.D. Smith, formerly Deputy County Architect, Leicestershire County Council, 6 July 1983.
42. MASON, *op. cit.*, p. 7.
43. COX, C.B. and DYSON A.E. (1969), *Fight for Education: a Black Paper*, London, Critical Quarterly Society.
44. SIMON, B. (1982) 'Why no pedagogy in England?', in SIMON, B. and TAYLOR, N. (Eds.)', *Education in the 80s: the Central Issues*, London, Batstone.
45. GALTON, M., SIMON, B., and CROLL, P. (1982), *Inside the Primary Classroom*, London, Routledge and Kegan Paul.
46. MASON, S.C. 'The changing face of the primary school', notes of an address delivered to teachers in the mid-1960s. Undated copy in the Mason papers.

Open Plan Schooling:
Last Stand of the Progressives?

Peter Cunningham

Introduction

'After the walls came tumbling down' was the sensational headline to a newspaper report of an unsensational national conference in 1984 celebrating twenty-five years of open-plan schooling.[1] 'Open-plan' is an emotive term. 'Open schooling' is often synonymous in use with 'informal teaching' or 'progressivism'. At the most general level of discourse, 'open-plan' schools are the outward sign of inward change, and are identified with what is supposedly 'new', 'unfamiliar' and somehow challenging to the traditional order. Pedagogy and building form are interwoven in both the professional and the public mind; Lowe (1979) has referred to the fact that 'society's image of 'schooling' was moulded by the buildings in which the process took place', and has pointed to the need for further investigation of this phenomenon.[2] Researching 'society's image' of schooling might entail investigation of popular reactions to school and school buildings, along the lines of Stephen Humphries' recent work on school refusal, or in a different way, Edward Blishen's exploration of children's ideals in *The School that I'd Like*.[3] The present chapter is concerned with professional discourse which constitutes one element of 'society's image', and draws on appropriate documentary sources for the advocacy of, and opposition to 'open-plan'.

Classroom research has made clear that an automatic association of 'open-plan' with 'progressive schooling' is misconceived, for however the detailed conclusions of Bennett and ORACLE may differ and be debated, the undisputed fact is that great varieties and mixtures of teaching methods are experienced in most classrooms. Moreover, in the strictly architectural sense of the ordering of space, 'open-plan' can incorporate wide variations in structure and internal organization. This point is well brought out in two recent issues of the *Times Educational Supplement*, where skilled sub-editors have exploited the emotiveness of the visual image. In one, an account critical of 'open-plan' classrooms was accompanied by a large picture, a curiously haunting image of endless space divided rigidly into rectangular 'sheep-pens' by bookshelves (most of them empty), the teachers' desks much in evidence and one in the foreground well loaded with sets of texbooks, children apparently much distracted — one holding up his hand for attention. In April, heading an account of Berkshire's enthusiasm for open-plan are pictures of children seemingly engrossed in their activity, including two boys working at an ironing board.[4]

Such images are not trivial. They are the visual slogans that inform debate even in the serious professional press. Their power reinforces and extends Lowe's point that buildings carry meanings. School buildings must be understood not only in terms of aesthetics, structure and function, but also as cultural symbols.[5]

The relationship of architectural provision to ideology and to practice is complex, and this short chapter can begin to explore only a few of the many themes which call out for study. Open plan schools were not simply the vehicle for a different form of classroom organization, even though research has tended to concentrate on this aspect: in designing open plan schools there was, for example, the ideal of an aesthetic classroom environment, traceable to particular Victorian sources; another feature was the response to certain curricular emphases and to various pedagogical and environmental factors; then there was also the growth of reaction within the profession against open-plan. Where previous studies have drawn largely on 'official' sources, such as Building Bulletins and Ministry publications, the study of professional discourse requires reference to a wider variety of 'unofficial' sources.[6]

Classroom Environment as a Pedagogical Concern

An exploration of the complex relationship between architectural form, ideology and practice in the primary school, should begin by considering how the quality of environment emerged as a pedagogical concern. For the period following 1945, this will require a look at inherited ideals, for some of these environmental ideals had a considerable history, too easily forgotten in current debate.

Edward Thring, whose centenary is celebrated in 1987, is of

particular significance to the post 1945 generation since he was so frequently invoked by one of the most influential promoters of innovation in primary schools, Sir Alec Clegg, Chief Education Officer in the West Riding of Yorkshire from 1945–1974. Clegg had a good sense of history; the first decennial review of educational development in the West Riding was laced with quotations from the seventeenth century schoolmaster, Charles Hoole, and in embellishing the second decennial report, Clegg turned to Thring, whom he also quoted in a number of other contexts.[7] Clegg's father and grandfather had both been teachers, and would doubtless have encountered in their professional lives the writings of Thring, as these had for many years been regarded as standard works.[8]

Heading a chapter on school cleaning (which a superficial eye might mistake for the most trivial administrative detail), Clegg cited the great Victorian headmaster:

> Another grave cause of evil is the dishonour shown to the place in which the work is done. Things are allowed to be left about, and not put away when finished with, great roughness is permitted in the treatment of the room and its furniture. Yet there is no law more absolutely certain than that mean treatment produces mean ideas, and whatever men honour, they give honour to outwardly. It is a grievous wrong not to show honour to lessons, and the place where lessons are given.[9]

In his collection of primary school teachers' writings, Clegg again quoted Thring on the condition of buildings:

> Unfortunately when all has been said, the conditions under which the work has to be done affect the possibility of doing the work.[10]

Victorian sources for careful attention to the school environment are also relevant when studying the influential work of Robin Tanner, HMI and professional artist. Tanner's contribution of primary education has been lyrically celebrated by W. van der Eyken, especially his encouragement of arts and crafts in the primary school curriculum.[11] His intense interest in arts and crafts, in the design of useful artefacts, extended to a concern for the quality of the classroom environment and its influence on children's work. In both respects his ideals were drawn from the principles of William Morris, the great Victorian craftsman and socialist. Robin Tanner was born less than a decade after the death of Morris, and his own father

was a craftsman in wood. As a young schoolteacher at Ivy Lane
School, in Chippenham, during the 1930s he was not far distant
from the home of William Morris at Kelmscott Manor in the neighbouring county of Oxfordshire, and he followed the spirit of Morris
in encouraging his pupils to improve and beautify the classroom.
Dusty ornaments and old photographs were thrown out and replaced with good pots and the children's own paintings, the var-
nished desks were scraped with pieces of glass to reveal their grain
and the natural texture of the wood, and walls were decorated with
murals designed and executed by the children themselves.[12]

In his later work as an HMI Robin Tanner deployed much
energy and ingenuity drawing teachers' attention to the importance
of the classroom environment and advising on techniques for improvement. This was effected through national HMI courses at
centres such as Dartington Hall, chosen with the consent of the
Elmhirsts for the beauty of its environment. But Tanner had a
particular influence in Oxfordshire after his appointment as HMI
for that area in 1956. Here he found a fellow spirit in Edith Moorhouse, the Senior Primary Adviser, who has described the work
which she undertook brightening the interiors of primary classrooms in the 1950s.[13] The well documented new open-plan schools
drew much professional attention, but an important part of the
building programme in a 'progressive' rural county such as Oxfordshire was the creation of open-plan environments within old
buildings by the demolition of interior walls and the building of
extensions.[14]

One device which had singular impact in Oxfordshire schools
was Robin Tanner's introduction of corrugated card, which could
be used to model space and as a background, and could make the
meanest classroom rather good. He used it at Dartington and introduced it to Oxfordshire in 1956, putting up displays of children's
work.[15]

So Thring (through Clegg) and Morris (through Tanner) were
powerful sources of influence regarding interest in the environment
of the primary classroom. In their common intellectual world loom-
ed the figure of John Ruskin. By contrast with the very active
engagement of Thring the schoolmaster and Morris the craftsman,
Ruskin's was a life devoted more exclusively to writing and to social
criticism, and therefore less of a direct inspiration to innovators
in primary education, yet in the context of primary school building
it would be mistaken to underestimate his stature as a source of
principles concerning the 'morality of architecture'. David and Mary

Medd were Ministry of Education architects who exerted considerable influence in the building of post-war primary schools; the
application of the 'Arts and Crafts' principle of 'truth to materials'
informed their work, for instance in seeking to

> express the inherent quality of materials within the physical
> environment of the classroom: the woodiness of wood, the
> whiteness of white, and the softness of a carpet.[16]

This Ruskinian principle has recently been described by one
architectural historian as

> the transference of the principle of human morality to inani-
> mate objects ... on the grounds that because man should
> not tell a lie, buildings should not.[17]

Architectural Response to Curricular, Pedagogical and Environmental Factors

Educational development cannot be explained simply by tracing
back a lineage of thinkers. There must also be current circumstances
which promote innovation. Seaborne (1971) has related the changing
architectural form of the primary school to some of the developments in pedagogy, but there were three aspects of the curriculum
in particular which focused attention on the school environment,
namely arts and crafts, movement and nature study. In practical
terms, these three curriculum areas made demands on space and
environment which resulted in characteristic features of the new
primary schools.

Arts and crafts began to assume a central part in the curriculum
for many primary school teachers. Exhibitions in England of children's art produced under the tutelage of Cizek from 1921 encouraged widespread acceptance of the value of child art and of the view
that children were artists in their own right, and Marion Richardson's conviction of the importance of children's self-expression received ever wider recognition through her work as an art inspector
for the London County Council (LCC), her exhibition of children's
drawings at County Hall in 1938, and her publications.[18]

It followed from identifying the creative spirit which lay, often
dormant, in every child that good paintings could not be produced
to order, as had often formerly been required, on a Friday afternoon
when all desks had been cleared and buckets of water introduced

into the classroom. Spontaneous creativity required access to facilities at most times of the school day, so a 'dedicated' area, with piped water and a floor suitable for wet activity was called for. In at least one Oxfordshire school, this became known as the 'studio', indicating the seriousness with which the children's painting and clay-modelling were regarded. Furthermore, the 'craft' philosophy demanded access to specialized tools and equipment, for the making of books and printing designs on paper or fabric, and the timescale of craft whereby an object is worked over a considerable period, required a space where work in progress could be safely left. Thus some new schools, such as Eynsham in Oxfordshire where Robin Tanner's influence ran particularly strong, had a craft studio for printing with oil-based inks, quite distinct from the painting studio or wet area. A considerable degree of open-planning was a natural consequence of this specialist provision; space limits required the sharing of such facilities between more than one class, and small groups of children working in these areas had to remain reasonably accessible to the teacher.

John Blackie HMI was an assessor to the Plowden Committee and an eloquent advocate of 'child-centredness'; in his view this approach had emerged earliest in art and physical education.[19] 'Physical Education' changed both its name and its nature under the influence of Rudolf Laban, the German emigré, and some of his notable followers, such as Lisa Ullman who ran the Art of Movement studio in Manchester (recognized by the Ministry of Education for one-year courses for women), and Diana Jordan, an adviser in that most progressive of local education authorities, the West Riding, and author of *Children and Movement*. Alec Clegg had met Laban when working as Deputy Education Officer in Worcestershire, and was instrumental in bringing Diana Jordan to work in the West Riding.

Where art and craft might be pursued by individuals and small groups, 'movement' made different demands. This was seen as a class activity. In fact the tradition of school assemblies and of physical exercise through drill had already established the large hall as a central feature of elementary schools. But the introduction of apparatus to encourage a more varied and creative approach required additional flexibility, and the expressive elements of dance and drama brought aesthetic criteria to bear on this space, that it might provide a sympathetic and inspiring environment. The Ministry's *Building Bulletins* referred to the hall as an extension of normal working space in which the natural energy of young children was to find an outlet in such activities as swinging, jumping and climbing, and as the centre of life in the school, it should maintain a welcoming atmosphere. Children's growth through movement was not seen as confined to formal lesson time, so that the external environment of the school had to provide appropriate facilities for use at 'playtimes'. The traditional asphalt yard was replaced by more irregular areas of lawn and hard surfaces for wet weather, in the best instances landscaped to provide a variety of spaces, and furnished with apparatus for scrambling and climbing.

Nature study was a third important focus of the curriculum with architectural implications. In the 'progressive' scheme of things, nature study had a special significance; for the Froebelians, who were an influential force in the 1950s, it was a means to understanding the unity of creation. The arguments for it were eloquently expressed in a Froebel Foundation pamphlet:

> Let us first think what country children have that is denied to their town cousins. Country children grow up in an environment of farms and gardens where there is birth, life, death, life re-born year in, year out in a wealth of examples ... the whole seasonal rhythm of nature that mirrors the rhythm of life itself.
>
> This, in its wholeness, is not experienced by the city child. We cannot recreate it in the classroom, but we must seek whatever instance we can to illustrate this cycle of life ... to develop an appreciation of the beauty, purposefulness and slow sureness of natural growth.[20]

However, the author emphasized that nature study in town schools was not to be a poor imitation of that which was possible in a village school, but something rich and beautiful in its own way. Children must *do* nature, and not just listen to or watch programmes; the example was given of a school within sight of Big Ben which used window boxes, tubs, sink gardens, a bomb-site, and visits to park, zoo or country. Therefore the exterior space had also to respond to the curricular demands of nature study. Country schools had often enjoyed gardens where 'rural studies' were considered appropriate for 'rural children', but nature study for all children, and especially the urban child, required that living things, plants and even animals, should be accommodated in the school environment. The inclusion of such work within a flexible curriculum also suggested a more flexible interaction between inside and outside than implied by the solid exterior wall.[21]

Other pedagogical developments than these curriculum innovations also drew attention to the school environment. Relationships between home and school received increasing attention in educational theory as a result of sociological research in the 1950s into the distribution of educational opportunity. A classic text in this respect was the longitudinal study by the Medical Research Unit under the direction of J.W.B. Douglas[22], and the problems identified were acknowledged by compensatory policies proposed in the Plowden Report published three years later. In more subtle ways, however, the regimes of home and school were already beginning to overlap in the 1950s. The relationship of the teacher towards her pupils was increasingly stressed as one of love, an interesting new twist given to the doctrine of *in loco parentis*, and arising from the attention paid to maternal affection as an important factor in children's early development.[23] Boys and girls were officially acknowledged to need

> the security and support of a home and the affectionate care of adults whom they trust. Throughout school-days the teacher shares with parents this place of importance in a child's life.[24]

The changing relationship was not simply one of compensating for 'inadequate' homes, but also of attempting to establish a sense of continuity and greater harmony between the school environment and that of the home. With increasing prosperity and growth of the consumer industry after the post-war economic recovery, improved standards of child-care and home comfort were to some extent two aspects of a single phenomenon.

This changing relationship between school and home was perhaps epitomized by the use of carpets in school, an innovation in domesticating and softening the school environment. In 1965 an article in *The Times* entitled 'Carpeted floors throughout the home — and in the schoolroom' illustrated the fitted carpets in an infants' school in Saffron Walden, and referred to the statistic that three out every five bedrooms were now fully carpeted. The intention at Saffron Walden was

> to provide a quiet home-like floor covering which, so the experts say, is going to have an effect on the behaviour pattern of children between 5 and 7.[25]

In 1967 the Midland Region of the BBC thought it sufficiently newsworthy to make a feature of a carpeted school.[26] The salient innovations in carpet technology had been the use of wool and

nylon mixtures, and Eveline Lowe school in London, a project by
the DES Architects and Building Branch Development Group, was
used for experimental purposes, different qualities of carpet being
applied to different areas. The *Building Bulletin* revealed however
that traditional institutional asceticism was not to be totally abandoned, as the carpet fibres were to undergo a special hardening,
noticeable only to touch and not to sight, in order to achieve

> the effect of removing an excessive sense of softness and
> luxury which may, in some circumstances, seem inap-
> propriate.[27]

Technical developments played an important part in improvement of the physical environment in schools. Early twentieth century pioneers of child-centredness, had laid emphasis on the need
for physical comfort and good health as a necessary prerequisite to
sound intellectual and emotional growth in the child, and it may
be seen as a natural extension of the school health services and school
meals that close attention was paid to the lighting and heating of
schools. In the period after 1945, the application of the minimum
daylight factor (applying at first only to schools) was one example
of such development. Attention to the aural environment was
another, whereby developments in furnishing, flooring and ceiling
materials such as acoustic tiles, and the application of sound absor-
bent materials to walls, reduced the sources of noise and the level of
reverberation, thus diminishing some of the environmental discom-
forts that might otherwise have followed from open-planning.

In practice, of course, mistakes were made in such experimental
conditions. For example the application of the daylight factor sometimes led to over-large windows and resulted in 'flat' lighting and
overheating in summer. Also designers of schools had to be on
guard against the blinkering effect of technology. As the Medds put
it:

> Education needs to resist the pressures of the engineers of
> interior space who would have our buildings offer all protec-
> tion and no connection. The buzz of the fan, the hum and
> flicker of the fluorescent light, are no compensation for the
> sound of the wind or the flickers of passing light and
> shadow.[28]

What underlay this statement may be interpreted as an unresolved tension between on the one hand, the aesthetic criteria
already referred to, which were highly traditional, and on the other,

the technical innovations which were incorporated into contemporary building. Unit building methods such as those adopted by the consortia were in conflict with the traditional 'arts and crafts' ideals which were upheld by the educational innovators. At Eynsham in Oxfordshire, some compromise was reached by the incorporation of a high-quality hand-made brick at various points, which was left exposed on internal surfaces as well as on the exterior. There was wooden weatherboarding too, which was troublesome to maintain and which rotted within fifteen years, to be replaced with a plastic facsimile. The flat roofs and glass expanses of the same building testify to the continued predominance of the 'international style' which had its roots in the Bauhaus, in an age of mechanized building. Of the visual deterioration of primary school environments, Manning noted in 1967 features such as pattern staining and leaks in flat roofs:

> Some deterioration is inevitable, for building is in a transitional stage between craft and industrialization, and it is in the nature of change and experimentation that there should be failure.[29]

The design of Eveline Lowe School had probably dealt with this problem more successfully than many, with its pitched roofs and pine interiors.

A tension between building and pedagogical ideals is tellingly illustrated in Chris Jarman's book on display.[30] An Oxfordshire primary adviser from 1874 to 1980 who as a young teacher had come under the influence of Robin Tanner, Jarman reflected the ideals to be found in that county whereby

> Good display and presentation can act as a focus for the whole activity of the school.
>
> We may not be able to do much about the structure of the building, but we can still do a great deal to make our working environment artistically useful.[31]

Two illustrations in Jarman's book reveal teachers masking off expanses of glass wall to provide a more intimate space for display. Corrugated card, introduced originally for the purposes of improving the dreary environments created by Victorian forebears, was now being used to soften the harshness of modern architecture and to allow the children and teacher to exert their influence on an environment otherwise imposed by the architect.[32]

Doubts and Discontents

The problematic nature of innovatory building forms was unconsciously reflected in the tendency of some teachers to reduce the
scale of teaching spaces and to screen off areas, but doubts about
open plan also emerged in other professional quarters.

The enthusiasm and support for open plan schools and for the
work of the Ministry's Development Group is well documented,
but reservations within the professions of architecture and education
were being expressed as early as 1967. In considering reactions
against open-plan schools in this context, it must be emphasized that
the present chapter is more concerned with the nature of the discourse than with the validity of different positions.

The architect Peter Manning concluded from his research project that the high reputation of English primary school architecture
had been earned by a small proportion of untypical schools and
levelled the criticism that:

> the purpose and function of primary schools are nowhere
> adequately defined — at least, not in a form usable by
> designers — and it is therefore virtually impossible to
> appraise the performance of a particular school building
> against objective criteria.[33]

The lack of objective criteria was a challenge also issued to the
Plowden Report, and the continuing problem of identifying such
remains high on the agenda of measuring school effectiveness in the
1980s. As for the style and content of the *Building Bulletins*, it is
true that no. 16 (1958) deliberately eschewed traditional analysis in
favour of a more narrative description of the Development Group's
own discoveries:

> It is not a memorandum on the planning of junior schools,
> and it gives no standard recipes or schedules of accommoda-
> tion. It merely tries to describe how the clients and designers
> tackled the problem, the questions they found themselves
> asking . . . The aim of the designers was to look more deeply
> into educational requirements than time usually permits.[34]

Maclure has cited the 'impressionistic reporting of new methods'[35]
of this particular *Bulletin*, and no. 36 (1967) on Eveline Lowe
Primary School was similarly coloured by enthusiastic descriptions
of informal learning, but it is fair to comment that these, like the

earlier Bulletins on primary schools, included also a great deal of technical data and commonsense application, such as basic anthropometric research on appropriate furniture sizes for young children.

Another criticism of the Development Group voiced by Manning concerned their failure to appraise designs after a few years' use. Perhaps the group took this criticism to heart as a later *Building Bulletin* was dedicated to the appraisal of Eveline Lowe School, after four years of use.[36] Manning felt, perhaps a little unjustly, that the Development Group neglected their responsibility to some extent in failing to communicate educational philosophies and trends to architects generally, with little over thirty-six Bulletins in twenty years and insufficient coverage in the architectural press. Such neglect, he considered, gave rise to the danger of

> . . . substitution of new fashions for old. The forms are copied, though the educational reasons for them may not be understood very adequately . . .[37]

Despite the influential voices of certain individual HMI such as John Blackie and Eric Pearson,[38] in favour of the new school architecture, a report from HMI in 1972 based on a survey of fifty-three open plan primary schools, though it acknowledged the benefits for children, teachers and communities, also entered a number of reservations. Some teachers with experience of other systems had found difficulty in adjusting, and some schools were deserting the important pastoral responsibility of one teacher for each child.[39] Above all good planning and careful monitoring were seen to be essential and despite the excellent tone of the great majority of schools visited, the sound work and curricular variety that was widely apparent,

> Nevertheless some children were working at less than capacity. This happened both in the schools where the children were allowed considerable freedom and those where they were allowed little.[40]

HMI referred to one class where one third of the children queued idly to await their turn with an occupied teacher.

> In another school, busy teachers, lacking the advantage of the greater detachment of HMI, failed to note the 6 year old girl who neatly packed her books together and moved off to another area when any one of the teaching team approached her; she did about 15 minutes work in a morning. So did the

two 8 year-old boys who took nearly two hours to write out first every 6th and then every 7th number up to 99. Another 7 year-old, standing in the middle of a shared teaching space saying 'There is so much to choose from I don't know what to do' was giving a clear indication that too much was being expected of her powers of organization.[41]

With these cautionary notes, the conclusion of the survey was measured in tone. It was felt that the schools visited met the teachers' needs 'reasonably well'. Equally important, the teachers were generally able to choose their own organizational patterns and teaching methods 'without being unduly inhibited by the design of the building'. Clearly the question of building form was not yet settled, for HMI hoped that their research would contribute to 'the continuing search for the most suitable conditions for the education of children of primary school age'.[42] The HMI survey of primary schools undertaken between 1975 and 1978 found that one-tenth of the classes in their sample of 542 schools were accommodated in open or semi-open working spaces. In one-fifth of the classses conditions inhibited the range of work, and the most common shortcoming in these cases was lack of space. Recommendations were made for the use of spare rooms as school rolls fell, but the problem of proper supervision was acknowledged where accommodation was based on individual classrooms.[43]

The National Union of Teachers had provided a considerable quantity of professional comment on primary school building since 1945, and a report published by th Union in 1974 offered valuable documentation of professional teacher reaction to open planning, cautiously welcoming some of the principles involved but seeking at the same time to safeguard the teachers' professional independence. Focusing on a fundamental conflict of interest, the report opened by drawing attention to the danger of open-plan schools being imposed from above, whereas the Union had constantly upheld the view that curriculum and internal organization were matters for the teachers.

> The Union regards it as one of its major responsibilities to protect the traditional rights of teachers to exercise their judgment in the fields of organization, curriculum and method, in freedom from outside dictation.[44]

Their claim that HMI, the DES, LEAs, governors and managers had always paid due regard to this principle lacked a little in historical accuracy and was even more poignant coming only two years before the saga of the DES Yellow Book, Jim Callaghan's Ruskin speech and a new campaign against teacher autonomy.

Explicitly, the Union committed itself to no opinion on the organizational and curricular merits of open planning. Implicitly, the tone of the report was favourable to many aspects, although in resisting the imposition on its members of a particular educational method, it noted that this was one still untested and whose effects were not yet known.[45] As if to reinforce their claim for teacher autonomy, the document emphasized that 'open planning' was essentially a philosophy rather than a building form, and moreover, in an educational system that had evolved by adaptation and experiment the concept of open planning and its execution had been pioneered by individual teachers following their own pedagogical or educational needs. Open planning was not a new or unique phenomenon but part of the continuing spectrum of teaching method and educational philosophy. Teachers in primary and even before that in elementary schools had always struggled to expand their curriculum from the somewhat arid necessities of the three Rs, and even while the selection system exerted its influence many schools had worked towards integrating the curriculum.[46]

An inevitable consequence of this argument was the demand for teacher consultation in planning new schools. Such consultation had been minimal and sporadic in practice as a survey of LEAs, attached to the report, revealed. The Union had, long before, succeeded in convincing a House of Commons Committee of the need for local authorities to set up panels of teachers to assist with the planning of new school buildings, but very few LEAs had responded.[47] Admitting the legal responsibility of the local authority to provide, and to determine the general character of schools, the report appealed to the tradition of leaving internal organization and matters of curriculum and method to its teachers. It followed logically that the profession ought to be consulted early in the process of designing a school building.

Further consequences of professional autonomy included the need to consider the training, experience and knowledge of teachers required to work in open plan schools, and ultimately, a respect for their convictions. More appropriate initial training had to be developed, more in-service opportunities were required to facilitate transfer to new methods and new situations. In particular, team teaching, though not synonymous with open-plan schooling, was frequently a feature and required adaptation of professional skills.

For the purposes of its report, the Union conducted a survey of teacher opinion through its local associations. Particular concerns and reservations are of interest in revealing some common concerns expressed about open-planning. Teachers with experience of formal classrooms found the output of visible work very much less in the open-plan school, leading to possible interpretation by parents as lack of progress. Noise level was a factor which clearly concerned teachers, over half of the local associations stressing the need for really quiet areas, and one teacher referring to possible exhausting effects of noise, although no member of the Working Party responsible for the report had felt that noise levels were unacceptable or even perceptible as a separate factor. More mental strain on teachers was another factor.

High pupil-staff ratios and overcrowding were considered to militate against successful open-plan operation and there was a concern that open plans were produced merely to reduce costs. Some local associations felt that there was no substitute for the enthusiastic teacher whatever the type of school building and that any direction of teachers into methods in which they lacked faith would be a retrograde step. A flexible environment rather than rigid open-plan was considered by some more suitable for a child-centred approach, and interestingly one or two replies considered that open-plan building was a passing phase, so that child-centred education would develop in the future in a more traditional type of building.

Conclusion

In the period of Plowden it might have seemed that 'the almighty wall' had indeed been demolished. The Plowden Report itself made much of Eveline Lowe school and by 1967 one quarter of all primary schools in the country were housed in post-war buildings, but as we have seen from the HMI Survey, in 1975 only one tenth of their sample were open-plan classrooms. Jericho had not fallen, after all. Nor had the New Jerusalem arrived. The pace of change in educational building is bound by its nature to be gradual, and the decentralized nature of the British educational system results in a great variety of building forms.

Yet the open-plan school, however various its realization, appeared to symbolize certain approaches to education such as integration of the curriculum, a stress on activity, and some freedom of choice for the child. Some architects, as we have seen, were concerned that the environmental consequences were insufficiently monitored; HMI worried about the possibilities of children escaping the notice of their teachers; teachers as a profession saw the limits which architects and administrators might be placing on their professional autonomy. In the climate engendered by the debacle of William Tyndale, the open-plan school stood as an outward symbol of the curriculum and teaching methods that might be pursued inside; ironically, and perhaps not insignificantly, the William Tyndale School itself was housed in an old Victorian building. In the Schools Council study published in 1980 it was implied that historians have to choose simply between finance and pedagogy as the salient factors in the introduction of open-plan schools.[48] Yet the truth is much more complex as a particular architectural form acquired so many meanings in the context of professional debate.

Notes

1. HAGEDORN, J. (1984), 'After the walls came tumbling down' in *Education Guardian*, 8 May.
2. LOWE, R.A. (1979), 'Studying school architecture' in *Westminster Studies in Education* v. 2, p. 47.
3. HUMPHRIES, S. (1984), *Hooligans and Rebels*, Blackwell; BLISHEN, E. (1969), *The School that I'd Like*, Penguin.
4. *TES* (1986) 14 February and 25 April.
5. MANNING, P. (1967), *The primary school: an environment for education*, Liverpool, Pilkington Research Unit p. 59 noted that the 'cultural significance' of the primary school, as well the social consequences of its design, are incalculable, as the young people using it are at such an impressionable age of development.
6. Acknowledgment must be made to three pioneering accounts of school architecture in this period: SEABORNE, M. (1971), *Primary School Design*, Routledge and Kegan Paul, SEABORNE, M. and LOWE, R. (1977), *The English School, its Architecture and Organization*, Routledge and Kegan Paul, and MACLURE, J.S. (1984), *Educational Development and School Building: Aspects of Public Policy 1945–1973*, Longman. Each in its own way has provided a clear account of the main lines of development in primary school building, and has placed these developments in an administrative context, drawing largely on official sources. SEABORNE, M. (1971), has additionally drawn attention to some of the changes in pedagogical theory which encouraged developments in architectural form, and to the reactions of some teachers to new school buildings.
7. Goldsmiths' College. n.d. (1974) *The changing school, a challenge to the teacher*, Report of a one-day conference.
8. CLEGG, A.B. (1980), *About our schools*, Blackwell, p. vii.
9. WEST RIDING EDUCATION AUTHORITY (1964) *Education 1954–64*, p. 72.

10. CLEGG, A.B. (1972), *The Changing Primary School,* London, Chatto and Windus, p. 90.
11. VAN DER EYKEN, W. (1969), *Adventures in Education,* Allen Lane, pp. 103–24.
12. Illustrated in VAN DER EYKEN (1969), *op. cit.* A collection of the children's original paintings is preserved by Wiltshire local education authority.
13. MOORHOUSE, E. (1985), *A personal story of Oxfordshire primary schools* (privately printed), pp. 37–47, 127–35.
14. For examples see MINISTRY OF EDUCATION, (1961), *Building Bulletin* no. 3 2nd ed., 'Village Schools'.
15. Robin Tanner in conversation with author, June 1986.
16. MEDD, D. and MEDD, M. (1972), in *Designing Primary Schools.* London, National Froebel Foundation, p. 11.
17. WATKIN, D. (1977), *Morality and Architecture,* Oxford, Clarendon press, p. 38.
18. CARLINE, R. (1968), *Draw they Must,* Edward Arnold, pp. 158–173; RICHARDSON, M. (1948), *Art and the Child,* University of London Press.
19. BLACKIE, J. (1967), *Inside the Primary School,* HMSO, p. 8.
20. HUTCHINSON, M.M. (1961), *Practical Nature Study in Town Schools,* National Froebel Foundation, p. 1.
21. It is not without significance that the *Building Bulletin* which described the development of the Eveline Lowe School in London, emphasized the desire of the architects to incorporate the qualities of the village school within the city. DES (1967), *Building Bulletin* no. 36, p. 3.
22. DOUGLAS, J.W.B. (1964), *The Home and the School, a Study of Ability and Attainment in the Primary School,* Macgibbon and Kee.
23. As an index of prevailing interests and ideas, John Bowlby's *Child Care and the Growth of Love,* first published by Penguin in 1953, was reprinted in 1955, 1957, 1959, 1961, 1963 (twice), before the appearance of the second edition in 1965, which was then reprinted almost annually until 1974. A fashionable account of teaching published in 1960 was Francesca Enns' *All My Children,* Hamish Hamilton, which revealed a concern for the emotional development of the children in her class, and their inter-personal relationships.
24. MINISTRY OF EDUCATION, (1959), *Primary Education, Suggestions for the Consideration of Teachers and Others Concerned with the Work of Primary schools,* HMSO, p. 23.
25. *The Times,* 20 November 1965.
26. 17 April 1947 *Midlands Today:* interview with headmaster of Wigston Primary School 'which is open-plan and has fitted carpets throughout'.
27. DES, (1967), *op cit.* para. 99.
28. MEDD, D. and MEDD, M. (1972), *op. cit.,* p. 10.
29. MANNING, P. (1967), *The Primary School, an Environment for Education,* Pilkington Research Unit, University of Liverpool Department of Architecture, p. 24.

30. JARMAN, C. (1976), *Display and Presentation in Schools* 2nd ed. A. and C. Black, (1st ed. 1972).
31. JARMAN, C. (1976), *op. cit.*, p. 5.
32. JARMAN, C. (1976), *op. cit.*, pp. 11, 24.
33. MANNING, P. (1967), *op. cit.*, p. 15.
34. MINISTRY OF EDUCATION, (1958), *Building Bulletin* no. 16, p. 8.
35. MACLURE, J.S. (1984), *op. cit.*, p. 129.
36. DES, (1972), *Building Bulletin* no. 47.
37. MANNING, P. (1967) *op. cit.*, pp. 21, 64.
38. BLACKIE, J. (1967), *op. cit.*, pp. 12–14; PEARSON, E. (1972), 'Trends in School Design', in *British Primary Schools Today: Vol. 2*, Macmillan.
39. DES, (1972), *Open Plan Primary Schools, Education Survey* no. 16, pp. 2, 4.
40. DES, (1972), *op. cit.*, p. 11.
41. DES, (1972), *op. cit.*, p. 11.
42. DES, (1972), *op. cit.*, p. 15.
43. DES, (1978), *Primary education in England, a survey by HMI*, HMSO, pp. 9, 110.
44. NUT, (1974) *Open Planning, a Report with Special Reference to Primary Schools*. London, National Union of Teachers, para. 36.
45. NUT, (1974), *op. cit.*, para. 21.
46. NUT, (1974), *op. cit.*, paras. 4, 7, 11.
47. House of Commons Select Committee on Estimates, 1952–53 (186) v, para. 43 and Recommendation 11, was reiterated by the same committee ten years later, 1960–61 (284) vi, para. 50 and Recommendation 19. The Minister's less than enthusiastic response to this recommendation was reported in the Second Special Report from the Estimates Committee, 1961–62 (17) v.
48. BENNETT, N. and others (1980) *Open plan schools*, NFER for Schools Council, p. 27.

The Plowden Philosophy in Retrospect

R.F. Dearden

The Plowden Report, published in 1967 in two volumes, was the product of three years of deliberation by the Central Advisory Council for Education (England).[1] Two such central advisory councils (CACs), one for England and one for Wales, were established by section four of the 1944 Act, to replace the previous Board of Education Consultative Committees. The Act apparently envisaged standing committees, but in the 1960s at least the CACs were *ad hoc* committees. Four years prior to the publication of the Plowden Report, which was actually entitled *Children and their Primary Schools,* there had appeared the Newsom Report, entitled *Half Our Future.* This was also a product of the CAC, but the two sittings had only Sir John Newsom as a common member. In 1967 the CAC for Wales produced *Primary Education in Wales* under the chairmanship of Professor C.E. Gittins, after whom that report became known, just as *Children and their Primary Schools* became known by the name of its CAC chairman Lady Bridget Plowden.

The duty of the CACs was very broadly defined as being 'to advise the Minister upon such matters connected with educational theory and practice as they think fit, and upon any questions referred to them by him.' And broad indeed were the terms of reference of the Plowden Committee: 'to consider primary education in all its aspects, and the transition to secondary education'. Volume One, as distinct from the tables of data constitutive of Volume Two, was very comprehensive. It ran to thirty-two chapters in nine parts, 555 pages and 197 recommendations. One looks back with nostalgia at the then resented price for Volume One of twenty-five shillings (£1.25), perhaps after just having paid £24 for the 1985 Swann Report. Incredulity increases when one recalls that the earlier CAC

Newsom Report, *Half Our Future,* had a cover price of eight shillings and sixpence (42½p).

On no fewer than twenty-one occasions the Plowden Committee looked back appreciatively to the three reports of 1926, 1931 and 1933 produced by the earlier Consultative Committee of the Board of Education under the chairmanship of Sir Henry Hadow, and especially to the 1931 report *The Primary School,* with its famous statement of curricular principle that the curriculum should be thought of 'in terms of activity and experience rather than knowledge to be acquired and facts to be stored'.[2] Though the Plowden primary schools are often thought of in terms of a 'revolution', and indeed the Report itself uses that term in one place (para. 739), nevertheless the Report saw what was happening in the 1960s as the fulfilment of Hadow rather than something totally novel.

The Report was called for by Sir Edward Boyle in 1963 but by the time that it was presented both minister and government had changed. Thus it was Anthony Crosland who in November 1966 expressed his gratitude to the Committee. While not actually saying that he welcomed the Report he did say, non-committally, that it would be studied with great care and that it would enable more informed decisions to be made. It is reasonable to suppose that he was somewhat preoccupied with his Circular 10/65 (12 July 1965) calling for the submission of plans for the full introduction of comprehensive secondary education. In this connection it is interesting to recall that the last of the six possible patterns for comprehensive reorganization listed in Circular 10/65 referred to middle schools, whether 8–12 or 9–13. These had been made possible by section one of the 1964 Education Act. They were not a new concept distinctive of the Plowden Report though it endorsed them, especially in the 8–12 variant, in its chapter on the ages and stages of primary education.

Upon publication in January 1967, Lady Plowden became spokesman for the Report. Something of the sense of excitement which surrounded its completion can be gathered from Lady Plowden's foreword to a little book called *Inside the Primary School,* also published by HMSO in 1967 and written by HMI J. Blackie, himself an assessor on the Committee. She wrote 'there has been a great wind of change in the primary schools since most of the adults of today were primary school children and many of the old beliefs have been blown away'.[3] A revolution was evidently under way comparable to the decolonization of Africa. But although Lady Plowden became spokesman for the Report, according to Kogan she did not herself draft any of the chapters, though she made her own decisions on the range and style of the Report.[4]

Although the Report refers to a 'recognizable philosophy of education' that was emerging as a quickening trend, only 109 schools in the fully approved first of nine possible categories had been identified. Almost the last sentence of the Report was that 'our review is a report of progress and a spur to more' (para. 1233). How far the revolution was promised rather than actual may be judged by the reported facts that in 1962 only 4 per cent of junior schools had rejected streaming and 85 per cent of teachers still favoured it. This was directly at variance with the Report's strong advocacy of the individualization of teaching. Another relevant contemporary fact was that the primary schools were short of 20,000 teachers, in spite of a great expansion in college places, and very many teachers were inexperienced. However, England was still thought of as an affluent society and the preoccupation with vocational preparation which was to become so pervasive in the 1980s was still to come. The Report comments, for example, upon the 'increased diversity of occupations available to school leavers' (para. 735).

The Report's vision of the future as it should affect children at school is a curious and even contradictory one. Paragraph 494 is worth quoting in full:

> One obvious purpose is to fit children for the society into which they will grow up. To do this successfully it is necessary to predict what that society will be like. It will certainly be one marked by rapid and far reaching economic and social change. It is likely to be richer than now, with even more choice of goods, with tastes dominated by majorities and with more leisure for all; more people will be called upon to change their occupation.

Yet within the same short chapter on aims the apparently contradictory claim is made that a school 'is a community in which children learn to live first and foremost as children and not as future adults'. The school, it is said, sets out 'to allow them to be themselves and to develop in the way and at the pace appropriate to them' (para. 505). Contrast this with the 1985 White Paper *Better Schools,* which urges that 'it is vital that schools should always remember that preparation for working life is one of their principal functions.'[5] A desperate but ultimately doomed attempt to reconcile these two strands in the chapter on aims might be found in seeing the vocational view as a failure 'to understand the best preparation for being a happy and useful man or woman is to live fully as a child' (para. 506).

Herself looking back on the Report after ten years, Lady Plowden identified four main themes in it.[6] First was the importance of the early years, upon which she reported some success especially with the establishment of playgroups. The second was the importance of treating each child as an individual, because individual differences are so great. Third was multiple deprivation and the embodiment of 'positive discrimination' in the concept of an 'educational priority area'. On this she found that the stimulus and the vision had vanished. Fourth was the bringing of home and school into closer partnership, and here she reported that schools had indeed become more open to parents.

There were many other themes in the Report, of course, such as the stillborn proposal to institute 'teacher aides' and the much more successful recommendation to establish middle schools, though it seems likely that these were introduced more as an economical way of introducing comprehensivization within exisiting buildings than for any of the educational arguments that were put forward (falling rolls are now putting this policy into reverse, again for economic reasons). But the aspect of this most wide-ranging report that I would like to focus upon is its 'recognizable philosophy of education'. What was it? What happened to it? Does anything of it survive in the flood of documents on the curriculum which since 1977 has issued from HMI and DES? By 'philosophy', of course, is not meant anything like academic philosophy, or even philosophy of education as it was then practised as one of the 'foundation disciplines'. All that is meant is the general principles or overarching conception which govern some practical enterprise.

A Recognizable Philosophy of Education

I take the essence of a school to be that it is a set of arrangements for learning to take place under the guidance of teachers. Two questions which therefore have a certain priority over many others that could also be asked are concerned with what is going to be learned and how the process of learning is going to be guided. As to the first question, Plowden may seem initially obscure, principally because the Report constantly reiterates that knowledge does not fall into rigidly separate compartments. In spite of that, however, chapter seventeen discusses aspects of the curriculum under eleven fairly conventional subject headings. But the most direct answer to the question of what the children are to learn is that they are to learn whatever is involved in developing their intrinsic interests. But this does not imply the complete withdrawal of the teacher or his or her reduction merely to the role of minder. The teacher has vital functions to perform in setting up the school environment, in choosing locations out of school to visit and in selecting materials and books for use not only in developing interests but also in stimulating them. 'From the start', we are told, 'there must be teaching as well as learning' (para. 754) for children are not free to develop interests of which they have no knowledge.

Certain passages do, if taken out of context, give the impression that the teacher's role is rather minimal. For instance one of the 'danger signs' is that 'much time is spent on teaching', while elsewhere it is said that the teacher must 'lead from behind' and must follow up the interests of children 'who, either singly or in groups, follow divergent paths of discovery' (para. 544). But such things are also said as that the teacher must keep in mind potentials for further learning, must awaken interest in the passive or apathetic, must provide an environment which challenges but does not exceed the children's reach and he or she must focus enquiry on useful discovery. The teacher must secure a balance in learning, whether across the day or some longer period such as a week. A need for consolidation, practice and direct instruction is recognized, though only after conceptual understanding has been achieved (para. 530). It is recognized that discovery may be trivial and inefficient and that not all learning can wait upon it (para. 544). While the teacher should not help too soon, he or she should not leave children to flounder, and while readiness for new learning is important to judge, this can be left for too long as well as being too early (para. 534).

Sketches of such a school in progress are given in paragraphs 277–289. A typical scene is described in which a group of children, with their teacher, are:

> clustered round a large square box full of earth. The excitement is all about an earthworm, which none of the children had ever seen before. Their classroom door opens onto the playground and inside are the rest of the class, seated at tables disposed informally about the room, some reading books that they have themselves chosen from the copious shelves along the side of the room and some measuring the

quantities of water that different vessels will hold. (para. 279)

In another class:

> One group was gathered round their teacher for some extra reading practice, another was at work on an extraordinary structure of wood and metal which they said was a sputnik, a third was collecting a number of objects and testing them to find out which could be picked up by a magnet and two boys were at work on an immense painting (six feet by four feet) of St Michael defeating Satan. They seemed to be working harmoniously according to an unfolding rather than a preconceived plan. Conversation about the work that the children were doing went on all the time. (para. 287)

At the end of these descriptions the Report comments that 'in these schools, children's own interests direct their attention to many fields of knowledge and the teacher is alert to provide material, books or experience for the development of their ideas' (para. 289).

Though the phrase is nowhere used in the Report, these practices came to be known as the 'integrated day', the essential characteristic of which was that a variety of different activities went on simultaneously, without interruption by bells or timetables. Change of activity apparently took place spontaneously according to the natural flow of interests. The ideal was the complete individualization of learning, but the Report recognized that this would imply only some seven or eight minutes of teacher time per day for each child, so group work was recommended as an economical way of coping with this situation when individualization became too difficult. By contrast with this positive picture, there is an interesting list of 'danger signs': 'fragmented knowledge, creative work limited, much time spent on teaching, few questions from children, too many exercises, concentration on tests' (para. 503).

Plowden also contains comments on some recent preoccupations, such as the use of specialists, written guideliness and assessment. Specialist teaching on a secondary model is nowhere countenanced, though older pupils in middle schools might with benefit be treated as a large group for which two or three teachers share responsibility. The idea of the teacher expert, who can give advice to colleagues and help the Head draw up schemes of work, is present. There is said to be little place for guidelines which write down exactly what is to be covered or what skills are to be acquired, though brief schemes for the school as a whole which set out the course of development might be useful. Any statement of the final standards that might be hoped for was said to be inappropriate because it would not allow for individual differences, but there was some place for standardized tests, secondary school comparative feedback and HMI advice.

It is a curious fact that this 'recognizable philosophy' is no-where mentioned in the 197 formal recommendations. The four-page spread on the Report in the *Times Educational Supplement* mentioned this philosophy only in one paragraph and that was a quotation.[7] But it is implicitly recommended and indeed Part Five, which contains the main statement of it, was said to be 'the heart of the report'. As the animating spirit of the Report, perhaps it did not need formal and specific recommendation. Yet it was this animating spirit which caught the imagination of the educational world, attracting hostile criticism from some while others flocked in droves from distant parts of the world to see this new wonder. A degree of competitiveness even emerged as to who had had the most visitors. There even appeared the globetrotting head, carrying his winged message of revolution across the skies for brief educational insemi-nation in distant places.

What was the justification for this philosophy? That lay in chapter two, on the growth and development of children. The chapter opened with the by now well known statement that 'at the heart of the educational process lies the child. No advances in policy, no acquisitions of new equipment have their desired effect unless they are in harmony with the nature of the child, unless they are fundamentally acceptable to him' (para. 9). The implication of this is spelled out in the introduction to Part Six, on the role of the teacher: 'our study of children's development has emphasized the importance of maturation to learning. The corollary is not to make the teacher's role passive but to underline the importance of di-agnosing children's needs and potentialities' (para. 874).

Perhaps two main theses can be distinguished here. First is the claim that children develop at very varying rates along different lines of development. With this went a coupling of the idea of readiness with various observations on critical or sensitive periods for learning specific things. The implication of this was that 'individual differ-ences between children of the same age are so great that any class, however homogeneous it seems, must always be treated as a body of children needing individual and different attention'. Again, 'until a child is ready to take a particular step forward, it is a waste of time to try to teach him to take it' (para. 75).

The second main thesis was that children have a natural desire to learn, which shows itself in interest, curiosity and a desire to master their environment. Piaget's work on stages in cognitive development was appealed to here, though not in any simplistic or crude way. From this the conclusion was drawn that 'the great majority of primary school children can only learn efficiently from concrete situations, as lived or described' (para. 531). The two points combined in a requirement that there be abundant opportunities for interaction with concrete materials. Both this and the previous thesis were present in Froebel's teaching in *The Education of Man,* and arguably what was happening was that Froebelian thought forms were finding apparent confirmation in contemporary empirical research. Thus it was concluded that finding out has 'proved' to be better than being told and 'the child is the agent in his own learning' (para. 529). This justification is a psychological, if not a biological one. An early comment upon it from a psychologist, namely Brian Foss writing in Richard Peters' edited *Perspectives on Plowden,* was that it concentrated over much on the first five years of life with little attention to the social pressures of later years.[8] Foss also went so far as to say that the recommendations could have been made quite apart from reference to the psychological evidence. However, the theory did not seem to be much referred to in the propagation of the Plowden ideas which followed.

One interesting venture which followed publication of the Report, and which arose in part from the great American interest which was shown, was the joint Schools Council and Ford Foundation publication in 1971 of a series of twenty-three booklets. Under the general title *British Primary Schools Today,* they described many aspects of informal schooling and its implications for various curricular areas. Joseph Featherstone wrote a shrewd introductory booklet for the series in which he linked the primary 'revolution' with the open education movement in the USA, associated with such names as John Holt. Featherstone caught the essence of the Plowden philosophy rather well when he wrote that it involves 'an emphasis on active learning, and an engagement with materials; teaching starts with children's experiences and moves towards more disciplined effort; there is a stress on expressiveness and a variety of means of communicating knowledge, including the kind of knowledge we associate with the arts; and finally, work in one area of the curriculum spills over into other areas'.[9]

How widespread was the take-up of these ideas? Kogan and Packwood, writing in 1974, said that while the Report had achieved no great success in terms of immediate planning or social engineering, 'it undoubtedly refined and strengthened the liberating effects of progressive education in a large number of schools'.[10] But how large a number of schools? One answer to this came from Neville Bennett's book *Teaching Styles and Pupil Progress*. Though this work was university-based research which took place in the north-west of England, it rapidly came to be referred to as 'The Bennett Report'. It identified twelve distinct styles of primary teaching, the first two of which could be classed as Plowdenlike. Type one was described as teachers who 'favour integration of subject matter, and, unlike most other groups, allow pupil choice of work, whether undertaken individually or in groups. Most allow pupils choice of seating. Less than half curb movement and talk. Assessment in all its forms — tests, grading and homework — appears to be discouraged. Intrinsic motivation is favoured.'[11] Styles one and two accounted for only 17 per cent of the teachers in the survey. 25 per cent could, on the other hand, be described as 'formal', and the remaining 58 per cent were a mixture of styles.

But what was alarming to Plowden supporters in Bennett's work was not so much the restricted spread of the philosophy but the apparently adverse conclusions on its effectiveness in practice. With the exception of one very experienced informal teacher, the formal teachers' pupils produced superior scores on the chosen measures in such basics as reading, English and mathematics, and scores no worse than informal teachers in creative writing. In drawing his own conclusions on this, Bennett wrote that 'the central factor emerging from this study is that a degree of teacher direction is necessary, and that this direction needs to be carefully planned, and the learning experiences provided need to be clearly sequenced and structured'.[12] This was all music in the ears of those who had always rejected the Plowden philosophy. Criticisms of the findings and conduct of the research did little to dislodge the general impression that was created. It was a message that too many people were only waiting to hear. Another winged message thus sped across the skies.

Looking back after ten years, Lady Plowden herself had some interesting things to say about the reception of her committee's Report.[13] She began by commenting that although both Houses of Parliament had debated the Report, it had never been officially welcomed by any government. She took particular exception to those who equated the Report's philosophy with 'wild men of the left', thinking perhaps of those who took Tyndale to be typical of what was happening, though the Black Papers had also appeared by then. Lady Plowden identified two reasons for the faltering in the take-up of the Report's progressive or child-centred philosophy: first the inexperience of so many primary teachers due to the great expansion in numbers and the tendency for many women to leave after only about three years of service, and secondly the recognition, highlighted by James Callaghan's Ruskin speech, that we were moving into a tougher economic world in which progressive ideas might appear 'too soft'. She commented on this that technology must certainly find a place in the primary school, though the methods of learning should remain the same.

Plowdenism in Subsequent Documents

On 18 October 1976 the then Prime Minister James Callaghan called in his Ruskin speech for a public debate concerning standards in education. This speech was made against the background of a press critical of standards in the schools, and a declining economic situation. There were loudly voiced suspicions that basic areas of learning were being neglected, that the pupils were undisciplined and that the curriculum was out of touch with the real adult world, with much inclination to blame all this on 'progressivism'. But doubts concerning standards are importantly ambiguous. The concern may be that not enough pupils are reaching an agreed standard and that more should do so, or it may be that the criterion is itself wrong and needs to be altered. This ambiguity is clearly present in the 1985 White Paper *Better Schools*, which presses for a raising of standards in the first sense while denying that the objectives which even the best schools set themselves are 'always well matched with the demands of the modern world'.[14] Plowden wanted to see more schools accord with its conception of primary education, but what if this standard was itself open to objection, or was thought not in fact to be justified by the arguments given?

The official view was set out in the 1977 Green Paper *Education in Schools*. This commented that the primary schools had in recent years been transformed by a widening of the curriculum and by 'the rapid growth of the so-called "child-centred" approach'.[15] It fairly, if briefly, summarized this as taking advantage of each child's stage of development and of his interests and harnessing his natural enthusiasm for learning by his own efforts. It recognized that visitors had come from all over the world to see the 'primary school revolution'. But the qualification was then added that these methods called for careful planning of opportunities and monitoring of progress, whereas through inexperience many teachers drawn to these methods had not realized this. The result was a failure to achieve satisfactory results in the basic skills and a degeneration into lack of order and application. The challenge, then, was to restore rigour (this is not Keith Joseph's special word) 'without damaging the real benefits of the child-centred developments'.[16] What this was said principally to require was close attention to securing continuity and progression in work and especially safeguarding a protected core of certain skills.

In a general statement of aims which has remained substantially the same ever since, the Green Paper came closest to supporting child-centredness in its first aim: 'to help children develop lively, enquiring minds; giving them the ability to question and to argue rationally, and to apply themselves to tasks'.[17] Further aims were broadly liberal or vocational, or concerned with basic skills. Aim eight, on resources for the disadvantaged, was an odd one out, while aim five, on being taught to esteem the role of industry and commerce, was soon dropped, possibly as a result of criticisms that it smacked of indoctrination. 'Physical skills' were later somewhat incongruously added to aim one, but apart from those changes much the same list appears in the 1985 HMI document *The Curriculum from 5 to 16* and in the 1985 White Paper *Better Schools*.

In view of these developments, the 1978 HMI survey *Primary Education in England* was awaited with especial interest, though, owing to a dispute soon after publication, for a while copies became collectors' items. In broadest terms the survey found the schools for the junior range to be orderly places where a quiet working atmosphere obtained in most classes when it was needed. The basics were not neglected and, on the contrary, HMI began a long struggle to have it recognized that narrowing to some such 'protected core' was actually counter-productive. Interestingly, three quarters of teachers were found to use mainly didactic methods and only one in twenty to use mainly exploratory methods. About one fifth used an appropriate mixture of both.[18] Far from dismissing child-centredness, the survey complained of insufficient opportunity for children to incorporate ideas of their own or to make use of spontaneous incidents which arose. Pure Plowdenism emerged in such examples as the study of a meadow and capitalizing on a burst water main.[19] But the strongest pointers to action to emerge were that children were not being stretched enough, especially the more able, and that insufficient use was being made of the special curricular strengths of teachers. There was also an emphasis on securing structure and progression, which implicitly posed as a problem how this might be harmonized with Plowdenlike spontaneity.

The same uneasy alliance is to be found in the 1982 First School survey *Education 5 to 9*. Again more attention to planned progression is urged, but children are also described as learning from firsthand experiences relating to their interests and their surroundings, supported by books and other materials.[20] Schools are praised which achieve a balance between opportunities to find out for yourself and more formal teaching, and between work initiated by the teacher and work chosen by the children.[21] As with the 1978 survey, there is a drawing back from individualization of teaching and a drawing attention to the merits not only of groupwork but also of class teaching.

Other documents and papers on primary education have appeared in recent years, from both DES and HMI. Their aim is declared in *Better Schools* to be the raising of standards and securing the best possible return on the resources invested in education. What this means in practice is much greater control over teaching and learning. Teachers will be controlled by the more active curricular initiatives being taken by governors, LEAs and DES, as well as by assumed HMI expectations. Within their own schools they will be more controlled by calls for progression and continuity, since these will involve co-ordination across years and schools and with specialists. Objectives will need to be written down and schemes constructed.

This last requirement contrasts strongly with the HMI observation in Plowden that some of the most successful headteachers were least able to formulate their aims clearly and convincingly (para. 497). However, these two observations are not quite so contradictory as may at first appear, since the formulation and statement of aims is a skill distinct from having such aims ingredient in judgment born of much experience, or what Polanyi has called 'tacit knowledge'. A person may have knowledge at his fingertips without necessarily having it at the tip of his tongue.

Learning will be more controlled by Keith Joseph's modern quadrivium: breadth, balance, relevance, and differentiation. These are all formal criteria which do not themselves pick out any particular content. In relation to the primary stage, 'breadth' and 'balance' are generally taken to cover a rather traditional range of subjects, though with nature study developed into science and technology introduced. However, the important point is recognized that exclusive concentration on basic skills is counter-productive in relation to them. 'Differentiation' is not Plowden's individualization of learning, but securing a good match between a pre-planned curriculum and the diversity of abilities. Progression in work is much insisted upon, not only in basic areas of the curriculum but also in art, physical education and topic work.

Some hint of Plowdenlike notions remains. For example, *The Curriculum from 5 to 16* reminds its readers that active learning and firsthand experience are important and that work has been better matched to abilities by teachers who combine didactic and exploratory approaches.[22] *Better Schools* says that in about half of all classes pupils are given insufficient responsibility for pursuing their own enquiries and deciding how to tackle their work.[23] Whereas recent papers have given a broad impression of projecting some secondary teaching practices downwards, contrary to Plowden's projection of infant practices upwards, the following recommendation occurs in *The Curriculum 5 to 16*:

> secondary schools might more often try to adopt the exploratory styles of learning which are characteristic of good primary school practice. Children who have learnt to find information for themselves, to make judgments about the direction their work should take and to pursue an interesting line of enquiry as it presents itself, lose an important element of enjoyment and pleasure in their education if such opportunities are suddenly denied them. (para. 131)

Plowden's light is thus not completely extinguished, though there remain unresolved questions as to how this greater degree of control over teaching and learning can harmonize with spontaneity and opportunism. But we may still ask whether Plowden's was indeed a light after all, or was it an aberration? After all, never more than a minority substantially adopted Plowden's philosophy.

An Assessment

There is no doubt that, in one sense of 'could', many more could have followed Plowden than did. The formal freedom of schools in relation to curriculum and methods was made much more real by the disappearance of the 11+ test. The Plowden philosophy became as it were the official ideology, in that it was supported by HMIs and very vigorously encouraged by some LEA chief education officers. Some schools but not others in the same area adopted its practices, as did some teachers but not others within a single school. Indeed, reforming heads were advised by Plowden to watch and wait for their opportunity where staff were recalcitrant. Individual conviction of the merits of the Plowden philosophy, or else the lack of such conviction, must be part of the explanation.

A fundamental question is raised by Plowden's educational values. These were presented as being derivative from child development studies, now assumed to be putting on a firm empirical basis what had previously been recommended in a more intuitive way by a long line of educational reformers, especially Froebel. But psychological and indeed biological factors can never suffice to establish such values. If such factors are universally operative, then they must be compatible with the diversity of child-rearing practises which actually exists, so that no choice between those practises is uniquely indicated. If these factors are not universal, then they are relative to a particular preferred ideal, which preference needs to be supported. The point can in fact be illustrated from Plowden itself, for when commenting on ethnic minorities and their problems the Report says that, though many of the children are eager to learn, 'this eagerness sometimes proves an embarrassment when it is for the disciplined book learning and formal instruction of their own culture and when the language barrier prevents the school explaining fully to parents the different way we go about education in England, (para. 183).' But, quite apart from ethnic minorities, there existed amongst many teachers and parents educational values different from Plowden's. Examples would include the place which should be given to the future in what we do now, and authority relations between adults and children.

The relative neglect of social factors was quickly noted by sociologists. Bernstein and Davies commented that the Report ignored the variety of home backgrounds from which children come and the differing parental understandings which exist of what the school is trying to do.[24] A later sociological study of a would-be Plowden school detailed the ways in which differing parental perceptions frustrated the school's philosophy.[25] In 'Mapledene School', as in the Report itself, such resistance was seen as pathological and not as stemming from alternative value-systems. The Report speaks of violent, unloving and broken homes as the standard case of deviance from its norm (para. 741), whereas at 'Mapledene' it was precisely caring parents who resisted the school and who taught their children at home, as it were to compensate for what was perceived as a poor school background. They valued something different. It must be said, however, that one of the strong themes in the Report was that the school should attempt to win the cooperation of parents in what it is setting out to do.

There were also some difficulties in accepting the Report's assertion that 'finding out has proved to be better for children than being told' (para. 1233). Discovery methods permit very different degrees of structuring and guidance, and their suitability depends not only on learners' expectations and teachers' skills but also on the nature of what is to be discovered. Children can discover a great deal, even in the freest situations, but not certain kinds of knowledge. Particular difficulties are raised by things which are true only by a set of social conventions, such as linguistic truths. French accordingly posed a particular problem for Plowden's approach to learning. Religious education presented other sorts of difficulty, in the end theological, for a discovery approach. The Report was very lukewarm about French, and in religion it solved the difficulty in its experiential approach in terms of 'getting faith established', a didacticism which produced notes of reservation.

Other problems affect discovery possibilities even in such apparently favourable cases as mathematics and science. Discoveries can indeed be made here, but some of them need genius, or at the least an imaginative theory, if they are to be made. Increasingly for the older children, who are advancing further into subject knowledge, awareness of a whole set of concepts and principles may be necessary even to see the problem let alone discover its solution. The idea of providing a structured environment to stimulate discovery works well enough at the level of relatively superficial properties, but teacher-led discussion and instruction become increasingly necessary the further you penetrate into a subject. Another feature which emerges with such penetration is that knowledge, as opposed simply to information, requires the recognition of some degree of separateness in the kinds of thing that can count as evidence, explanation or justification. Plowden's insistence that knowledge does not fall into rigidly separate compartments misses an important point here by taking its position to a simplistic extreme.

A further difficulty for many teachers was undoubtedly that of classroom management. How was one to cope with thirty pupils all following divergent paths of discovery, and developing at different rates, not only compared with each other but also between different facets of themselves? How was one in this situation to maintain a balance in learning over a day or week, or to ensure that enquiry led to worthwhile discovery, and all very often within an overcrowded classroom? Sharp and Green concluded that the Plowden teacher could be 'successful' only by producing a quite unmanageable situation.[26] The ORACLE Project, which ran from 1975 to 1980 and which produced much more detailed empirical sketches of teacher behaviour than had Bennett, concluded that 'given contemporary class sizes, the Plowden "progressive" ideology, based essentially on individualization, is impractical; and, we would claim, our data bear this out beyond question'.[27] Plowden teaching, they found, hardly exists in practice. They found individualized teaching, but it was 'factual and managerial'. Exploratory work, leading to discovery, went on in the course of class teaching, not individual work. This was quite the reverse of Plowden's prescriptions. ORACLE also found that although groupwork was apparently practised, as Plowden had recommended, it was individual and not collaborative work that took place in the group.

An unresolved problem to which I have already referred concerns the harmonizing of planning and spontaneity. The ideal learning situation, according to Plowden, is one in which apparently spontaneous interests arise which the teacher then artfully develops in profitable directions. Indeed his art has already been exercised in setting up a situation which will make more likely the emergence of interest. One can see this working with the youngest children, but with developing knowledge there are going to come difficulties of presupposed understanding and the emergence of problems at an appropriate level of difficulty. This runs back to difficulties already mentioned over discovery methods.

The Report did itself recognize that its recommended approach presented great demands for teachers. It needed teachers 'of great personal qualities, strong character and a deep understanding of children, and it also needs first rate organization' (para. 739). After a survey of the way in which a Plowden child would learn, it says that 'the demands made on teachers have appeared frighteningly high' (para. 875). Then did it make sense, especially at a time when there was a very high proportion of inexperienced teachers in the primary schools, to have as the key requirement of the recommended practice teachers of superb quality? Some there were. They were to be found in 109 schools (para. 270).

Conclusion

It would seem, then, that both theoretical and practical objections to Plowden would account for much of the reluctance to adopt its prescriptions in anything like their pure form. What remains of the Plowden 'philosophy' then? How much has been found to be acceptable and has been integrated into the evolving tradition of primary practice? As was noted earlier, the Committee did to a considerable extent give endorsement to many trends which were already spontaneously developing in the schools anyway. And many of these trends can stand independently of Plowden's justification or pure doctrine. These trends were probably due to no single cause so much as the going of the 11+ examination. For with the demise of the 11+ came mixed ability classes and a freeing of the curriculum. This put strong pressure on a move towards some variant of the integrated day, or at least some form of group work, simply because the teacher could not simultaneously cope with a teacher-demanding activity being engaged in by a wide diversity of pupils all at once.

Other changes also found favour. Classrooms became much more colourful places as more time was found for creative work. Topic work flourished, though sometimes for no better reason than that it kept children engrossed while the teacher attended to something else, or left the room. The contribution of educational publishers to making possible some of these changes also deserves note. Teacher-pupil relationships became more relaxed and friendly, though not merely permissive, and parents became more welcome in schools. Plowden's ideal of the individualization of work and of artful opportunism may have proved practical only for a few paragons, but something of the spirit of Plowden has found a permanent place.

But arguably Plowden had a more important, more elusive, effect than these discrete endorsements of emerging trends alone would suggest. Prior to Plowden, primary education had been in many ways the Cinderella of the education service. Especially under the 11+ it was very much orientated towards and subservient to the purposes of secondary education. But now were not visitors coming from abroad just to view primary education and to learn from it? What they expected to see and what they actually learned from it may be a matter for conjecture, but this attention did much for the sense of pride and the self-confidence of primary teachers. Certain educational values were finding embodiment in primary practice in a way that secondary schools themselves might profitably emulate. Cinderella was beginning to find a voice of her own.

Notes

1. CENTRAL ADVISORY COUNCIL FOR EDUCATION (ENGLAND), (1967), *Children and their Primary Schools, Vol. 1 Report, Vol. 2: Research and Surveys*, London, HMSO.
2. CONSULTATIVE COMMITTEE OF THE BOARD OF EDUCATION, (1931), *The Primary School*, London, HMSO.
3. BLACKIE, J. (1967), *Inside the Primary School*, London, HMSO.
4. KOGAN, M. and PACKWOOD, T. (1974), *Advisory Councils and Committees in Education*, London, Routledge and Kegan Paul.
5. DES (1985), *Better Schools*, London, HMSO.
6. PLOWDEN, LADY B. (1977), 'Recurring themes' in *Education 3–13*, 5, 2, pp. 27–30.
7. *Times Educational Supplement*, (1967), 'Plowden on primary schools', 13 January, pp. 97–100.
8. FOSS, B. (1969), 'Other aspects of child psychology', in PETERS, R.S. (Ed.) *Perspectives on Plowden*, London, Routledge and Kegan Paul.
9. FEATHERSTONE, J. (1971), *Introduction* to the series *British Primary Schools Today*, London, Macmillan.
10. KOGAN, M. and PACKWOOD, T. (1974), *Advisory Councils and Committees in Education*, London, Routledge and Kegan Paul.
11. BENNETT, N. (1976), *Teaching Styles and Pupil Progress*, London, Open Books.
12. *Ibid.*, p. 162.
13. PLOWDEN, LADY B. (1977), 'A decade of Plowden', in *Times Educational Supplement*, 14 January, pp. 17–8.
14. DES (1985), *Better Schools*, London, HMSO.
15. DES (1977), *Education in Schools*, London, HMSO.
16. *Ibid.*, para. 2.3.
17. *Ibid.*, para. 1.19.
18. DES (1978), *Primary Education in England*, London, HMSO.
19. *Ibid.*, para. 3.22–3.
20. DES (1982), *Education 5 to 9*, London, HMSO.
21. *Ibid.*, para. 3.11.
22. DES (1985), *The Curriculum from 5 to 16*, London, HMSO.
23. DES (1985), *Better Schools*, London, HMSO.
24. BERNSTEIN, B. and DAVIES, B. (1969), 'Some sociological comments on Plowden', in PETERS, R.S. *Perspectives on Plowden*, London, Routledge and Kegan Paul.
25. SHARP, R. and GREEN, A. (1975), *Education and Social Control*, London, Routledge and Kegan Paul.
26. *Ibid.*, Ch. 6.
27. GALTON, M. *et al.*, (1980), *Inside the Primary Classroom*, London, Routledge and Kegan Paul.

Training the Teachers: The Colleges of Education and the Expansion of Primary Schooling

Joan D. Browne

McNair and the Institute System

Following the recommendations of the McNair Committee, 1944,[1] the training of teachers was organized through Institutes of Education, attached to universities, from 1947–1975. This succinct and far-seeing report condemned the parsimony with which many colleges were equipped and run, and the cramped nature of the two-year course into which personal and professional education had to be squeezed. It recognized several fundamental problems, such as the narrow parameters of student recruitment from low birthrates and limited opportunities for secondary education, and difficulties of staffing where both academic standing and appropriate school experience were required. In its scrutiny of the curriculum a distinction was made between professional and 'general subjects' for the students' personal equipment but the hope was expressed that staff would be able to weave a seamless coat for student wear — not a very easy garment to design in practice. A generous injection of resources, a three year course of training, including a continuous term's practice in school were the proposed remedies on which all members agreed.

Unanimity was not reached in the report as to the exact form of the university connection but by 1951, of the sixteen Area Training Organisations set up, thirteen gave a central responsibility to the Institute of Education within the university, with representation to local authorities, voluntary bodies, the organized teaching profession and the training institutions, including colleges of Art and Music where they had training programmes. HMI had a watching brief but no longer had any part in the assessment of teaching.[2]

The McNair plans were well received by the professionals, the authorities, and the educational press, and with some misgivings by universities, but their doubts lay dormant under the enthusiasm of college and Institute staff. The new organization seemed to fit into the post-war determination to improve the lot of ordinary people and the prospects of their children and to back up with a unified training programme the implementation of the 1944 Act which aimed at putting an end to the two systems of education, elementary and secondary. Few believed that it would be an easy task to make the post-war dream a reality, but it was in the primary school that success seemed most likely.

The pattern of studies in the colleges attached to Institutes of Education differed in detail but always comprised the Principles and Practice of Education, including teaching practice, the study of one or two main subjects, and a range of professional studies usually including, for primary students, the teaching of number, reading and English, physical education, arts and crafts, and Religious Education with a conscience clause.

The Principles and Practice of Education was based on the study of developmental psychology and was supported by visits to notable schools and by special studies of individual children. The work of a particular group, the infant or junior group, would be in the hands of an education tutor who would also be responsible for the teaching of reading and preparation for experimental work such as centres of interest. A historian might be called in to deal with the recent history of education and its connection with social change while a tutor with a philosophical turn of mind might assist with the exploration of individual and social goals, but the age of the specialist in educational disciplines had not dawned.

The main subjects were described as being for the personal education of the student and aimed at notions of excellence and the creation of habits of independent study. They were not confined to the age range of the children to be taught but the needs of the schools played a part in the selection of topics to be covered, and in some instances grouped courses such as environmental studies or a combination of the arts introduced intending primary teachers to novel combinations and methods. It was not implied that educational studies did not contribute to personal education as it was well understood that it might be in contact with children that students would mature most rapidly.

In view of later misgivings[3] about the status of the studies related to the school curriculum it would be true to say that their somewhat disconnected nature was recognized and tutors were concerned at the time taken in a short course, in filling in deficiencies in the students' own knowledge, but the brevity of the two year course was held responsible for these shortcomings and there was little demand for less time to be spent on main subjects or on education.

While only a few Institutes started journals or promoted research in the early days, all set up libraries for the use of teachers, held conferences, and participated in in-service training by offering courses, some award-bearing. These Advanced Diploma courses, open to teachers and teacher trainers on a whole or part-time basis, could be followed by a higher degree, in some cases open to non-graduates, making it possible for the first time for experienced primary teachers to take a university backed qualification with professional relevance. Previously the only qualification open to those aiming at teacher training was the Froebel Trainers' Diploma, which was and continued to be a valued qualification, but even the venerable name of Froebel did not carry the university's undoubted cachet. Many who took Advanced Diplomas and MEds entered training work, but even if they did not, they tended to become sympathetic to ideas current in training institutions at the time.

These are usually described as progressive education[4] but although its advocates in the state system knew of the private progressive schools such as Summerhill or the Malting House School, practice in the colleges owed more to the Hadow Reports of 1931 and 1932, with their emphasis on 'activity and experience'. It also had its roots in Froebelianism, particularly in its belief in the importance of play as the foundation of learning. The potential of children in the ordinary schools was to be fostered by allowing them more freedom for individual development, including artistic development, than they had hitherto experienced. It aimed at giving all children, as the White Paper preceding the 1944 Act had put it 'a happier childhood' but the rest of the sentence 'a better start in life' was held to entail mornings devoted to the tool subjects, the basic skills, essential to life and the 11+.

There is evidence to show that there was common ground between the more advanced teachers in the schools and teacher trainers in the late forties and fifties. It can be seen in subjects offered for dissertations, in journals started under Institute auspices, and in college syllabuses. In the papers set for the Diploma in Child Psychology of the University of Birmingham,[5] the preoccupations of the first ten years of Institute life were mental measurement, attainment testing, backwardness in the basic subjects, activity methods, the exploration of the environment, assessment and cumulative records, children's vocabulary, personality factors, studies of perception applied to the teaching of reading and towards the end of the fifties studies of Piaget, and also of the relation of learning difficulties to social deprivation. A similar list, couched in simpler and more practical terms appears in syllabuses and papers for initial training and formed the basis for students' special studies. Similarly, the first ten years of the Education Review[6] deals with the same subjects with the addition of descriptive articles on activity methods, and on work in drama, art and movement and in environmental studies emanating from schools and colleges.

It was possible to find schools in most areas where some aspect of progressive work could be seen in action, or where tutors and students, anxious to start up some project, would at least be tolerated, but conditions for the regular school practice of 110–20 half days, enjoined in most Institutes, were not ideal. The schools were at the sharp end of the problems that arose from shortage conditions after the war and the beginning of the birthrate bulge, so that often books and apparatus for teaching of number and reading on an individual basis were not available and even space was in short supply.

If the schools were suffering from a glut of pupils, a dearth of candidates for training was the problem of the colleges who found themselves drawing on the low birthrate of the thirties, with limited pre-war secondary education, especially for girls, and wider post-war opportunities for employment for women. Insufficient candidates came forward with either the old School Certificate or the five O levels deemed to be the minimum standard of entry in the new General Certificate of Education established in 1951. It was possible to put up cases for special admission to the ATO, a practice rightly opposed by the Teachers' Unions where school leavers were concerned, but which brought in a large number of mature students, generally married women, many of them excellent recruits, academically and personally, who rapidly climbed the promotion ladder to become Heads of infant and junior schools, sympathetic to new methods.

The first attempt to deal with the post-war teacher shortage was by the one year emergency scheme for teachers from the Forces[7] and many local education authorities who had maintained colleges for the first time under that scheme were encouraged to continue. McNair had shown that of the eighty-three recognized training colleges, fifty-four belonged to voluntary bodies and twenty-nine were provided by LEAs. The majority were small in size. In 1938 twenty-eight had fewer than 150 students and twenty-eight had less than 100.[8] By 1950, thirty-four new colleges had been founded, thirty for women, though many became co-educational later, situated in stately homes, former war-time hostels, or hotels; they were larger in size than most established colleges and were all provided by LEAs. The transformation of the system had begun.

Questions of Supply

The institutions that train primary teachers are particularly vulnerable to demographic factors, as changes in the birthrate are felt first in the primary schools, and as the majority of the teachers are women, social trends such as early marriage and childbirth, or attitudes to birth control have the maximum effect. The supply of women teachers was a main concern of the first report of the National Advisory Council for the Training and Supply of Teachers, NACTST,[9] set up in 1949 and which played a crucial role in its early years in the expansion of the colleges and the establishment of the three year course. Some improvements in grant, in staying-on in the sixth form, in methods of selection, and conditions of service, together with the increased output from the new colleges began to take effect, so that from the mid-fifties the profession appeared to be growing at a rate of over 5000 a year. The NACTST, under its Chairman, Sir Philip Morris, recommended the adoption of a three year course,[10] as envisaged by McNair and advocated unceasingly since 1938 by the Association of Teachers in Colleges and Departments of Education, ATCDE. The main arguments were educational but a supplementary reason was the belief that unemployment among teachers would result if the course was not lengthened. Hardly had the Minister agreed, in June 1957, to adopt the recommendation to implement the three year course in 1960, than the wastage figures revealed that the year's increase of 7000 teachers had been cut to 4300 by their operation. Analysis of the figures showed that wastage was likely to increase as the age of the profession dropped; the birthrate was also higher than forecast. Nevertheless the promise of a three year course was adhered to, so that expansion of the colleges became a necessity and pressure secured 12,000 new places by 1958, 4000 more by 1959 and a further 6000 in 1960.[11] Thus was the expansion of the colleges set on foot. Besides urging the increase in college numbers, the NACTST set out criteria for expansion, advising the establishment of larger colleges near universities or other cultural centres and more co-educational establishments. The result of these changes was that from the length and nature of the course, and the size and character of the institutions, the training colleges became for the first time likely candidates for recognition as establishments of Higher Education.

Some senior civil servants had other ideas as to how the shortages should be solved. They proposed Box and Cox plans to utilize college premises to the full and in a circular dated October 1st 1960, *The Balance of Training*,[12] enjoined on the colleges the production of 85 per cent primary students in their yearly intake, with 15 per cent secondary students, limited to specialist courses in certain colleges for shortage subjects, mathematics, science and physical education to which music, Religious Education and English were later added. The argument was that other specialists would be produced by universities. Although recognizing their obligation to train most of the teachers for the primary school, training institutions did not wish to see the careers of their students limited, and suspected that if their work was confined to the primary school, it would not be over-resourced. Some concessions were secured in that a course could be designated infant/junior or junior/secondary, provided that the first named in the age range was a genuine feature; in fact this insistence on some flexibility helped the supply situation as not enough graduates to meet the needs of the schools did apply from universities. Indeed, when from 1972 onwards, training for graduates intending to teach in the primary school was made compulsory, there was also a rapid growth of PGCE courses offered in colleges.

The Three Year Course and the BEd Degree

There was no lack of advice as to how to run the three year course as every professional association of teachers produced a pamphlet on the subject as did the Directors of Institutes and HMI. In view of the present intervention of HMI in the training programme it is interesting to note the contents of the latter, subtitled *Suggestions for a three year course*,[13] as it laid stress on main subject study as a professional as well as an academic experience and on the importance of encouraging habits of independent study, rather than adding short courses to the already heavy load. They believed that the three year course would reveal a wider spread of ability among students but hoped that the weaker candidates could then be dropped. The largest Teachers' Union, the NUT, saw the three year course as a step likely to bring graduate status in its train and so, together with the teacher trainers, stressed the need for academic excellence. The National Association of Head Teachers, NAHT, advocated more genuine collaboration between schools and colleges on school practice, but no-one came forward with plans for greater school responsibility or for longer practices, probably because it was realized that neither were possible in the circumstances of expansion.

The structure of the three year course followed the two year pattern closely, and it may be said at this juncture, that the first BEds, introduced as a consequence of the Robbins Report, for a selection of students, did not alter this structure. But there was a change in the balance and content of the course, for a higher proportion of time was allotted to the study of the main subjects, although a short methodological treatment was added to such subjects as history and geography which had not generally attracted a compulsory method course — perhaps in deference to the HMI viewpoint.[14] A more fundamental change was the way in which education was tackled, as there was a move away from the 'all purpose' education tutor towards the specialist in one of the educational disciplines, that is psychology, sociology, philosophy, and history as applied to education, often a well qualified young academic recently appointed to meet the needs of the expanding colleges. There were gains in this change as the integration claimed for the earlier system could leave rather a blurred picture in the minds of students, an impression easily erased by forcible re-education in the schools. Insights from psychology had always provided the stiffening for primary educational studies, and those current in the sixties were based on the work of Jean Piaget[15] and followers such as Jahoda[16] and Goldman[17] who applied his work on the normal development of children's concepts to the wider curriculum. Piagetian studies provided a more relevant theoretical base for work in the contemporary primary school than the mental measurement or more general developmental psychology that had preceded them. However, especially when taught in a simplified form, they did tend to reinforce the idea that there were strict limits beyond which a child could not go at a particular stage of development and certain concepts that he could not grasp.

'Readiness' and 'sequencing' are essential concepts for a teacher to be aware of, but not to follow slavishly to the exclusion of trying to stretch children, to follow up individual enlightenment, or give help in the mastering of difficult concepts. Again, the educational sociology of the period dealt largely with problems relating success in learning to family background and social class and was often responsible for sympathy among students for children of problem families and the inhabitants of inner cities increasingly from overseas, and gave some scientific backing to the beliefs of a generation which tended to be anti-establishment and on the side of the under-dog. However, it is true that, the carefully stated theories of, for example, Bernstein,[18] relating language learning to patterns of language acquisition in different types of home led to too ready an acceptance of some children's difficulties as inevitable and insurmountable. There was also a danger that the experience of the practitioner would be diminished as compared with the research finding of the expert. Where the primary tutor survived, even if a member of a discipline team, the change was not so marked, and was also tempered in those institutes that relied more on assessment and less on university set examinations. Examination tended to increase with the coming of the BEd, but in the fourth year students were more likely to have the time and maturity to deal with such issues.

In the search for academic and theoretical substance for main subject study and in the educational field, a search which had to be undertaken if the colleges were to grow in status as well as stature, that part of the course referring to the school curriculum became less important and took up a smaller amount of time relative to the rest. It is not easy to find colleges that neglected the teaching of reading to primary students, or failed to see that they mastered methods of teaching the new mathematics to primary children but the pursuit of higher academic standards may have given these studies less cachet in the students' eyes. Curriculum theory, based on the work of Bloom[19], Phenix[20] and Bruner[21] was beginning to be studied in colleges but its relevance to the students' pressing need to prepare for the actual work of the classroom was hard to establish. School practice was pursued with genuine seriousness but the fact that large numbers of new tutors had to be inducted into their work at the same time as the schools were suffering from a glut of probationers may have made its supervision less effective.

The difficulties must not be exaggerated for a period of expansion is a period of hope, but as one hears so much in the eighties of the problems of falling roles, it is as well to remember that rising roles posed some questions, too. Several experiments were set on foot, of which the best known was that initiated at the University of Leicester[22], applying some of the techniques of social work training to school practice supervision, and many colleges, through the use of more specific criticism forms, sought to involve the class teacher in helping students in a more meaningful way, but it was difficult to secure any relief in teaching time for primary class teachers.

The appointment of the Committee on Higher Education under Lord Robbins[23] was the signal for the ATCDE[24] to press for the granting of a BEd degree to selected students. The Association was confident that the improving intake would yield enough candidates capable of reaching the required standard. That all teachers should eventually have a degree had the backing of the Teachers' Unions and the LEAs, although the latter were more immediately concerned to challenge university control over Higher Education, teacher training included, a conflict which destroyed the unity of the NACTST which had secured the three year course.

The Robbins Committee's report recommended that a proportion of students of Colleges of Education[25], as they were to be called, should read for a four year BEd, and that there should be a further increase in numbers to 40,000 a year, calculated to produce 111,000 students by the mid-seventies. It also put forward a scheme for the government of colleges through Institutes of Education, which was turned down, to no-one's surprise. For reasons connected with the development of Higher Technical Education the Committee also recommended that the National Council for Technological Awards should become the Council for National Academic Awards, CNAA, with power to award degrees, thus providing an alternative route for the colleges. The CNAA made no move to take on Certificate work but began to set up machinery for the award of a BEd.

The training institutions were highly delighted at the degree recommendations of the Robbins Committee although some tutors were worried about the divisive effect that might ensue. This was a common attitude among primary teachers who thought that the BEd would be chiefly a qualification for secondary teachers, a belief that proved not to be true in the long run. Although the expansion of the colleges and the differentiation in their type of work in some ways put an end to the intimate relationship that had existed between them and local schools, the resources in staffing and equipment that expansion brought did benefit the schools indirectly.

The larger colleges were able to appoint specialists in handicapped pupils, in teaching English as a second language, in educational technology and in the teaching of French in the primary school, and set up courses for teachers in some of these fields or offered the use of well-equipped facilities, often before the LEAs were able to supply them for the schools. A few research projects were started with the support of, for instance, the Nuffield Resources for Learning project[26], and the experience that some teachers were beginning to have with Schools Council projects made them more open to a research approach, especially if geared to the production of school materials.

The Plowden Committee's Relevance to Teacher Training

The primary schools received their report in 1967 when the investigations of the Plowden Committee[27] were published, and on the whole it was a favourable one. It is fully described elsewhere in this volume but one or two points which have reference to training must be mentioned here. The description of the teachers' task as:

> to provide an environment and opportunities which are sufficiently challenging to children and yet not so difficult as to be outside their reach. There has to be the right mix of the familiar and the novel, the right match to the stage of learning

proved very influential, especially when developed by HMI, for both colleges and schools. Their establishment of progressive education as an orthodoxy likely to increase its hold was welcomed in colleges, though with some surprise as being rather contrary to experience, and with disappointment that it did not carry any very favourable account of the colleges which had presumably produced the teachers who had won such international acclaim. Two recommendations, one concerning the involvement of students in the Educational Priority areas, and the other on the compulsory training of graduates intending to teach in the primary school were useful; the first reinforced a process already begun on Merseyside[28], the Midlands, and some parts of London while the second finally galvanized the Secretary of State into action long recommended by the professional associations and the NACTST. The large majority of the graduates for primary and middle schools came to be trained in the Colleges of Education — the present, 1986, percentage is 80 per cent in public sector institutions and 20 per cent in universities including two which absorbed large colleges. Even trained graduates were at first regarded with suspicion in the primary school, and in the colleges the work was at first seen as peripheral, until the high potential of graduates for the future, concentrated the minds of all on the problems of switching from a highly specialized degree course to one which emphasized the needs of young children, and the wide range of the primary school curriculum — all in one short academic year.

The first dissenting voice as to the excellence of primary education came barely two years after the Plowden Report in the first Black Paper, 1969, dealt with in Chapter 6. The ludicrous assertion that the social ills of the time originated in the child centred approach of the primary school found no supporters in the Colleges of Education, though there was agreement with the later ORACLE[29] investigation that learning might be impeded by lack of genuine interaction between pupil and teacher. In any case the Training Institutions were fully occupied in defending their own patch.

Criticism of the Colleges and the James' Report

The training of teachers and, in particular, the BEd, came in for severe criticism in the late sixties and seventies from the teachers' organizations, certain university professors, and individual non-university Higher Education spokesmen, backed by politicians. A proportion of teacher trainers, including the General Secretary of the ATCDE, were disenchanted with the attitude adopted towards the BEd in some Universities, in particular those that were unwilling to make an Honours degree available or reluctant to recognize subjects not universally studied in universities such as music, art, craft and physical education as main degree subjects, thus leading to great unfairness between college and college. Several LEA colleges made plans to turn over to the CNAA for validation. There was too widespread awareness that the rapid expansion had not allowed the time for reflection that would have been appropriate to the adoption of so many new roles, and confrontation with unusual educational problems. In the new degrees the primary curriculum had not been dealt with at a deep enough level and the involvement of the class teacher in training had been often discussed but seldom realized.[30] Nevertheless the chorus of criticism that was expressed at the Colston conference[31], 1969, or emanated from the Select Committee of the House of Commons,[32] seemed inappropriate, bearing in mind the scale of the changes that had occurred.

The Secretary of State, Edward Short, was pressed to set up an enquiry, pressure which he tried to turn aside by instituting a series of ATO investigations, which produced some interesting material but were not able to allay the demand for an independent appointed Committee. This was set up in 1971, under the chairmanship of Lord James of Rusholme[33], a known opponent of the Institute system. When the report was published, a year later, as had been required, its proposals for a third cycle of enhanced in-service training, and of a planned and meaningful induction for young teachers was well received in all quarters. However, its degree scheme, which envisaged a two-year academic course which could lead to a DHE, followed by a year of professional study in college and a year's further training in school, *after* which a degree of BA(Ed) would be awarded, foundered, almost as soon as it was launched. This was chiefly because of the proposal to set up a third validating body and organizational structure, repudiated by the teacher trainers on the Committee, although the difficulties of starting a degree in one area and finishing it elsewhere, and the objections of the Teachers' Unions to the ambiguous status of the trainees played a part in its rejection. It became clear, moreover, that quite different issues were in the mind of the government as the birthrate fell and the funds grew shorter.

Contraction and Merger

These were the drastic cutting down of the teacher training system and the merging of its resources with those of the public sector as a whole. The White Paper, *A Framework for Expansion*[34] outlined this policy of contraction, although its scale was not at first clear. A choice appeared to be offered either to remain monotechnic with an increased role in in-service training, to diversify as a free standing institution, or to merge with a Polytechnic or other FE institution or, it was reluctantly conceded, join with a university. However, it transpired in the Circular 7/73[35] that called on LEAs to submit plans, that training places would fall from 114,000 to 70,000 or

60,000 — the lower figure was fixed by 1975. By 1977, this had been reduced to 40,000, 35,000 in colleges and polytechnics and 5000 in universities, and a list of college closures was announced. By 1982 several other institutions lost their teacher training intake and the process of contraction of the number of training institutions is still going on,[36] although the number of *places* is beginning again to increase, in response to the needs of the primary school.

Changes of the Decade 1975–1985

It is inappropriate here to lament the circumstances of the contraction of the teacher training system as these only affected the primary school indirectly; it is better to concentrate on the positive elements that came out of the reorganization.

First, the drop in numbers required for the profession made it possible to insist on a two A level entry, the minimum standard for degree study, to take effect in 1975.[37] The Certificate in Education was phased out and replaced by a three year, pass, or four year, honours degree. In 1978 passes at O level in mathematics and English were also made compulsory qualifications. These measures did not guarantee gifted or imaginative teachers but did mean that a certain level of attainment could be taken as a base. Moreover colleges catering for degree work and the PGCE need no longer feel themselves to be 'only doubtfully recognized as part of the system of Higher Education' (Robbins).

In fact the qualifications demanded caused some difficulties as BEd courses could not reach even their much reduced target in the late seventies, so that more places were allocated to the PGCE, and for the first time more teachers were recruited by that route than through the concurrent course.

Secondly, there were quite considerable changes in the degree course offered, for the BEds of the post-James era tended to be more consecutive in approach than previous models, especially in those institutions that were hoping to attract non-teacher applicants for a general degree. Modular structures were often adopted to achieve this end and were also used to introduce a more thematic approach to educational issues, embracing such topics as — the organization of work in the primary classroom, educational problems of the inner city, or the educational needs of ethnic groups, rather than concentrating on a disciplinary analysis. The procedures of the CNAA encouraged thorough course planning and although colleges absorbed in, or validated by, universities could work more by personal academic contact, the necessity to respond to the needs of the schools and to explain what was on offer to potential students, together with the insecurity of the future, made it a period of constant examination of course objectives in all training institutions. But it was also a period of quite fundamental institutional change, so that the degrees devised for one type of future had to be modified as the realities of the actual mergers became clear. In fact, the choices of students were often dictated by falling numbers and staffing difficulties, consequent on early retirement, and restrictions on staff recruitment, rather than course planning.

In 1981, the CNAA launched an enquiry into the BEd[38] and came down on the side of a four year honours concurrent degree and this was also the form adopted in the eighties in institutions within, or validated by, universities.[39] The teaching profession was now supportive of the BEd especially for primary teachers, and HMI also reported that it was more successful in training in the mastery of classroom skills[40] for the primary school than the PGCE. Several smaller colleges, Charlotte Mason, Bishop Grossteste, Lincoln, and Scarborough, devised four year BEds for primary and middle school teachers only, and either dropped or diminished the main academic subject in favour of applied educational studies which aimed at combining the consideration of selected subjects of the school curriculum with educational topics, and an emphasis on school based work.[41] In all institutions secondary BEds were confined to the shortage subjects so that the needs of the primary teacher were borne strongly in mind.

The seventies and eighties were also a period when the way in which curriculum studies were tackled, long a matter for debate, was the subject of experiment and change. This was spurred on by the Bullock Report (1975), on language across the curriculum, and backed up by the later Cockcroft Report on Mathematics,[42] which both criticised the thoroughness of preparation for teaching the basic skills — a theme also, of course, of the 'Great Debate'. The training institutions responded by increasing the number of hours spent on the basic skills, and by initiating conferences and surveys on the nature and quality of curriculum courses as a whole. These lead to some illuminating discourse on the subject, laying stress on process, skills and attitudes rather than informational content, but did not entirely solve the problem of how to achieve the sought after depth in studies still regarded by students as a way of survival in the classroom.[43]

The difficulties were particularly obvious in the case of the PGCE for primary students, whose numbers had increased dramatically in the late seventies. Both CNAA[44] and HMI[45] surveyed these courses, and a particularly thorough and illuminating report emanated from UCET.[46] It took as essential elements in the course, techniques, professional knowledge, curriculum knowledge, interpersonal skills and qualities, and constructive revaluation (of the curriculum) and showed how the disciplines of education could illumine current problems of the schools for these graduates. Time seemed the only element with which it did not get to grips.

Many new kinds of school/training institution co-operation have been tried or more widely adopted during the last ten years, and have taken the form of school based studies as part of school experience, or of courses in the training institution in which serving teachers have played a significant part. The much greater involvement of the training institutions in in-service training in the form of award-bearing courses, BEd, or other more advanced studies, has created a pool of teachers, familiar with current aims in training, and well able to give help in appropriate and informed ways. There is still a strong tendency, however, owing to problems of 'covering' work in school, to use headteachers, or recently retired teachers, rather than those actually handling children as a day to day experience.

The ATCDE used to complain that there were no policies for teacher training, only for teacher supply, but there has been a significant change in this respect. The first advisory body set up after the issue of the White Paper, the Advisory Council for the Supply and Training of Teachers, ACSTT, was chiefly and inevitably, concerned with questions of supply but its successor, the Advisory Council for the Supply and Education of Teachers, ACSET[47], has taken an active interest in the curriculum offered to students. The fact that these advisory councils are appointed for a short term and dissolved when their immediate work is done, seems to point to the fact that the real influence on the curriculum lies elsewhere and its source appears to be government policy with regard to the schools as interpreted by HMI[48] in their surveys and report.

In view of the weakness that HMI's primary school survey detected in the subject knowledge of primary teachers, it is not surprising that stress is laid on its acquisition, either in first degree courses or in at least two years' concentrated study in the BEd. It is conceded in the criteria, agreed to by ACSET[49], which every course must satisfy in the future, that this subject study may be a broad curriculum area, such as language, and in the case of primary teachers it must be related to the learning of young children; the primary teacher is seen as a consultant in his or her specialism which it is hopefully stated in the White paper[50], may be in science, mathematics or music, although it is noted that the expertise of primary teachers, at present, is heavily weighted towards the arts and humanities. No indication is given as to how this state of affairs is to be remedied.

Reliance may be being placed, more than is admitted, on the substantial courses in mathematics and language, and more recently science, that have become a feature of the college curriculum. Emphasis is laid on the necessity of covering the full range of the curriculum in first schools, though the teachers of older primary and middle school children, can be more selective, presumably filling the gaps by in-service courses. The curriculum requirements are heavy, but it is envisaged that the third group of courses to be included, 'studies closely linked with practical experience in school', involving the active participation of practising school teachers, will give reality to short courses, as it has always done in the best practice. This partnership will supplement the 'recent, substantial and relevant experience' in schools that a sufficient proportion of the training staff are in the process of acquiring by teacher/tutor appointments, secondments, and exchanges.

Educational Studies appear only in the guise of a formidable list of topics and problems that institutions may be expected to offer, ranging from class management to the values of society and its cultural heritage, and including those concerns that are the refrain of every educational discourse, the multicultural society, children with special needs and preparation for the world of work. It is no doubt intended that the professional will gauge the most appropriate disciplinary approach to illumine these matters for young graduates in a coherent way and link them with the primary school child whose needs must remain the central concern of teachers, whatever the prescription.

Lest it should be thought that there is a return to the situation castigated by McNair, the 'survival by hurrying' syndrome, the HMI discussion paper advised that:

Courses for intending teachers should be based on guided study and experiment and therefore undertaught rather than overtaught[51] and referred to good selection methods as the best way to secure teachers with the personal qualities, including the ability to form good relationships, which are of first importance to teaching success. Emphasis on the need to match a teacher's training with the post taken up, and the recent indictment of insufficient resources at the teachers' disposal[52] indicate that it is not always deficiency in training that is the root of the problem.

It is early days yet (August 1986) to judge with what degree of flexibility these criteria will be applied by the Advisory Council for the Accreditation of Teacher Education, CATE[53]. The personnel of the Committee gives grounds for hope of a professionally valid approach, but its hand seems tied by previous pronouncements. It is the job of HMI to report on observed strengths and weaknesses, and to encourage best practice, but there is a danger in the conversion of this advisory role into the power to say 'yea' or 'nay' to a course and thus end the argument, not on grounds of financial or administrative efficiency but on controversial academic considerations, for example on the amount of time to be spent on subject study and its relation to performance in the primary classroom. However, there should be sufficient experience and integrity in the training institutions, backed, as they now appear to be by the profession as a whole, to achieve a working solution, allowing for the student in training to develop as a person as well as a professional — for these outcomes are related but not the same thing. If this is not achieved, the painful experience of the last decade will have been in vain, and one would be tempted to ask, 'What were the mergers for?'

Notes

1. BOARD OF EDUCATION, (1944), *Teachers and Youth Leaders*, London, HMSO.
2. NIBLETT, W.R., HUMPHREYS, D.W. and FAIRHURST, J.R. (1975), *The University Connection*, Winds or NFER.
3. ALEXANDER, R.J. (1984), 'Teacher education and the primary curriculum in RICHARDS, C. *New Directions in Primary Education*, Lewes, Falmer Press.
4. SELLECK, R.J. (1972), *English Primary Education and the Progressives 1914–1939*, London, Routledge and Kegan Paul.
5. University of Birmingham Institute of Education. See papers set for the Diploma in Child Psychology, 1950–60.
6. *Education Review*, Vols I-XII 1948–60, University of Birmingham.

7. *Challenge and Response*: (1950) Ministry of Education Pamphlet No. 17, London, HMSO.
8. *Teachers and Youth Leaders, op. cit.* para. 36.
9. NATIONAL ADVISORY COUNCIL FOR THE TRAINING AND SUPPLY OF TEACHERS, (1951), *First Report*, HMSO.
10. *Three Year Training for Teachers*, (1956) Fifth Report of the NACTST, HMSO.
11. *The Demand and Supply of Teachers 1960–80*, (1962) Seventh Report of the NACTST, HMSO.
12. *Balance of Training*, Letter 14/60 Ministry of Education.
13. *The Training of Teachers*, (1957), *Suggestions for a three year Training College course: Pamphlet No. 34*. Ministry of Education, HMSO.
14. University of Birmingham Institute of Education, Syllabuses 1960–1.
15. For example, PIAGET, J. (1950), *The Psychology of Intelligence*, London, Routledge and Kegan Paul; PIAGET, J. and SZEMINSKA, A. (1950), *The Child's Concept of Number*, London, Routledge and Kegan Paul.
16. JAHODA, G., (1962–3) 'Children's concepts of time and history' in *Education Review*, Vol. 15, No. 2.
17. GOLDMAN, R. (1964), *Readiness for Religion*, London, Routledge.
18. For example, BERNSTEIN, B., (1967) 'Social class differences in the relevance of language to socialization' in *Sociology*, 13, pp. 1–20.
19. BLOOM, B.S., (1956) *Taxonomy of Educational Objectives*, London, Longmans.
20. PHENIX, P.H. (1964) *Realms of Meaning*, New York, McGraw Hill.
21. BRUNER, J. (1966), *Towards a Theory of Instruction*, Cambridge, Harvard University Press.
22. CASPARI, I. and EGGLESTON, J. (1965), 'A new approach to the supervision of teaching practice' in *Education for Teaching*, 68, November, pp. 47–52. See also COPE, E. and BRIMER, A. (1971) 1965–68, *School Experience in Teacher Education*, Occasional Publication, University of Bristol.
23. DES, *Higher Education*, (1963), a report of the Committee on Higher Education under the Chairmanship of Lord Robbins.
24. *Memorandum*, (1961) prepared by the ATCDE for submission to the Committee on Higher Education, July.
25. *Higher Education. op. cit.* paras. 324–341, 481–485, 344–360, 429–434.
26. TAYLOR, L.C. (1971), *Resources for Learning*, Harmondsworth, Penguin. See also KEFFORD, C.W. (1970), *Approaches to Environmental Studies*, an account of work involving programmed learning and parental participation in a Coventry primary school, originally funded through the Resources for Learning Project.
27. CENTRAL ADVISORY COUNCIL FOR EDUCATION (ENGLAND), (1967), *Children and their Primary Schools*, London, HMSO. See Chapter 25 and paras. 163 and 969.
28. MIDWINTER, E.C. (1971), *Priority Education*, Harmondsworth, Penguin.

29. GALTON, M. and SIMON, B. (Eds.) 1980, *Inside the Primary Classroom*, London, Routledge and Kegan Paul.

30. For discussion of these issues at the time see BROWNE, J.D., 'The curriculum,' and EVANS, A. 'College and school relationships', in HEWETT, S. (Ed.) *The Training of Teachers — a Factual Survey*, London, University of London Press; also: RENSHAW, P. (1971) 'A curriculum for teacher education', in BURGESS, T. (1971) *Dear Lord James*, Harmondsworth, Penguin.

31. *Towards a Policy for the Education of Teachers*, Colston Papers, (1969), Vol. 20, Butterworth.

32. WILLEY, F.T. (1971) *An Enquiry into Teacher Training*, London, University of London Press.

33. DES (1972), *Teacher Education and Training (James Report)*, London, HMSO.

34. DES (1974), *Education — a Framework for Expansion*, London, HMSO.

35. DES (1973), *Development of Higher Education in the Non-university Sector*, Circular 7/73.

36. *Times Educational Supplement*, 1986, 27th June. See also *Times Higher Educational Supplement*, 1986, 20th June.

37. *A Framework for Expansion, op. cit.*

38. CNAA (1981) *Report of the BEd Working Party*, London.

39. For example, The University of Warwick, *University prospectuses 1980–2*. A modular degree had been devised in the period of uncertainty that preceded the merger of Coventry College of Education with the University. This was modified then replaced during 1981–82 by an Honours only four year degree.

40. DES (1982), *The New Teacher in Schools: A Report by HMI*, London, HMSO.

41. ROSS, A.M., MACNAMARA, D. and WHITTAKER, J. (1977), *An Experiment in Teacher Education*, Guildford, Society for Research in Higher Education.

42. DES (1975), *A Language for Life: The Bullock Report* London, HMSO, and DES (1982), *Mathematics Counts: Cockroft Report* London, HMSO.

43. ALEXANDER, R.J. and WORMALD, E., (Eds.) (1979), *Professional Studies for Teaching*, Guildford, Society for Research Higher Education.

44. CNAA, (1984) *Perspectives in Postgraduate Initial Training*, London.

45. DES, (1980), *PGCE in the Public Sector: An HMI Discussion Paper*, London, HMSO.

46. UCET (1982), *Postgraduate Certificate in Education courses for Teachers in Primary and Middle Schools: A Further Consultative Report*, London, University Council for the Education of Teachers.

47. ACSTT, (1973–78), ACSET (1979–84).

48. DES, (1978), *Primary Education in England: A Survey by HMI*, London, HMSO.

49. ACSET, (1983), *Advice to the Secretaries of State — Criteria for the Approval of Initial Training Courses and the Mechanics of Accreditation*, (mimeo).

50. DES, (1983), *Teaching Quality*, Cmd, 5833, HMSO.
51. DES, (1983), *Teaching in Schools — The Content of Initial Training: An HMI Discussion Paper*, London, HMSO.
52. DES, (1986), *Report by HMI on the Effects of Local Authority Expenditure, Policies on Educational Provision in England in 1985*, London, HMSO.
53. Appointed 13 April, 1984.

The author was involved in the training process from the middle of the 1939–46 war until 1975, in two colleges and in the professional organization of teacher trainers, it, therefore, seems appropriate to draw on personal experience rather than to rely solely on the research literature, especially as for the early part of the period it is sparse. Nevertheless, the work contained in the bibliographies of the following publications has been thoroughly consulted. CANE, B. (1986), 'Teachers, teaching and teacher education' in BUTCHER, H. (Ed.) *Educational Research in Britain*, London, University of London Press; TAYLOR, W. (1978), 'Recent research in the education of teachers', in *Towards a Policy for the Education of Teachers*, London, Butterworth. ALEXANDER, R.J., (1984), 'Innovation and continuity in initial teacher education curriculum', in ALEXANDER, R.J., CRAFT, M. and LYNCH, J. (Eds.), *Change in Teacher Education*, London, Holt, Rinehart and Winston, (an invaluable source of information).

The Black Paper Movement

Frank Musgrove

Themes 1969–1977

The Black Papers melodramatically announced a death. The victim was educational standards and the culprit 'progressivism'. The primary school was deeply implicated: it had embraced the 'new mathematics', vertical grouping, look-and-say. 'Creativity' and 'self-expression' in the primary school were chief suspects. These highly technical matters were addressed with assurance by literary dons. What they may have lacked in technical competence they more than made up in moral rectitude.

The Black Paper movement spanned almost a decade. The first issue was in February 1969, the fifth and final issue in 1977. The early issues appeared as special supplements of the literary journal, *Critical Quarterly*. The Black Papers were intitiated, sustained and managed throughout by literary scholars who had taken degrees in English mostly at Cambridge but sometimes at Oxford. These publications stand firmly in a long literary-moral tradition which extends back through Leavis and Tillyard to Arnold, Sidgwick and Coleridge. This has been one of the most powerful and disastrous demodernizing impulses of our age.

But the timing of Black Paper One is a little odd. It appeared in the wake of two reports of the Central Advisory Council for Education (England) which were highly reassuring and proclaimed a postwar success story. The 'Newsom Report', *Half Our Future*, was published in 1963 and dealt with the education of 'average children'. Four national reading tests of fifteen-year-olds which had been carried out between 1948 and 1961 provided an important yardstick for the report. There was evidence of considerable variation in standards among secondary modern schools, and progress in the early postwar years may simply have been making good lost ground, 'But the later tests of 1956 and 1961 show that we are now going forward into new territory.'[1] On the basis of good, technically competent surveys the Report was able to claim: 'Today's average boys and girls are better at their books than their predecessors half a generation ago. There are reasons to expect that their successors will be better still.'

The 'Plowden Report', *Children and their Primary Schools*, appeared four years later. It was able to draw on five national reading tests of eleven-year-olds, the last undertaken in 1964. HMI Peaker wrote an important technical appendix on the reading surveys and claimed 'a remarkable improvement in the standards of reading' among eleven-year-olds since the war. (The advance was on average seventeen months — a gain over sixteen years of almost twenty-four per cent.)[2] This report appeared in 1967. In 1969 Black Paper One announced the postwar collapse of standards.

There was other very impressive and authoritative evidence that attainment in 'basics' has improved quite dramatically since 1950 and probably since the thirties. Wiseman published his important and widely reviewed book, *Education and Environment*, in 1964. This gave the results of an extensive research programme in Greater Manchester in the 1950s. A survey of reading comprehension, mechanical arithmetic and verbal reasoning had been carried out with 14,000 fourteen-year-olds in 1951 and with a follow-up sample in 1957. It was quite clear that there had been 'a substantial improvement in standards of educational attainment in tool subjects from 1951 to 1957', that ground lost during the war had been more than recovered, and all the indications were that 'standards have gone well beyond the 1939 level'.[3]

The real occasion for Black Paper One was not the state of primary schools but university expansion and student unrest. Kingsley Amis triumphantly repeated his dictum that 'more means worse'. The relevant background is the Robbins Report (1963), *Higher Education*, and its implementation in the late 1960s, student unrest at the LSE and Hornsea College of Art and the events of 'Mai-Juin' 1968 at the Sorbonne and Nanterre. Black Paper One devoted 50 per cent of its articles and space to universities. Only one article (out of twenty-two) and a short note were devoted to primary schools.[4] But over the next four issues the primary school moved centre-stage and universities almost dropped out of sight. The Black Papers reached their climax in 1977 with only two articles on universities, eleven on primary schools, and Dolly Walker, a dissident teacher at the highly progressive and now notorious William Tyndale junior school reflecting on the awful lessons of the William Tyndale debacle.

Black Paper One was a lightweight affair by men who felt no need to produce evidence for the decline they alleged. The tone could be flippant: 'How unimaginably long ago it now all seems,' wrote Walsh, 'Good King Robbins' golden days. . .' Walsh, Dyson, Cox and Amis wrote as modern literary men who (as Lionel Trilling once said) see themselves licensed in emotion and intuition by the tradition of their subject, relatively uncommitted to method and to fact, inclined to moral indignation, and especially 'apt to assume that the intellectual life is dramatic'.[5] Black Paper One was high on theatricality. The contributions were stylish: Amis wrote on 'Pernicious Participation', Robert Conquest on 'Undotheboys Hall'. But the editors learned quickly that literary elegance, moral indignation, intuition and high drama are not enough. Henceforth even quantified evidence was patiently (even boringly) assembled and analyzed, contributions were sought from heavyweight behavioural scientists (like Eysenck and Burt), and in Black Paper Two Arthur Pollard, Professor of English Literature at the University of Hull, contributed an impressive amount of arithmetic to show the inferior O and A level results of comprehensive, compared with grammar school, pupils.[6] Later Black Papers presented examples of highly sophisticated research methodologies and data analysis like John Todd's reworking of statistics allegedly showing some adverse effects of selection (regression or wastage between O and A level in highly selective grammar schools). 'The true interpretation' Todd convincingly concluded, 'is fundamentally different from that given by the researchers.'[7]

The Black Papers soon shifted their focus from the university to the primary school as the symbol and source of contemporary decadence. But they sustained their attack on comprehensive reorganization and equality which began in Black Paper One with an article on 'Comprehensive Disaster' and became even more strident in Black Paper Two. The primary school was invoked at the outset principally to explain the perversity of university students' demands for 'relevance', 'participation' and the reform of teaching methods and exams. The influence of Froebel, Freud and Piaget on primary schools had promoted the notion that 'people should develop in their own way at their own pace'. This was clearly deplorable:

'Competition has given way to self-expression. And now this has worked its way up to the student generation. They don't want to be chivvied through exams on a career ladder; they want to be (what they conceive to be) themselves...'[8]

The Black Papers changed their particular focus and their style, but their general thrust remained constant throughout. They championed streaming, competition, external examinations, selection and elites; they deplored 'discovery methods', 'creativity' and 'self-expression'; but above all, perhaps, they showed a consistent concern for reading standards which they claimed had declined and only formal and structured teaching could restore. Order, structure, hierarchy, formality and decorum are the overriding concern of these literary men. They rejected 'participation', even 'dialogue', because they were the *literati*, inheritors of a sacred trust, guardians of eternal standards and truths. (Walsh, Amis and the Warden of All Souls were perhaps the most explicit on this score.) In the last resort the empirical evidence which they now so assiduously gathered was an irrelevance: their case was not empirical but moral.

Research on all these issues is beset with great technical (and often conceptual) difficulties and the results are at best tentative and commonly ambiguous or even contradictory. The research reviews which the editors obtained from distinguished psychologists were objective and painstakingly honest. Richard Lynn gave an authoritative and far-ranging account of the research on streaming; but the evidence from England, Utah and Stockholm was by no means clear and conclusive.[9] Barker Lunn's original research for the NFER pointed to the academic benefits of streaming in primary schools[10]; but a second large-scale, complex inquiry produced no clear results.[11] (Lynn speculates a little drily on the motives for conducting it.) Cyril Burt also pointed to the conflicting and inconclusive nature of research on streaming (and comprehensive reorganization), underlined the great range of circumstances, and highlighted the crucial importance of teachers rather than particular forms of organization.[12]

The debate on reading standards is also bestrewn with technical difficulties. The editors early enlisted the support of an eminent authority who had spent a life-time in studies in this field, Professor Sir Cyril Burt. In the second Black Paper, Burt claimed that standards in reading, spelling and arthmetic were 'appreciably lower' than in 1913. He refers the reader to a recent article in a professional journal[13] but gives no particulars. In their editorial 'Letter to Members of Parliament' Cox and Dyson made much of this 'alarming situation' as revealed by Burt. They also referred to other surveys which indicated a declining number of seven-year-olds able to read.

The article that Burt referred to was in fact a review article written by himself in which he makes only a very brief mention of surveys he had conducted in London since 1913. He concluded not that 'progressive' methods *per se* were to blame for any decline, but that we need 'a more discriminating use of concrete and practical procedures in place of purely verbal teaching...'[14] He refers the reader for further details to yet another journal, in which he is even more circumspect. There he gives a table of median scores (not the sharpest measure of general level) on standardized tests administered at intervals since 1914 (with 1920 as base score: 100). Reading comprehension in 1965 was 99.4, in 1920 100, in 1914 100.1; problem arithmetic was 97.6 in 1965 and 101.3 in 1914. Burt warns: 'All such comparisons are admittedly precarious'; and even on these data there was no evidence of really significant decline. His conclusion was this:

'The most striking feature that emerges is the zig-zag fluctuation in each of the subjects tested, never very large, and due mainly, it would seem, to the effects of the wars and the subsequent recovery in each case.'[15]

The Bullock Report, *A Language for Life*, was expected to support the alarmist claims; but long before its publication it was widely known that it did not. It was also known that one member of the Bullock committee, Stuart Froome, strongly, even passionately, disagreed with his colleagues and would write a 'Note of Dissent'. He was invited to contribute to Black Paper 1975. He claimed that standards were indeed falling, cited a number of disturbing surveys, and placed the blame squarely on 'activity methods', look-and-say, and John Dewey. He did not mention Bullock.

In Black Paper 1977 this was fully rectified: he accused the Bullock committee of dishonesty and fraud. There was damaging research which 'must have been well known to all members of the Bullock Committee, and yet it receives no mention in the Report'. Inconvenient research (by D. Cookson, educational psychologist for Staffordshire) had been sent to the committee and simply ignored.[16]

The Bullock Report was not alarmist, but neither was it euphoric: unlike the Newsom and Plowden Reports it did not proclaim a success story. It conceded probable decline in reading proficiency among seven-year-olds. But it was very alive to all the technical problems involved in testing and comparing, and it knew that 'progressivism' was on trial. It therefore conducted a large-scale survey of English teaching but found no different approach to or emphasis on 'basics' in schools with an integrated day and vertical grouping compared with more traditional schools.[17] A majority of the Committee approved mixed-ability grouping. Froome was incensed.

The Black Paper movement ended in 1977 on a triumphal note. The Bullock Report of 1975 was a disappointment; but 1976 yielded a rich harvest. The Auld Report on affairs at the William Tyndale school under its progressive headmaster Terry Ellis showed, in careful, balanced prose the bizarre consequences of some advanced (and socially motivated) educational theory[18]; and Bennett's 'Lancaster Report' on teaching styles showed more progress in primary schools, on all fronts, under 'mixed' or 'formal' than 'informal' teaching.[19] But Bennett, though finding the Plowden Report of 1967 seriously deficient, had scant regard for the excesses of the Black Papers: 'Their contributors took a swing at anything labelled progressive, permissive or egalitarian, often using the terms synonymously'. They wrote about educational standards; but their real fear (like Matthew Arnold's) was anarchy.

1958–9 The Collapse of the Postwar Settlement

The Black Paper movement was an attempt to restore the deeply conservative postwar educational settlement. This settlement — supported by a majority of both political parties — was based on the 1944 (Butler) Education Act.[20] It was characterized by rigorous rationing of opportunity, early selection and segregation and the preservation of minority culture. It was implemented and consolidated by two Labour administrations between 1945 and 1951 and remained substantially intact for some fourteen years. It began to collapse, really quite suddenly, in 1958 and rapidly after 1964. The first Black Paper, a shrill response to this collapse, appeared in 1969.

Before 1945 the vast majority of children received only an elementary school education and left school at fourteen. The great claim of the postwar settlement was to provide secondary education for all. This was quite fraudulent. Some 80 per cent of the nation's children still received an elementary education, now renamed 'secondary modern', and they still left at fourteen. What occurred in 1945 was a restoration of the *status quo ante bellum* with some tidying up and relabelling. County and municipal secondary schools were relabelled grammar schools and senior elementary schools were relabelled secondary schools; the grammar schools lost their small proportion of fee payers and the entire intake were now scholarship boys and girls. (The scholarship examination was now called the '11+'.) This highly conservative settlement lasted virtually intact for more than a dozen years, although the school leaving age was later raised first to fifteen and eventually to sixteen. Educational research was largely devoted to refining and sharpening the instruments of selection. The science of selection gave an air of legitimacy to a system of scholastic and social segregation that was morally repugnant and educationally indefensible.

Legitimacy was also conferred by the customary naiveté and idealism of 'educationists'. Secondary modern and grammar schools were to have 'parity of esteem'; but the secondary modern schools were to have a remarkable 'freedom' denied the grammar schools — freedom from external examinations. Educationists colluded in this cruel deception not out of deliberate malice but out of an invincible innocence.

Secondary modern school pupils were still taught mainly by nongraduates and the curriculum was essentially the old elementary school curriculum. Domestic science, woodwork and PE were somewhat more highly developed as specialist disciplines and English became more ambitious and far-ranging; but many teachers (72 per cent of some thousands of experienced teachers surveyed in 1955) thought the general level of attainment was lower than in the old elementary schools.[21]

And yet the secondary modern school, with its relatively undefined aims, became a focus of social idealism. In 1947 the Ministry of Education emphasized (in its pamphlet, *The New Secondary Education*) the freedom of the secondary modern school to develop along its own lines with due regard for the nature and interests of its pupils. Educationists had a vision of society beyond the school in which stress and competition were reduced 'and motives higher than those of profit and personal gain would direct human endeavour'.[22]

The purity of the secondary modern schools would be preserved by a simple device — the new GCE examination to be introduced in 1951 would be restricted to sixteen-year-olds while secondary modern pupils left at fifteen; when they were required to stay to sixteen the minimum age for taking GCE examinations would be raised to seventeen. A leading article in the *Times Educational Supplement* (1 May 1948) congratulated the Minister on placing temptation beyond the reach of the new modern schools and so getting them off to a good start. A storm of protest — mainly from grammar schools — forced the Minister to abandon the age restriction in April 1952. Educationists were scandalized that, by 1954, some 10 per cent of secondary modern schools were 'embracing the chains' of external examinations 'under which their grammar school colleagues have groaned for much of the past thirty-five years'.[23]

It has been argued that the postwar educational settlement, which in effect distinguished and perpetuated the elite and the mass, was a deliberately class-based settlement. All the talk of 'parity of esteem' was merely camouflage for an essentially class-based system. Raymond Williams linked the 1944 Education Act with the Taunton Commission's report on endowed grammar schools of 1868 and saw an 'essential continuity, despite changes in the economy, of a pattern of thinking drawn from a rigid class society...'[24] Ottaway had advanced exactly the same argument, tracing the postwar settlement from the Taunton Report through the Spens Report on secondary education of 1938: 'Can we not detect here the continuance of social class distinction?'[25]

It would be an exaggeration to regard the postwar settlement as a disguised and dishonest rehash of Victorian proposals which were frankly and explicitly based on class differences; but in spite of the utopian rhetoric it looked to a very traditional past rather than to a fluid, high-tech future. The Ministry of Education said that the secondary modern school could and should achieve parity of esteem by its own efforts, but systematically deprived it of the resources for doing so.[26]

There was a palpable shift in the nation's mood in 1958–9. The pinched postwar settlement cracked. Ian McLeod announced the last days of National Service and we ended a period of twenty years under arms. Galbraith published *The Affluent Society* and captured the sense of new possibilities in all Western industrial countries: 'affluence', it is true, meant more peace-time (non-crisis) inflation, less than 'full' employment (but more cushioned unemployment), youth as an economically redundant and yet very special social category, far less manual labour, far more leisure and the rise of a new education (rather than trade or property) based middle class. Michael Young published his devastating satire (of the kind of world that would be embodied in the Black Papers), *The Rise of the Meritocracy*, and S.C. Mason initiated his comprehensive high schools under the 'Leicestershire Plan'. C.P. Snow gave his Rede Lecture on 'The Two Cultures' and did much to shift perspectives from a tradition-based literary culture to a future-based scientific culture. The Labour Party rejected the 11+ and the secondary modern school (without quite accepting comprehensives). Gaitskell's 'New Year Message to the Labour Party' at the end of 1958 was emphatically in favour of abolishing the 11+ examination which 'slammed the door of opportunity' for the vast majority who had 'failed'; in Labour's policy booklet for 1959, *The Future Labour Offers You*, the aim was grammar school education for all. Postwar Britain had finally been born.

By 1958 both political parties knew that the secondary modern schools had failed in their impossible task, and that the electorate knew, too. It is true that by their own efforts the schools had developed advanced work and broken the examination monopoly of the grammar schools; the early ministerial efforts to keep them in their place had failed before the schools' determined 'upthrust'.[27] But self-generated upthrust was not enough. The mere existence of the secondary modern school was a moral affront.

By 1958 S.C. Mason, the Director of Education for Leicestershire, regarded selection as 'no longer tenable'. The problem was not educational but moral. Eccles, the Conservative Minister of Education, knew that it was untenable, too, but would have liked more, not less, selection leading by more diverse routes into a more diversified system of higher education (and well paid jobs).[28] Working class parents, who supplied most of the secondary modern school's pupils, were no longer simply voters: they were income tax payers, too (as they were not, in the main, before the war). They were fully paid-up members of the state; and they were paying for an educational system that consigned the great majority of their children to the dustbin at the age of eleven. The logic as well as the morality of war-time PAYE and lower tax thresholds had at last come home to roost.

The modernizing process over the next ten years was at first slow and tentative and is still far from complete: the move towards a more open, generous and egalitarian form of education and society which prepared its children for a science-based world; the expansion and diversification of higher education and the belated recognition and growth of the social sciences. The Black Papers were hostile to all these changes: Sociology and 'relevance' were as much the object of attack as the Plowden Report. Robert Conquest described Sociology as 'the bastion of barbarism' and Amis said of relevance: 'the teacher who wants to impart it is the enemy of culture'. It is not surprising that change should be resisted; what is, perhaps, surprising is that the resistance was mobilized and managed by literary men. Their aim was always the restoration of the past: only in Boyson's advocacy of 'educational vouchers' in the fourth Black Paper[29] is there any notion that the future should not be exactly like the past.

1869–1969 Modernity and English Literature

The year 1869 saw the publication of Matthew Arnold's *Culture and Anarchy*; 1969 saw the publication of Black Paper One. It was a fitting (though unwitting) centenary tribute, for there is a direct line of descent between the two. The crucial link-man who stands between Arnold in 1869 and Walsh, Bantock, Cox and Dyson in 1969 is F.R. Leavis who transmitted Arnold's high moral stance towards literature (and distaste for modern urban-industrial civilization) virtually intact in the English degree course at interwar and postwar Cambridge. The Black Papers like Arnold's book are centrally about anarchy, the passing of an established order, the loss of old disciplines and ancient pieties.

Both publications attacked what they saw as the collapse of standards in their day, although Arnold's critique was on a much broader social front. Both lamented the alleged levelling tendencies of their times (Arnold was very suspicious of democracy and contemptuous of the recently extended franchise, the Black Papers focus more narrowly on the dangers of equality in education and of using education to promote or 'engineer' equality). Three enormously influential books formed the intellectual climate out of which the Black Papers grew: to Arnold's *Culture and Anarchy* we must add Leavis's *Mass Civilization and Minority Culture* (1930) and *Culture and Environment* (1934). They are all of a piece; and they are among the most corrosive publications of our age. They have provided a remarkably potent inoculation against both justice and modernity.

Arnold, it is true, gave his inaugural lecture as Professor of Poetry at Oxford on 'The modern element in literature'. But for him 'modernity' meant Periclean Athens (infinitely more modern than Elizabethan England with its passion, barbarous magnificence and 'fierce vanities'): for modernity meant order, decorum, rationality and restrained taste. He entirely approved of modernity in this sense, conceded that his own age was quite modern, and recognized (like Freud) that it led often to depression, lassitude and *ennui*. This thin, tepid and bloodless texture of life was the hallmark of modernity.[30]

Not so large-scale industry, advanced technology, wealth-creation and the free market economy; and in *Culture and Anarchy* Arnold berates urban-industrial society and the middle-class 'Philistines', with their chapels and tea-meetings and narrow illiberal lives, who sustain it. In this facetious book written in highly convoluted prose, he returns again and again to pillory John Bright, who epitomized the new forward-looking industrial age: a northerner, an industrialist, a Quaker, an advocate of more democracy, greater equality and international free trade, he is derided at every turn. To see the greatness of England in coal, iron, great cities and extensive railroads was simply to prevent our 'fixing standards of perfection that are real'. Arnold's plea was against 'machinery' and all for 'inwardness'.

In 1930 Leavis wrote of 'mass society' in similar terms. His book *Mass Civilization and Minority Culture* opens with a quotation from Arnold (our modern world is 'mechanical and external and tends constantly to become more so') and is supported throughout with references to *Culture and Anarchy*. The machine is still producing standardization and social disintegration; but salvation lies with the tiny minority who alone are capable of 'unprompted, first-hand (literary) judgment', who 'keep alive the subtlest and nost perishable parts of tradition', and upon whom 'fine living depends'. The mass-and-the-elite is the paradigm of England's postwar educational settlement.

The values that must be kept alive are those of the 'organic community'. Leavis and Denys Thompson in *Culture and Environment* sneer at 'progress' and improved standards of living for the poor and commend the village world described by 'George Bourne' (George Sturt) in *The Wheelwright's Shop*. The master-servant relationship as well as the craft skills of the old village life are held up for admiration. These literary men have scarcely a good word to say for today's school-bred literacy of ordinary folk.

There have been very senior and distinguished literary scholars who doubt the relevance of Arnold and Leavis to our times. The literary men who shaped and in large measure wrote the Black Papers have no such doubts. But Graham Hough[31] and Raymond

Williams[32] at Cambridge and Lionel Trilling[33] at Columbia University in New York have shown signs of alarm almost equal to those expressed in 1959 by C.P. Snow. The world has changed since 1869. And it has changed mightily for the better.

Bantock and Walsh say it has changed only for the worse, and in the direction that Arnold said. In 1952 Bantock recognized some of the limitations of Arnold's thought and work but maintained nevertheless that we should 'turn to him for light', for the situation that concerned Arnold 'has not only grown worse, but has grown worse along lines that Arnold indicated...' His thought is even more salutary and timely than when he was alive.[34] In 1963 he reaffirmed this view: 'Today we seem further than ever from the solution to the problems which Matthew Arnold in *Culture and Anarchy* so resolutely faced'.[35]

Walsh has insisted into the 1980s on the continuing relevance of Leavis's concept of elites and his posture towards industrial society. In 1956 he placed Leavis firmly in the company of Coleridge and Arnold ('his name can without incongruity be joined with theirs') and said the argument for a small, highly moralized literary elite still stood[36]; in 1980 he saw the change from 1934 as merely to greater materialism: 'So that the passage of time has made Leavis's essential intention the more necessary and the more relevant'.[37] And always there is in Walsh and Bantock the tireless invocation of D.H. Lawrence (Leavis's 'great discovery') to justify the attack on industrial society, on equality, and on literature or even literacy for the mass. Walsh in 1956 cites Lawrence (and notably Birkin in *Women in Love*) to support his attack on equality which means not only 'a debasement of standards' but 'also involves the supposition that all are theoretically capable of intellectual culture. This is a very dangerous assumption which generates in a large number a profound contempt for education and for all educated people'.[38]

The suspicion of literature and even literacy for the masses runs deep through the Cambridge literary establishment and was clear long before Leavis's time. It is true that English literature had been pioneered as a subject of study in the mid-nineteenth-century Working Men's Colleges and in university extension courses[39]; but perhaps for this reason was seen by the end of the century as inappropriate for general consumption. E.M. Forster had taught at the Working Men's College at Great Ormond Street but in 1910 presented a very disparaging picture of the lower-class Leonard Bast in *Howard's End*, made him ridiculous in his quest for culture and admirable only in his bid for authentic, real-life experience. Forster shows the characteristic literary man's distaste for machines and industry; but he married off the highly cultivated Schlegel girl to the wealth-creating Mr Wilcox who lived in a world of anger and telegrams — for which Leavis never forgave him.[40] D.H. Lawrence was far more reliable in his rejection of the urban-industrial world.

C.P. Snow instanced Lawrence as the supreme literary Luddite (in contrast to the men of science who 'have the future in their bones').[41] First Bantock[42], then Leavis[43], rose to Lawrence's defence (essentially as a corrective in a scientific-rationalist age). But it was Lawrence's approval of hierarchical pre-industrial social relationships (the squire might be arrogant but a 'curious blood-connection held the classes together') which placed him firmly within the Leavisite world.[44]

Better scholars, more worldly and more deeply informed men, knew what terrible, sentimental rubbish this was. Raymond Williams knew that 'it is foolish and dangerous to exclude from the so-called organic society the penury, the petty tyranny, the disease and mortality, the ignorance and frustrated intelligence which were also among its ingredients';[45] Snow was quite right to point out in his Rede lecture that scientific-industrial advance, urban life and more complicated and large-scale forms of social organization meant enormous gains for the poor and their main hope for dignity and independence; and Lionel Trilling knew that Matthew Arnold's ideal of order was 'achieved at the cost of extravagant personal repression, either that of coercion or that of acquiescence'.[46]

The Leavisites have made some effort to adapt to today's urban-industrial world[47]; but even the most 'revisionist' see the curriculum for the majority of children as a curriculum for a kind of urbanized peasantry. Even Brian Jackson quotes Matthew Arnold at length (and with complete approval both of his sentiments and, incredibly, of his 'magnificent prose') before commending the traditions of working-class life in Husdersfield as a basis for education[48]; Hoggart described a new peasantry in working-class Leeds, with a tightly-knit back-street life, but regretted the corrosive effects of mass-literacy and mass-entertainments which 'are in the end what D.H. Lawrence described as anti-life'.[49] But it was in Black Paper 1977 that Bantock described a new folk culture and spelt out an 'Alternative Curriculum'.

He had already argued that what we require today is an education that relates to 'the sort of reality that George Bourne depicts his peasantry as facing … only translated into twentieth-century terms. What, in fact, is required is a new folk culture…'[50]

In Black Paper 1977 he argues that although industrialization has destroyed the old folk culture, the new folk culture, like the old, should be based on action and not on books. This is a remarkably Forsterian view. Bantock follows it through: after the primary school books will play little part and education will draw on 'a more primitive kinaesthetical potential'. Dance, drama, ritual, music, painting, sculpture and crafts will be the main curriculum. 'To put it in its broadest terms, I suggest that we place a greater emphasis on action than on reflection and that such powers of reflection as these lower academic achievers are capable of should spring out of such activity'.

The difficulties that Matthew Arnold saw around him in 1869 have not got worse: they are infinitely better. We are not a mass society but highly plural and remarkably diversified; the middle class is not sunk in torpor but is highly cultivated: it throngs into theatres and classical concerts and reads great literature; indeed, according to Pierre Bourdieu it is defined by its literary cultivation, has appropriated the world of letters as 'cultural capital' which it uses to reproduce itself.[51] The highly moralized English degree course as it has existed at Oxford since 1894 and Cambridge since 1917 is now otiose. As Trilling has said, the study of English literature 'evolved in circumstances in which one could attribute to literature a function which it may no longer have'. Arnold and Sidgwick[52] saw middle-class England in a state of sodden immobility, but 'Neither foresaw the modern mobility, the contemporary suffusion of mind by ideas of a benign, enlightened, moralized, liberal kind. Neither foresaw the contemporary diffusion of artistic culture and its simulacra, a society drenched with art and with newspaper gossip about the arts'.[53] In fact English literature degrees have been another great success story.

But they have been taught by remarkably conservative men and they have turned the attention of the young to a highly traditional past. Lionel Trilling has described literary study and activity in America as an 'adversary culture', and with a far greater concentration on twentieth-century authors this may well be the case. But literary culture in England has not been subversive but massively conservative not only because of its content but because of the character of those who have taught it.

The early years of the degree at Oxford were dominated by the Merton Professor, Sir Walter Raleigh, and the early years of the Cambridge degree by the occupant of the King Edward VII Chair, Sir Arthur Quiller-Couch. Both were outstanding snobs. 'Q' always lectured in correct morning dress; his activities were primarily social or rhetorical[54]; and everything he thought or said presupposed, in Basil Willey's view, 'the old class structure of society, the old sense of decorum, propriety and ceremony in human relationships as in literature'.[55] Sir Walter Raleigh was a notable social reactionary who had 'an unquestioning belief in the virtues of good mixing in the best company'.[56]

His successor in the Merton Chair, George Gordon, was even worse: a singularly odious man, formerly Professor of English at Leeds, he gloated over the collapse of the General Strike. He thought it of supreme importance to enjoy a good dinner and know the right people. He was Professor of Poetry and finally President of Magdalen.

Levis, it is true, had no gentry pretensions: he was a Cambridge townsman and his father was in trade. And he remained an outsider at Cambridge until the end of his days. More representative of his generation of literature tutors were C.S. Lewis and J.R.R. Tolkien. Lewis was a difficult, reactionary man (neither Betjeman nor the future novelist Henry Green survived their degree courses with him) and according to Bowra he 'did not much like young aspirants to literature and was much more at home with the past than the present'.[57] His friend Tolkien was himself something of a 'hobbit' who disliked mechanical farming and foreign travel, was opposed to democracy, and believed that each man belonged to a specific 'estate'.[58] He was the Merton Professor at Oxford from 1945 to 1959.

The study of English literature in English universities appears to have attracted very socially conservative and perhaps socially insecure men. (In postwar Oxford students of English were by far the largest group proportionately of those requiring some kind of psychiatric help: 15 per cent of all students referred but only 8 per cent of the population at risk.[59]) Twitchy, difficult, reactionary men, Larkin was perhaps a fair example.

In the Black Papers they have characteristically emphasized tradition, order, decorum. For his course on modern (twentieth-century) literature at Columbia University, Trilling required his students to read Frazer's *Golden Bough* and Nietzche's *The Birth of Tragedy* to alert them to the influence of disorder and unreason in modern, subversive literature. From Nietzsche they would learn something of the nature of the Dionysiac impulse and this is the key to understanding modernity. This is precisely what Dyson, in Black Paper One, would guard all students against. In his article, 'The sleep of reason', he reiterates the traditional moral aims of education and deplores 'self-expression', for 'civilization is, after all, dependent on man's rational control'. Character-building is still the key to our world: 'It is the foundation of much that was great in public and grammar schools. Apollo demands his due as much as Dionysus'. This is still the authentic voice of Arnold a hundred years on, without concession to a radically changed world or any real understanding that change has occurred.

1976–7 A Movement Vindicated?

The year 1976 appears at first sight to be the climax of a widespread reaction against postwar progressive education. Robin Auld Q.C. published his strictures on progressivism as implemented at the William Tyndale junior school in 1974 and 1975; Bennett's 'Lancaster Report' gave details of the superior progress of junior school children over a period of one school year under formal rather than informal or progressive teaching; and Flew published a blistering philosophical attack on the new wave of sociologically inspired progressivism especially as it found expression in the book *Knowledge and Control* edited by M.F.D. Young.[60]

The attack came from sociologists, too. The previous year had seen Sharp and Green's study of 'child-centred' education at 'Mapledene Lane' junior school which exposed some of the shams of progressivism and concluded that 'modern child-centred education is an aspect of romantic radical conservatism';[61] Kate Evans was also publishing her research on some of the pretences and conservative consequences of spatial 'openness' in junior schools[62]; and the following year saw Punch's devastating evaluation (in *Progressive Retreat*) of 'classical' progressivism at Dartington Hall. Black Paper 1977 was cleverly timed, a triumphal publication referring to some of these events (notably the Auld and Bennett reports) as vindication of a long, hard-fought campaign.

And yet it would be wrong to see the Black Paper movement 1969–77 as part of a more general reaction against (real or imagined) postwar progressivism — which had never been really extensive (seriously influencing the practice of perhaps one-sixth of all primary school teachers)[63] or particularly radical. Progressivism was now getting its second wind and a much sharper ideological and political edge. In fact the year 1976 also saw the publication in America and England of an enormously influential book by Samuel

Bowles and Herbert Gintis which presented a powerful Marxist critique of traditional schooling.[64]

The Black Paper movement had coincided with a new wave of sociologically inspired and politically sophisticated progressivism which appeared to give powerful support to an 'invisible' (child-centred) pedagogy. It was associated with the London University Institute of Education and the Education Faculty of the Open University and was based on a potent and unlikely brew of Marxism, 'phenomenology' and some hitherto neglected aspects of Durkheim's sociology. The Black Papers did not react to this until quite late, although Bernstein's widely cited 'Open schools, open society?' had been published in 1967.[65] It was Bantock in Black Paper 1975[66] who saw clearly and accurately how the new thinking in the field of the sociology of knowledge underpinned the new progressivism and promoted a deeply subversive attack on so-called middle-class values and knowledge, middle-class institutions and middle-class 'hegemony'.

It is curious that the Black Papers had quite failed to understand the nature of Sociology and its very conservative influence on postwar education: the more conservative aspects of Durkheim's thought (on moral education and the external and obligatory character of 'social facts') mediated by Fred Clarke to support a deeply conservative and highly authoritarian approach to the curriculum.[67] (A 'progressive' like Ottaway, who had turned late in life to sociology, was deeply embarrassed by this Durkheimian legacy.[68]) The 'new' sociology of the 1970s drew on quite other aspects of Durkheim's thought (*The Division of Labour* and *The Elementary Forms of the Religious Life*) to make a very intellectually dubious case for 'openness' in the school curriculum: the alleged symbolic replication of the social state. The older, authoritarian strand in Durkheim is now being revived by Hargreaves.[69]

The 'new sociology' (of M.F.D. Young, Keddie and Esland) was making its threat to traditional schooling and standards precisely at the point where the Black Papers imagined they had triumphed. (Keddie's *Tinker, Tailor . . .* was published in 1973,[70] Hammersley's *The Process of Schooling* in 1976.[71]) The most bizarre illustration was Terry Ellis, with his advanced diploma from the London Institute of Education, at the William Tyndale school. But the influence ran deep through the initial and more especially the further training of teachers throughout the seventies. It could now be seriously proposed not simply that education should be 'child-centred', but that a class of schoolchildren constituted an 'epistemic community' capable of constructing (or perhaps 'negotiating') its own reality.[72]

By 1977 the Black Papers had been overtaken by the new progressivism and had certainly not refuted the old. The empirical evidence which seemed at last to support their case was far from conclusive. Bennett's evidence on progressive methods was certainly not the last 'scientific' word on the matter, just as it was not the first. It was technically interesting in being a longitudinal or follow-up, and not a correlational, study. But it was published without any mention of powerful and authoritative correlational studies by Warburton which pointed to a totally opposite conclusion.[73]

Bennett also tried to produce evidence on 'creativity' (imaginative writing) but admitted that this was the weakest part of his study. It led to no clear conclusion.[74] But highly competent studies of teaching and creativity in junior schools had in fact shown a strong connection between child-centred, 'self-initiated' learning and high scores in tests of divergent thinking.[75] It is true that Hudson had suggested that progressive education probably hindered rather then helped creativity (because it made pupils happy)[76], but this was an unwarranted inference from his own research which was not about teaching and learning but personality. The Black Papers had waged a consistent campaign against the pursuit of creativity in junior schools. Their main objection was that this undermined 'basics'. But in 1977 the argument that competently applied progressive methods helped both creativity and basics still rested on powerful empirical support.

But empirical evidence was not of primary importance. The Black Paper movement occurred not because progressivism was rampant and there was strong evidence for the collapse of standards: it occurred at the point of intersection between the powerful Arnold-Sidgwick tradition of highly moralized literary studies and a belated wave of postwar modernization. The movement was initiated and managed throughout by literary scholars, who have constituted a very influential demodernizing force in our times. The moral impulse and indeed the academic networks which sustained them are now probably much weaker than they were; but on many fronts of contemporary life this tradition keeps us anchored in a past which is now a gigantic irrelevance.

Notes

1. A Report of the CENTRAL ADVISORY COUNCIL FOR EDUCATION (1963), *Half Our Future*, London, HMSO.
2. PEAKER, G.F. (1967), 'Standards of reading of eleven year olds 1948–1964' in A Report of the CENTRAL ADVISORY COUNCIL FOR EDUCATION *Children and their Primary Schools*, London HMSO.
3. WISEMAN, S. (1964), *Education and Environment*, Manchester, Manchester University Press.
4. JOHNSON, C.M. (1969), 'Freedom in junior schools' and BROWNE, G.F. (1969), 'Notes from a junior school headmistress' in COX C.B. and DYSON, A.E. (Eds.) *Fight for Education: A Black Paper*, The Critical Quarterly Society.
5. TRILLING, L. (1967), *Beyond Culture*, Harmondsworth, Penguin Books.
6. POLLARD, A. (1970), 'O and A level: Keeping up the standards' in COX, C.B. and DYSON, A.E. (Eds.) *The Crisis in Education: Black Paper Two*, The Critical Quarterly Society.
7. TODD, J. (1971), 'Comprehensive statistics' in COX, C.B. and DYSON, A.E. (Eds.) *Goodbye Mr Short: Black Paper Three*, London, Davis-Poynter. The research which Todd reinterpreted was published by CHRISTIES, T. and GRIFFIN, A. (1970) in *Educational Research* 12, 3.
8. Editorial comment (1969) in *Fight for Education: A Black Paper*.
9. LYNN, R. (1971), 'Streaming: Standards or Equality?' in COX, C.B. and DYSON, A.E. (Eds.) *Goodbye Mr Short: Black Paper Three*, London, Davis-Poynter.
10. BARKER LUNN, J.C. (1967), 'The effects of streaming and non-streaming in junior schools: Second interim report' in *New Research in Education* 1, pp. 46–75.
11. BARKER LUNN, J.C. (1970), *Streaming in the Primary School*, Slough, NFER.
12. BURT, C. (1971), 'The organization of schools' in COX, C.B. and DYSON, A.E. (Eds.) *Goodbye Mr Short: Black Paper Three*, London, Davis-Poynter.
13. *Journal of the Association of Educational Psychologists*
14. BURT, C. (1969), 'Recent studies of abilities and attainment' *Journal of the Association of Educational Psychologists*, 2, 4, pp. 4–9.
15. BURT, C. (1969), 'Intelligence and heredity: some common misconceptions' *Irish Journal of Education* 3, 2, pp. 75–94. For 'Reading Accuracy' the scores were: 1914 101.4; 1945 90.8; 1965 96.7; for Mechanical Arithmetic 1914 103.2; 1945 88.9; 1965 97.7. The marked improvement since 1945 is abundantly clear from Burt's figures.
16. FROOME, S. (1977), 'The Bullock Report' in COX, C.B. and BOYSON, R. (Eds.) *Black Paper 1977* London, Temple Smith.
17. CECB, (1975), *A Language for Life* Report of the Committee of Inquiry appointed by the Secretary of State for Education and Science under the Chairmanship of Sir Alan Bullock, London, HMSO.
18. AULD, R., Q.C., (1976), *William Tyndale Junior and Infants Schools Public Inquiry*: London, ILEA.

19. BENNETT, N. (1976), *Teaching Styles and Pupil Progress*, London, Open Books.
20. Although the Butler Education Act of 1944 was widely heralded as a new dawn both at the time and for long afterwards, historians of education are beginning to recognize its conservative, even reactionary, character: see WALLACE, R.G. (1981), 'The origins and authorship of the 1944 Education Act', *History of Education*, 10, 4, pp. 283–9 and SIMON, B. (1986), 'The 1944 Education Act: A conservative measure' *History of Education*, 15, 1, 31–43. Simon concludes: 'The threat of radical change had been held at bay. The "New Order" in English education ... turned out to be the old order in a new disguise', p. 43.
21. TAYLOR, W. (1963), *The Secondary Modern School*, London, Faber and Faber.
22. TAYLOR, W. (1963), *Ibid*.
23. See WHITEHEAD, F. 1956, 'External examinations examined' *Journal of Education*, 88, 1039, pp. 47–50. 357 out of 3480 secondary modern schools had entered 5585 candidates in 1954. Whitehead concluded that some form of examination for secondary modern schools might be desirable, but it should not be O-level GCE.
24. WILLIAMS, R. (1961), *The Long Revolution*, Harmondsworth, Penguin Books.
25. OTTAWAY, A.K.C. (1953), *Education and Society*, London, Routledge and Kegan Paul.
26. For the gap between financial support for secondary modern and grammar schools see VAIZEY, J. (1958), *The Costs of Education*, Allen and Unwin and TAYLOR, W. (1953), *The Secondary Modern School*, London, Faber and Faber.
27. LUKES, H. (1959), 'The pedigree of the modern school' *British Journal of Educational Studies* 7, 2, pp. 125–139.
28. WALKER, D. (1986), 'Specialist choice: Tory answer to comprehensives' *Times Educational Supplement* 10 January, p. 5.
29. BOYSON, R. (1975), 'The developing case for the educational voucher' in COX, C.B. and BOYSON, R. (Eds.) *Black Paper 1975* London, Dent.
30. See ARNOLD, M. (1960), 'On the modern element in literature' in SUPER, R.H. (Ed.) *Matthew Arnold: On the Classical Tradition*, Ann Arbor, University of Michigan Press. The lecture was given on 14 November 1857 and first published in *Macmillan's Magazine* February 1869.
31. See HOUGH, G. (1964), 'Crisis in literary education' in PLUMB, J.H. (Ed.) *Crisis in the Humanities*, Harmondsworth, Penguin Books for a criticism of the Arnold-Leavis claim for literary studies and broad support for C.P. Snow's view of literary culture as deeply destructive. His criticism of literature-as-morality is more fully developed in HOUGH, G. (1963), *The Dream and the Task. Literature and Morals in the Culture of Today*, London, Duckworth.
32. WILLIAMS, R. (1961), *Culture and Society 1780–1950*, Harmondsworth, Penguin Books.
33. TRILLING, L. (1967), *Beyond Culture*, Harmondsworth, Penguin Books.

34. BANTOCK, G.H. (1952), *Freedom and Authority in Education*, London, Faber and Faber.
35. BANTOCK, G.H. (1963), *Education in an Industrial Society*, London, Faber and Faber.
36. WALSH, W. (1956), 'The literary critic and the education of an elite' *British Journal of Educational Studies* 4, 2, pp. 139–151. 'The true elite is characterized by a deep sense of the gravity of moral issues as well as by a fineness of other discriminations...'
37. WALSH, W. (1980), *F.R. Leavis* London, Chatto and Windus.
38. WALSH, W. (1956), 'D.H. Lawrence as teacher', *Journal of Education* 88, 1049, pp. 513–7.
39. See PALMER, D.J. (1965), *The Rise of English Studies*, London, Open University Press and BACON, A. (1980), 'Attempts to introduce a school of English literature at Oxford: The national debate 1886 and 1887' *History of Education*, 9,4, pp. 303–313.
40. LEAVIS, F.R. (1952) *The Common Pursuit*, London, Chatto and Windus.
41. SNOW, C.P. (1964), *The Two Cultures*, Cambridge, Cambridge University Press.
42. BANTOCK, G.H. (1963), *Education in an Industrial Society*, London, Faber and Faber.
43. LEAVIS, F.R. (1962), *Two Cultures? the Significance of C.P. Snow*, London, Chatto and Windus.
44. See BANTOCK, G.H. (1952), *Freedom and Authority in Education* London, Faber and Faber. See especially chapter six: 'D.H. Lawrence and the nature of freedom'.
45. WILLIAMS, R. (1961), *Culture and Society 1780–1950* Harmondsworth, Penguin Books.
46. TRILLING, L. (1967), *Beyond Culture*, Harmondsworth, Penguin Books.
47. See INGLIS, F. (1975), 'Attention to education: Leavis and the Leavisites' *Universities Quarterly* 30, pp. 94–106.
48. JACKSON, B. (1962), *Education and the Working Class*, London, Routledge and Kegan Paul.
49. HOGGART, R. (1958), *The Uses of Literacy*, Harmondsworth, Penguin Books.
50. BANTOCK, G.H. (1963), *Education in an Industrial Society*, London, Faber and Faber.
51. BOURDIEU, P. (1977), 'Cultural reproduction and social reproduction' in KARABEL, J. and HALSEY, A.H. (Eds.) *Powder and Ideology in Education*, New York, Open University Press.
52. For Sidgwick's views of the importance of English literature as a (Public) school subject see SIDGWICK, H. 1868, 'The theory of classical education' in FARRAR, F.W. (Ed.) *Essays on a Liberal Education* London, Macmillan. More than Arnold — or Leavis — Sidgwick emphasized enjoyment and the stimulation of sluggish imaginations and minds.
53. *Beyond Culture, Ibid.*
54. TILLYARD, E.M.W. (1958), *The Muse Unchained*, London, Bowes and Bowes.

55. Quoted in HOWARTH, T.E.B. (1978), *Cambridge Between the Wars*, London, Collins.
56. LEAVIS, Q.D. (1943), 'The discipline of letters' *Scrutiny* 12, 1.
57. BOWRA, C.M. (1966), *Memories 1878–1939*, London, Weidenfeld and Nicolson.
58. CARPENTER, H. (1977), *J.R.R. Tolkien*, London, Allen and Unwin.
59. DAVIDSON, M.A. and HUTT, C. (1964), 'A study of 500 Oxford student psychiatric patients', *British Journal of Social and Clinical Psychology*, 3, pp. 175–185
60. FLEW, A. (1976), *Sociology, Equality and Education*, London, Macmillan.
61. SHARP, R. and GREEN, A. (1975), *Education and Social Control*, London, Routledge and Kegan Paul.
62. EVANS, K. (1974), 'The head and his territory', *New Society*, 24 October. EVANS, K. (1979), 'The physical form of the school, *British Journal of Educational Studies*, 27, p. 29.
63. In Bennett's sample of primary schools in Cumbria and Lancashire 'a fairly generous estimate is that some 17 per cent of teachers teach in the manner prescribed by Plowden': see BENNETT, N. (1976), *Teaching Styles and Pupil Progress*, London, Open Books. Bennett concluded from his own survey and other relevant research that there is 'little evidence for a wholesale movement towards informality'.
64. BOWLES, S. and GINTIS, H. (1976), *Schooling in Capitalist America*, London, Routledge and Kegan Paul.
65. BERNSTEIN, B. (1967), 'Open schools, open society?' *New Society*, 14 September, pp. 351–3.
66. BANTOCK, G.H. (1975), 'Progressivism and the context of education' in COX, C.B. and BOYSON, R. (Eds.) *Black Paper 1975*, London, Dent.
67. See CLARKE, F. (1948), *Freedom in the Educative Society*, London, University of London Press. See also CENTRAL ADVISORY COUNCIL FOR EDUCATION (1947) (Chairman: Fred Clarke): First Report, *School and Life*, London, HMSO.
68. OTTAWAY, A.K.C. (1955), 'Educational sociology of Emile Durkheim' *British Journal of Sociology* 6, pp. 213–227.
    OTTAWAY, A.K.C. (1968), 'Durkheim on education' *British Journal of Educational Studies* 16, 1, pp. 5–16.
    OTTAWAY did his best to give a sympathetic account of Durkheim's thought but was forced sadly to concede that Durkheim was not really a progressive ('Yet he knew about the methods of Pestalozzi').
69. HARGREAVES, D.H. (1980), 'A sociological critique of individualism in education' *British Journal of Educational Studies* 28, 3, pp. 187–198.
70. KEDDIE, N. (Ed.) (1973) *Tinker, Tailor ... The Myth of Cultural Deprivation*, Harmondsworth, Penguin Books.
71. HAMMERSLEY, M. *et al.* (Eds.) (1976), *The Process of Schooling*, London, Routledge, and Kegan Paul.
72. ESLAND, G.M. (1971), 'Teaching and learning as the organization of knowledge' in YOUNG, M.F.D. (Ed.) *Knowledge and Control*, London, Collier-Macmillan.
73. WARBURTON, F.W. (1964), 'Attainment and the school environment' in WISEMAN, S. *Education and Environment*, Manchester, Manchester

University Press. Warburton's intensive research was based on 48 secondary modern and all-age schools in Salford: 'Attainment ... is consistently higher in the more progressive schools'. There was a particularly strong connection between progressiveness and reading comprehension, but also with scores on intelligence tests ('the most surprising single finding').

74. BENNETT, N. (1976), *Teaching Styles and Pupil Progress*, London, Open Books.
75. HADDON, F.A. and LYTTON, H. (1968), 'Teaching approach and the development of divergent thinking abilities in primary schools' *British Journal of Educational Psychology* 38, 2, pp. 171–180.
76. HUDSON, L. (1966), 'Lieben und arbeiten — a case of cake and eat it' in ASH, M. (Ed.) *Who Are the Progressives Now?*, London, Routledge and Kegan Paul, and *Contrary Imaginations*, London Methuen.

Toward Central Control: Government Directives on the Primary Curriculum

Jayne Woodhouse

Summary

From the mid-1970s onwards, in the context of widespread public criticism of education, government moves to assert control over what was taught in schools became increasingly apparent. Direct attempts to influence the curriculum took the form of policy statements from the DES, together with surveys of existing practice and discussion documents from HMI. This chapter aims to examine the effect of these central directives on primary education, and to offer a personal viewpoint of their impact on the classroom.

Towards Central Control

Government intervention in the school curriculum, although regarded as an innovation in the 1970s, has a long-established history. During the nineteenth-century central control over elementary education was exerted through codes and inspection. This was intensified after the introduction of the Revised Code in 1862, when the 3Rs became the basic grant-earning subjects. When payment by results ended, the Board of Education laid down the subjects which should be taught in the official elementary Code, abolished in 1926. The Code was interpreted in the *Handbook of Suggestions for Teachers*, published from 1905 onwards and last reprinted in 1948. However, the *Handbook* was permissive, and stressed the responsibility of the teacher for determining what went on in the classroom:

The only uniformity of practice that the Board of Education desire to see in the teaching of Public Elementary Schools is that each teacher shall think for himself and work out for himself such methods of teaching as may use his powers to the best advantage and best suited to the particular needs and conditions of the school. Uniformity in detail of practice is not desirable.[1]

The view that curricular policy should be left to the professional judgment of teachers was enshrined in the 1944 Act, where the word 'curriculum' does not appear. Under the Act, responsibility for what is taught in schools (with the exception of Religious Education) rests with the local authority and school governors, but in practice is delegated to Heads and teachers. The legal framework, therefore, determines that the Secretary of State for Education has no direct financial control over educational provision, nor any statutory authority over the curriculum. The result has been to establish a system of schooling where the needs of the locality are paramount, and to devolve to individual schools a level of autonomy unique in Western Europe. However, it is important to remember that this professional independence is a relatively recent concept, overlying a far longer period of direct government intervention.

Attempts by the Ministry to reassert control over the content of education have been well documented, particularly by Kogan,[2] Salter and Tapper,[3] and most notably Lawton[4] who has analyzed in detail the methods by which the DES has sought to exert its authority. The following consideration of some of the issues raised by these authors aims to provide a wider context for the discussion of directives on the primary curriculum.

Signs that the DES was growing dissatisfied with its role as a Department with responsibility but no effective power became apparent from 1960. At this time, David Eccles, Conservative Minister of Education, indicated in a subsequently much-quoted phrase the Ministry's desire to enter the 'secret garden of the curriculum'. The establishment of a 'commando-type unit' — the Curriculum Study Group — was a move in this direction. The CSG met with hostility from teachers' associations and LEAs who saw it as an attempt to exert control over the curriculum. In the face of such opposition it was disbanded and replaced in 1964 by the more acceptable Schools Council on which teachers held a majority.[5]

This early attempt at intervention by the Ministry was unsuccessful, but there were indications that a decade later the government was beginning to reassert itself. Warning signs can be seen in the establishment of the Assessment of Performance Unit (APU) in 1974 to monitor performance in schools through a system of national testing. The following year, HMI enquiries into primary and secondary education were begun, and the Taylor Committee was instituted to consider ways in which the management of schools could be broadened. Finally, a clear statement of government intent was contained in the 'Yellow Book'. This was a confidential memorandum prepared by the DES for the Labour Prime Minister James Callaghan and leaked to the press:

> It will also be good to get on record from Ministers and in particular the Prime Minister, an authoritative pronouncement on the division of responsibility for what goes on in school, suggesting that the Department should give a firmer lead... The climate for a declaration on these lines may now be relatively favourable. Nor need there be any inhibition for fear that the Department could not make use of enhanced opportunity to exercise influence over curriculum and teaching methods.[6]

With Callaghan's Ruskin College speech on 18 October 1976, and the subsequent Great Debate, the content of education entered the wider political arena. At the end of the Debate the government issued a consultative document *Education in Schools* — the 'Green Paper' — which marked a turning point in the role of the DES. Although the paper purported to deny any moves towards central control, it was in fact an unequivocal statement of active government intervention:

> It would not be compatible with the duty of the Secretaries of State to 'promote the education of the people of England and Wales', or with their accountability to Parliament, to abdicate from leadership on educational issues which have become a matter of lively public concern.[7]

The Green Paper was followed by Circular 14/77[8] requesting local authorities to report on the curricular arrangements in their areas, signifying that they were to take a stronger lead in curriculum development.

One result of the move towards government intervention was to unleash a flood of central guidelines from the DES, and also from HMI who were closely involved in formulating policies. Official statements in *A Framework for the School Curriculum*[9] and the subsequent *The School Curriculum*[10] repeatedly confirmed the DES' intention to determine national educational policy as part of its statutory responsibility under the 1944 Act. The directives were aimed towards establishing a common area of the curriculum or 'core', together with agreed aims and objectives for all stages of compulsory schooling. In order to achieve this, LEAs were instructed to implement curricular policies at local level, and schools required to set out their aims in writing and regularly review them.

More recently there has been a period of renewed activity by the DES and HMI following Sir Keith Joseph's speech at Sheffield in 1984. This called for 'clear objectives' in order to raise standards through a curriculum which is broad, balanced, relevant, and differentiated.[11] The subsequent DES note[12] shows the government taking an increasingly hard line on the necessity to produce a 'broad consensus' on curricular objectives. As a result of this initiative, further HMI guidelines will focus on the various subject areas which will contribute to a national curricular policy. The latest government statement, the White Paper *Better Schools*[13], is a reworking of official policy as it has emerged since the Great Debate. It advocates a three-tier structure of responsibility for the curriculum, composed of the DES, the local authorities and the schools, with functions which are separate 'though interrelated'. The right of individual schools to determine their own programmes is clarified, as is the duty of the government to be actively involved in curricular policy.

The publication of official statements from the Green Paper onwards is one method by which the DES has sought to influence the school curriculum. However, the Ministry has also extended its authority by a number of additional, but no less effective measures which need only be considered briefly here. From 1977 HMI have been deployed as an information-gathering service, and their reports and surveys used to legitimize central intervention. The DES has secured greater control over evaluation through the increased activity of the APU. In 1984 the Schools Council was disbanded and replaced by two committees whose members are nominees of the Secretary of State. Successive measures have been used to intervene in initial teacher training which will have a major impact on the schools of the future. The eighties have also seen notable attempts to control local authority spending on education through the method of 'rate-capping'.[14] The establishment of Educational Support Grants, and financial assistance towards in-service training in 1984 will further direct funding towards centrally-determined projects. Most recently, as this chapter is written, the DES is securing additional means to render itself less accountable by the abolition of Central Advisory Councils for Education, and the Secretary of State's annual report to Parliament.[15] Although the DES has always publicly stressed the importance of its partnership with local authorities and schools, these measures are further substantial evidence of the 'tightening grip' of central control over both the structure and the content of education. It remains to consider the extent to which government intervention influenced the primary curriculum during the 1970s and eighties.

Primary Education and the Great Debate

In 1967 the Plowden Report[16] gave official support to child-centred methods of primary education. By the mid-seventies progressive teaching had become a term of abuse, and the question of standards a political issue. During the sixties, primary schools were able to enjoy a level of autonomy not granted to secondary schools with their emphasis on examinations. By 1976 the primary curriculum was the subject of national debate and a candidate for central intervention. It is important to consider why, in a relatively short space of time, primary education entered the political arena and came under the influence of central government initiatives.

The 1960s have often been regarded, in retrospect, as the 'golden age' of primary education. The abolition of the 11+ released the schools from one of their greatest constraints and provided the opportunity for progressive methods of teaching to develop. Classrooms where children could learn by discovery, and exercise personal choice over their activities became centres of international interest. The view that education should be based on the experiences of the individual child gained official endorsement in the Plowden Report. This glowing affirmation of primary practice, with its emotive and emotional language, confirmed the child-centred approach to teaching as the received orthodoxy:

> A school is not merely a teaching shop, it must transmit values and attitudes... The school sets out deliberately to devise the right environment for children, to allow them to be themselves and to develop in the way and at the pace appropriate to them. It tries to equalize and to compensate for handicaps. It lays stress on individual discovery, on first hand experience and on opportunities for creative work. It

insists that knowledge does not fall into neatly separate compartments and that work and play are not opposite but complementary. A child brought up in such an atmosphere at all stages of his education has some hope of becoming a balanced and mature adult.[17]

However, it was only two years later that this viewpoint was being criticized in the first Black Paper[18] as constituting the 'roots of anarchy'. Progressive methods in primary schools were claimed to be directly responsible for, among other things, student unrest, emotional disturbance and an increase in the crime rate. The report heralded a period of growing disenchantment with education which focused on the primary phase. Public disquiet was fuelled by the media and Black Paperites, whose emotional appeal and sense of conviction outweighed their lack of evidence. Concern was directed towards 'standards' and 'the basics' — elements believed to be missing from schools which resembled 'a factory for making decorations'.[19]

By the mid-seventies, criticism of primary methods had reached a peak. It gained credence from two official publications which seemed to suggest that current anxieties were justified. The Bullock Report[20] on language advocated a national system of monitoring pupils' performance to raise standards in literacy. Secondly, Bennett's work on teaching styles[21] was hysterically construed by the media as firm evidence that informal instruction was less effective in the classroom. While these reports cast 'official' doubt on progressive methods, the Tyndale case appeared to confirm that the so-called primary revolution was being enacted with disastrous results. William Tyndale Junior School became the cause célèbre of educational discontent as a result of the controversy surrounding the radical changes introduced by a number of teachers. The dispute spread beyond the classroom to involve parents, advisers and local government officials, and required a public enquiry to resolve. The Tyndale affair is particularly significant to this discussion for addressing many of the issues which would form the basis of subsequent debate and action. These included the question of curricular control, the role and responsibilities of LEAs, the accountability of teachers, and the assessment of effectiveness in education.[22] Gretton and Jackson were not alone in considering these 'proper subjects for consideration by the Secretary of State for Education'[23], and therefore a legitimate cause for government intervention.

The mounting criticism of education can be seen as a response to the social and economic pressures of the seventies. The climate in which Plowden had been conceived was characterized by full employment, economic growth and a commitment by both major political parties to educational expansion. In a period of inherent optimism for the future, schools were regarded as agents of social change which would help to secure a more egalitarian society. By the mid-seventies growth of the economy and public services was over. The 1973 oil crisis heralded the onset of a worldwide recession, resulting in major cutbacks in expenditure. Disenchantment with education followed the realization that large-scale investment had not made a major impact on social inequalities. Therefore, in a society threatened by economic depression, schools and teachers fulfilled their recurrent role as scapegoats for the state of the nation.

The backlash against 'modern' educational methods provided an area of public concern which could be exploited as a political issue. It has already been noted that by the mid-seventies signs that the DES intended to take a more active part in curriculum policy were apparent. On taking office, the Labour Party was faced with cutting back public spending on education, and contracting the service as a result of the declining birth rate. Government concern with standards could, therefore, be used, not only to legitimize central control, but also to justify reducing the education budget on the grounds of 'efficiency'. The ensuing Great Debate can be interpreted as a deliberately orchestrated political manoeuvre, both to gain votes by exploiting popular prejudices, while at the same time strengthening central authority over the curriculum.

The Yellow Book reveals the extent to which the DES took up the general attack on primary schools. One of the four aspects selected for comment by the Prime Minister was the teaching of the 3Rs. The Ministry's response was a sharp criticism of informal methods which 'could prove a trap to less able and experienced teachers'. The memorandum went on to call for a return to basic skills:

> As a result, while primary teachers in general still recognize the importance of formal skills, some have allowed performance in them to suffer as a result of the uncritical application of informal methods, and the time is almost certainly ripe for a corrective shift of emphasis.[24]

This reactionary document had much in common with the Black

Paper reports, especially in its generalizations and lack of evidence. By the time of Callaghan's Ruskin College speech, the most contentious statements had been toned down. Nevertheless, the Prime Minister emphasized the right of non-professionals to be involved in all areas of schooling where 'there is legitimate public concern', one of which was identified as 'new informal methods'.[25]

When the criteria for discussion during the Great Debate were formulated, Callaghan's simplistic '3Rs in primary schools' was replaced by the more rigorous heading, the 'curriculum 5–16'.[26] The main focus was firmly directed towards establishing a common core of subjects, progress in which would be monitored by diagnostic testing. The resulting Green Paper has been described as the 'first Departmental criticism of the effects of the developments in primary education, since these were set in train by the Hadow Report of 1931'.[27] The paper's findings were somewhat more muted than the Yellow Book. Concern for standards was mitigated by the statement that 'It is simply untrue that there has been a general decline in educational standards'.[28] There was also a highly qualified endorsement of the child-centred approach 'in the hands of experienced and able teachers', without whom it would deteriorate 'into lack of order and application'.[29] This was balanced by the view that primary schools must safeguard basic skills:

> There are some skills for which the primary schools have a central, and indeed over-riding responsibility. Literacy and numeracy are the most important of these: no other curricular aims should deflect teachers from them.[30]

The outcome of the Great Debate for the primary curriculum was to give progressive methods some almost grudging support, while at the same time confirming public anxieties by references to protecting 'reading, spelling and arithmetic'. Teachers could gain some reassurance from the general educational aims outlined in the Green Paper. For example 'to help children develop lively, enquiring minds'[31] is something that primary schools have always been attempting to do. However, the general impression given by the DES is that of a Department with little knowledge of the theory or practice of primary teaching. The Ministry's view reduces primary education, like arithmetic, to 'a series of targets'[32] at which children could be systematically aimed. This basically utilitarian concept of education as a means to an end would subsequently be a prominent feature of all central directives. It stands in stark contrast to the primary school philosophy which stresses the value of education as an end in itself.

In conclusion, the Great Debate was less of a public discussion than an opportunity to present government policy. By making a case that teachers should be more accountable for their actions in the interests of efficiency and the maintenance of standards, the DES had opened the way to restructuring the system.

The 1978 Primary Survey

Before 1978, government statements on primary schools had been made without any real knowledge of what young children were actually being taught. The survey by HMI, *Primary Education in England*[33], is a most important document for the issues raised in this chapter. It provided for the first time much-needed information on the curriculum, and offered a rigorous and professional analysis of current practice. The findings and recommendations of the report would make a major contribution to the development of curricular policy, and would inform many subsequent DES and HMI statements.

During 1975–7, the Inspectorate investigated a national sample of seven, nine and eleven-year-olds in 1127 classes from 542 schools. Their conclusions revealed that public anxieties about teaching methods were misplaced and many government criticisms unsubstantiated. The Survey was fundamental in exposing the myth of the primary classroom as a scene of riot and anarchy. Its findings indicated that standards had not fallen, that children were generally quiet and well-behaved, and were being taught in a largely didactic manner under the teachers' firm control. In particular, the Survey revealed that, far from having abandoned the basics, children were spending most of their time in the repetition of isolated tasks in literacy and numeracy. This picture of the primary classroom hardly conformed to the Black Paper image, or the government's impression of schools where modern methods had got out of hand. The Survey's findings suggested that the primary school revolution had barely fired its first shot, let alone progressed to threatening the social order.[34] The child-centred approach, though it had become the established theoretical orthodoxy, had clearly failed to percolate down to the grassroots level of education. 'The current curriculum is revealed as scarcely more than a revamped elementary school curriculum with the same major utilitarian emphases'.[35]

Additional findings in the Survey had important implications for curriculum development. Concentration on the basic skills was too narrowly conceived, with children not having enough opportunities to apply these skills in other subject areas. Furthermore, the pupils' ability level, especially for the more able, was not adequately 'matched' by the work provided, which was often too easy and repetitive. Certain subjects, such as history and geography, were only superficially taught, while science was largely neglected. In order to extend the curriculum, HMI raised the question of specialist teachers — a departure from the traditional practice of one teacher per class.

The HMI Survey marks a significant change in the approach to primary education since the Plowden Report, and characterizes the curricular policy of the seventies and eighties. While Plowden represented the 'liberal romantic' view of education, the Survey signifies a move towards 'liberal pragmatism'.[36] The needs of the individual child are still central to curriculum policy, but there is a growing recognition that schools should also take into account the wider demands of society. The contrast between the two reports is reflected both in the tone and in the content. The heady rhetoric of the sixties is replaced a decade later by sober appraisal. Where Plowden had been concerned with organization and method, HMI directed the emphasis towards the content of education and what should be taught in schools. While Plowden believed that 'At the heart of the educational process lies the child'[37], the Inspectorate qualified this by stressing the importance of the acquisition of knowledge:

> Curricular content should be selected not only to suit the interests and abilities of the children and to provide for the progressive development of the basic skills, but also because it is important in its own right.[38]

Although the Survey considered the skills and attitudes which underlie primary schooling, this concentration on the content of education is revealed by the discussion of the curriculum in terms of separate subjects.

Subsequent statements from the DES and HMI would return to many of the points raised in the Primary Survey. The problem of 'match', the development of science, and the deployment of subject specialists would be among the major issues incorporated into policy documents. In particular, official directives would have to take on board the evidence that traditional teaching methods emphasizing the basic skills dominated primary schools. Raising standards, therefore, would mean extending rather than restricting the primary curriculum.

Central Directives in the Eighties

With the change of government in 1979, initiatives towards central control of the curriculum continued against a background of swingeing cuts in the education budget. The view that the DES should offer leadership on the curriculum was reputedly given further support by the responses to Circular 14/77.[39] These appeared to show that there was little national consistency on curricular policy, and that LEAs did not know enough about what went on in their schools. However, the original questions in the Circular had been very open-ended, and it is difficult to see how concise conclusions could have been drawn from them, except as part of a deliberate policy. After receiving information from the local authorities, the DES and HMI published simultaneous views on the form that a national curricular policy should take in January 1980. The Department's document *A Framework for the School Curriculum*[40] failed to distinguish between primary and secondary education, and offered a general outline for the years of compulsory schooling. The emphasis was towards a traditional, subject-based approach. English, mathematics, science, and physical education were seen as essential parts of the curriculum, and approximate time allocations given to the first three. This crude simplification had little to offer primary schools, which warranted only a cursory mention. There was little to suggest from this document that the DES considered primary education as anything but an adjunct to the secondary school, or that the Department had considered the specific problems of developing a curriculum for younger children. *Framework* was received with much hostility, especially by the NUT, for both its unequivocal stance on government intervention, and its superficial means-end view of education. In contrast, the HMI report *A View of the Curriculum*[41] derived from a more professional appraisal which drew upon extensive experience of primary and secondary schools. In this publication, the primary curriculum received a separate consideration which went beyond division into subject areas. HMI stressed the need for all children to share 'areas of experience' which they identified as language and literature, mathematics, science, aesthetics, and social abilities — headings which had been established in the Primary Survey. There was also a consideration of the skills and concepts underlying the curriculum, showing a concern with the process as well as the content of education.

Comparison of *Framework* and *View* shows two very different opinions at work. On one hand, the DES was advocating more active intervention by LEAs in developing a curriculum which it saw as having a predominantly utilitarian function. Although the Ministry stressed the intention of giving a clear lead in national policy, it showed little evidence of any theoretical understanding of the issues it meant to direct. In contrast, HMI were attempting a more professional analysis based on a knowledge of existing practice. Their appraisal of the curriculum emphasized the wider role of education above and beyond the mere acquisition of information. Instead of imposing curricular change, the Inspectorate were seeking to develop existing practice through the schools and teachers.

Some move towards reconciling these conflicting viewpoints emerged in the DES' subsequent statement *The School Curriculum*[42], published in 1981. This highly significant document showed the government adopting an increasing role in determining what schools should teach. In the words of the Secretary of State (Mark Carlisle) it represented 'our own firm views. We want education authorities and schools to be guided by them'.[43] The main differences between this and the previous directives were the removal of the time allocations and the incorporation of HMI recommendations. *The School Curriculum* restated the broad aims of education contained in the Green Paper, and left them largely unchanged. A separate section followed on the primary phase, in contrast to the earlier publication. The influence of HMI can be seen in the consideration of skills, concepts and attitudes underlying the curriculum, and in the call for a move away from domination by the 3Rs: 'There is no evidence that a narrow curriculum, concentrating only on the basic skills, enables children to do better in these skills'.[44] Topic work, science, art and craft, and French were areas singled out for specific attention. In the light of the framework suggested by *The School Curriculum*, LEAs were requested to review their curricular policies, and schools to set out their aims in writing and regularly review them.

During the subsequent period of Conservative government, primary schooling was largely overshadowed by developments in secondary education. However, a number of significant reports increased the information on what primary children were being taught and the standards they were achieving. The Cockcroft Committee[45] made major recommendations on the teaching of mathematics, emphasizing the need to apply the subject in a variety of learning situations. HMI reports on First[46] and Middle Schools[47] confirmed the evidence of the Primary Survey in revealing a curriculum dominated by the basic skills. The results of APU tests in mathematics, science and language were available for the first time, and suggested areas in which performance could be improved. Finally, inspections of individual schools by HMI, published from 1983, showed a wide variation in primary practice. These diverse documents consistently highlighted key elements for the development of the primary curriculum. 'Continuity' and 'progression' were seen as vital areas needing attention, together with clear curricular planning by each school if these were to be achieved.

This growing body of detailed information helped to inform the most recent central initiatives towards the primary curriculum. Signs of renewed government interest in primary schooling were heralded by Sir Keith Joseph's speech at Sheffield in 1984. The *Times Educational Supplement* saw what it suggested could be the start of a 'Great Primary Debate' in the Secretary of State's reference to a need for clear objectives for 'each phase' of education in order to raise standards. This was interpreted as evidence that the government was 'now planning a more direct assault on the primary school curriculum than anything so far attempted'.[48] The DES response signalled a further stage of active intervention in the content of education. The note *The Organization and Content of the 5–16 Curriculum*[49] outlined official policy on objectives for the primary phase. The viewpoint expressed here was almost a backward step from the one contained in *The School Curriculum*. The earlier paper had considered the primary curriculum in terms of skills and areas of experience. While the DES note refers to the limitations of a subject-based curriculum, its following description consists entirely of subject areas. Some of the cruder statements would later acquire a more professional veneer: for example 'introduce pupils to computers' becomes in *Better Schools*[50] 'introduce pupils to the nature and use in school and in society of new technology'. However, the main objectives for the primary phase retain their view of the curriculum as essentially content-based.

The HMI response to Sir Keith Joseph's call for a broad consensus on objectives for the curriculum was published in the recently inaugurated *Curriculum Matters* series. Compared with the DES recommendations, a similar conflict of opinion emerges to the one seen previously in *View* and *Framework*. In the Inspectorate's guideline *The Curriculum from 5–16*[51], the emphasis is on areas of learning and experience, with reference to the underlying skills, concepts and attitudes. Subsequent documents in the series have progressed to considering the objectives which might be established for separate subject areas. It remains to be seen to what extent future DES directives incorporate the Inspectorate's recommendations.

What becomes apparent in a consideration of central publications in the eighties is how little has been achieved since the debate was initiated by Callaghan. There is still no clear formulation of what the precise aims and objectives for the primary phase should be, nor a general agreement on curriculum content. Official statements also consistently reveal two glaring omissions. The first is the lack of any practical guidance as to how schools are to implement national policy. Secondly, there is no reference to the allocation of extra resources. Demands to extend what is being taught in schools have implications for the provision of extra materials, as well as staffing above the traditional pupil-teacher ratio. The concept of curriculum-led staffing, with additional teachers to provide expertise in specified areas, is especially relevant if primary schools are to utilize subject specialists. Instead of an expansion of resources to meet these demands, LEAs and schools are being impelled to implement curriculum expansion at a time of severe and increasing cutbacks in the service. By ignoring these fundamentally important issues, official publications lose much of their credibility as educational guidelines. They are reduced instead to platitudinous political statements, designed to project official policy, but without any real regard for the quality of schooling.

Finally, brief mention should be given to some of the additional measures which have supported official publications in directing the primary curriculum. Eleven-year-olds have been the subjects of national monitoring by the APU in mathematics, science and language, the first results of which appeared during 1980–1. It is not proposed to offer a detailed account of the impact of the APU here, but its establishment was seen in many circles as a means of central intervention.[52] It was believed that national monitoring would encourage schools to teach to a set of pre-specified objectives determined by national criteria. Fears that the work of the APU would lead to the domination of an American-style system of testing have so far proved unfounded. Members of the Unit have stressed their independence, and their results have been presented neutrally.

However, the danger remains in attempting to evaluate educational achievement through children's performance in standardized tests. DES policy is to encourage assessment by LEAs, which has led to a growth of testing in schools. There is a risk at local level of creating a backwash effect on the curriculum, where 'what is taught is what is tested'.[53]

Government priorities for the primary curriculum will also be enforced through the allocation of resources to approved areas via Educational Support Grants, and the in-service grants scheme, established in 1984. These moves are likely to favour the development of science and technology. The tendency towards subject specialism will also increase with DES demands that students on initial teacher training courses should spend a large part of their time in subject studies. Therefore, for primary schools in the future, the effects of central control are likely to have an increasing influence.

Conclusion

Statements from the DES have repeatedly refuted the allegation that they represent a move towards central control. They have stressed the importance of 'partnership' between the Secretary of State, the local authorities and the schools, and denied any wish to make statutory changes to this relationship. However, by a rigorous interpretation of the legal framework, the government has affirmed both its obligation to determine national policy, and the duty of the local authorities to implement it. Policy statements have been issued as matters for discussion, or guidelines, or consultative documents, and the autonomy of the school in deciding individual programmes supported. Nevertheless, the DES has succeeded in determining the form that the debate on the curriculum should take, and establishing the parameters within which discussion is to be conducted. The view of the curriculum which has emerged during the eighties is essentially one defined by central agencies. The teacher's role, therefore, has been reduced to discussing 'questions set by others'.[54]

Some of the issues which have been raised by the DES are generally acceptable. The idea that the primary curriculum should be broad and balanced with opportunities for progression and continuity is a professional challenge. However, the national framework being promoted to secure these aims is very narrowly conceived. The emphasis on subject areas leads to the primary curriculum being viewed in terms of content rather than in relation to the development of the child. The move towards defining precise objectives for the curriculum, with statements about what pupils 'should know' at each stage, has the danger of reducing education to a linear sequence along which children are supposed to pass. The importance of the social aspects of the primary school and the value of the inter-disciplinary approach to teaching could be submerged in a national policy which stresses the outcome above the process of education. This seems far removed from the view of the primary curriculum expressed in the Hadow Report half a century ago:

> the curriculum is to be thought of in terms of activity and of experience rather than knowledge to be acquired and facts to be stored'.[55]

The Effect on the Classroom

My main credential for writing this section is that I was teaching in primary schools from 1974–85 — a period which encompasses most of the issues under discussion. What follows draws extensively on this experience and expresses an essentially personal viewpoint. Nevertheless, I hope that it offers a valid interpretation of some of the ways in which central initiatives influenced primary practice at classroom level.

Perhaps the most striking feature of the seventies and eighties was the need for teachers to adjust to enormous leaps in professional ideology. At the start of the period, the child-centred approach advocated that the individual's own experiences were fundamental to the learning process. This was shortly challenged by the belief that informal methods neglected the basic skills, only to lead to a further change of direction with the view that the 3Rs were, in fact, being taught to the virtual exclusion of everything else. The lack of consistency meant that teachers, even when following officially-endorsed methods, seemed to be always in the wrong. This view-point was compounded by the popular press who often distorted the findings of central publications in order to heap further invective on the teaching profession.

An additional characteristic of this period was the deluge of guidelines, discussion papers and directives from HMI and the DES which flooded the schools. The sheer quantity of material was sufficient to produce a 'shut off' effect due to the impossibility of assimilating all the literature being produced. I would suggest that the main impact on the classroom came, not directly from central government, but through the interpretation of these policy statements at local level through the LEAs. This was particularly apparent during the eighties when education authorities were directed by the DES to produce curricular policies. These were communicated to schools in the form of guidelines on curriculum development, and disseminated through the work of local authority advisers and in-service training. Schools were also required during this period to implement their own curricular reviews, and to state in writing their aims and objectives. From 1982 curriculum policy was incorporated into the compulsory school booklets produced by individual schools for distribution to parents. Although the initial demand to engage in curriculum development stemmed from the DES, schools were likely to determine their own policies in the light of LEA guidelines.

A major consequence of this activity was to extend greatly the professionalism of the primary teacher. Schemes of work and record books had always been a feature of the primary classroom, but the system was often haphazard and uncoordinated. Teachers were now required to engage in an appraisal of what was being taught in their schools, and to extend this into a structured programme across the curriculum. Of course, the production of written guidelines is no guarantee that these will be put into effect in the classroom. Nevertheless, I believe that the process of formally stating curricular objectives played an important part in helping teachers formulate and extend their work.

The developments which occurred as a result of this activity affected the content, rather than the organization of primary education. The HMI Primary Survey noted that by 1978 the major contemporary organizational change in junior classes — the abolition of streaming — had been effected in most schools. Policy from the mid-seventies was directed towards extending the curriculum in terms of the subjects taught, rather than through any change in teaching methods. One major impact on the classroom can be seen in the development of science and technology during this period. The priority afforded to science teaching by LEAs came as a direct response to the recommendations in central publications. Developments in technology also owed much to government influence in the form of grants towards the purchase of micro-computers. By the mid-1980s the anomalous situation could arise whereby primary schools, unable to afford basic reading books, could nevertheless provide their pupils with the latest software.

This question of resource allocation was possibly the most important issue to anyone working in schools during the 1970s and 1980s. Although additional demands were being made on teachers, the means to implement them were not forthcoming. This was particularly apparent during the period of Conservative government which saw the state system of education being virtually dismantled. Annual reports from HMI on the effects of cutbacks in local authority spending revealed a growing disparity in the service being provided by different LEAs. The effect on primary schools included loss of part-time teachers and ancillary help, falling capitation levels and widespread decay of school buildings. In order to provide even the most basic materials, teachers were forced to spend large amounts of time in fund-raising. Furthermore, as a result of falling rolls, there was widespread redeployment of teachers, so that many schools lost the specialist leadership being advocated by the DES and HMI. Heads and teachers were confronted with an inherent conflict between the growing demands facing them, and the lack of time, staffing levels, and materials to put these into effect. In addition, at a time when expectations of teachers were rising, their professionalism was increasingly under attack. Criticism of the profession by Sir Keith Joseph, together with his emphasis on methods to weed out weaker teachers, helped to create a loss of confidence in the Secretary of State. Attempts to restructure conditions of service, combined with major falls in salary levels, led to one of the longest and most acrimonious pay disputes on record. All of these issues contributed to the fall in morale among the teaching profession so evident in the 1980s. Moves towards developments in the primary curriculum were, therefore, incompatible with an educational service which was being run down, and a teaching profession which felt under threat.

At the beginning of the seventies, research, albeit limited, by Taylor and Reid[56] suggested that teachers considered Heads and themselves to be the major determinants of what was taught in schools. The Secretary of State and House of Commons ranked lowest in the scale as having very little influence. If this study were to be conducted today, the results might be considerably different. From the mid-seventies the freedom of the individual teacher came strongly under attack with the general demand that teachers should be more accountable for their actions. The growth of central control can be seen as part of this wider challenge directed against the autonomy of the teacher. By the mid-eighties the effects of central directives were being felt on the classroom through the efforts of local authorities to stimulate curriculum development. Interpretation of central policy at local level has, so far, avoided the utilitarian emphasis of DES directives, and actively utilized the professional contribution of teachers. However, the fact remains that primary schools are likely to be increasingly evaluated, not by the extent to which they meet the demands of the community which they serve, but by the success with which they conform to nationally-imposed criteria.

Acknowledgement

I should like to thank Malcolm Ogles for discussing many of the issues raised in this chapter.

Notes

1. Quoted in Gordon, P. (1985), 'The Handbook of Suggestions for Teachers: Its origins and evolution' in *J. Educ. Adm. Hist.*, January, 17, 1, pp. 41–8.
2. Kogan, M. (1978), *The Politics of Educational Change*, London, Fontana.
3. Salter, B. and Tapper, T. (1981), *Education, Politics and the State*, London, Grant McIntyre.
4. Lawton, D. (1980), *The Politics of the School Curriculum*, London, Routledge and Kegan Paul. And (1984), *The Tightening Grip; Bedford Way Papers 21*, London, University of London.
5. Kogan, M. *op. cit.*, p. 63.
6. *The Times Educational Supplement*, 15 October 1976.
7. DES (Welsh Office) (1977a), *Education in Schools: A Consultative Document: Cmnd 6869*, London, HMSO. (The Green Paper), para. 2:19.
8. DES (1977b), 'Local Authority Arrangements for the School Curriculum', *Circular 14/77*, London, HMSO.
9. DES (Welsh Office) (1980a), *A Framework for the School Curriculum*, London, HMSO.
10. DES (Welsh Office) (1981a), *The School Curriculum*, London, HMSO.
11. DES (1984a), *Press Notice 1/84*, Text of the speech by the Rt Hon Sir Keith Joseph, Secretary of State for Education and Science, at the North of England Education Conference, Sheffield, on Friday, 6 January 1984.
12. DES, (1984b), *The Organization and Content of the 5–16 Curriculum: A Note*, London, HMSO.
13. DES (Welsh Office) (1985a), *Better Schools, Cmnd 9469*, London, HMSO.

14. LAWTON, D. (1984) *op. cit.*, pp. 11–2.
15. *The Guardian*, 22 July 1986.
16. CACE, (1967), *Children and Their Primary Schools: The Plowden Report*, London, HMSO.
17. *Ibid*, para. 505.
18. COX, C. and DYSON, A. (Eds.), (1969), *Fight for Education*, London, Critical Quarterly Society.
19. *Times Educational Supplement*, 31 October 1975.
20. DES (1975), *A Language for Life; The Bullock Report*, London, HMSO.
21. BENNETT, N. (1976), *Teaching Styles and Pupil Progress*, London, Open Books.
22. RICHARDS, C. (1984), *The Study of Primary Education: A Source Book Vol. 1*, Lewes, Falmer Press, p. 45.
23. GRETTON, J. and JACKSON, M. (1976), *William Tyndale: Collapse of a School or a System?* London, Allen and Unwin, p. 125.
24. *Times Educational Supplement*, 15 October 1976, p. 2.
25. *Times Educational Supplement*, 22 October 1976, p. 1.
26. DES, (1977), *Educating Our Children: Four Subjects for Debate*, London, HMSO.
27. RICHARDS, C. (1984), *op. cit.*, p. 51.
28. Green Paper, para. 1.4
29. *Ibid*, para. 2.2.
30. *Ibid*, para. 2.3v.
31. *Ibid*, para. 1.19i.
32. *Ibid*, para. 2.3.
33. DES, (1978), *Primary Education in England. A Survey by HM Inspectors of Schools*, London, HMSO.
34. See also SIMON, B. (1980), 'The primary school revolution: Myth or reality?', in *Education in the Sixties*, History of Education Society Conference Papers.
35. RICHARDS, C. (1980), 'Demythologizing primary education' in *Journal of Curriculum Studies*, 12, 1, p. 78.
36. Definitions in RICHARDS, C. (1982), 'Primary education 1974–80', in RICHARDS, C. (Ed.) *New Directions in Primary Education*, Lewes, Falmer Press, p. 12.
37. CACE, *op. cit.*, para. 9.
38. DES (1978), *op. cit.*, para. 8.25.
39. DES (1979) *Local Authority Arrangements for the School Curriculum*, London, HMSO.
40. DES (1980a), *op. cit.*
41. DES (1980b), *A View of the Curriculum*, London, HMSO.
42. DES (1981a) *op. cit.*
43. *Times Educational Supplement*, 27 July 1981.
44. DES (1981a), para. 35.
45. DES (Welsh Office) (1982), *Mathematics Counts; the Cockcroft Report*, London, HMSO.
46. DES (1982), *Education 5 to 9*, London, HMSO.

47. DES, (1983), *9–13 Middle Schools: An Illustrative Survey*, London, HMSO.
48. *Times Educational Supplement*, 13 January 1986, p. 21.
49. DES (1984b), *op. cit.*
50. DES (1985a), *op. cit.*, para. 61.
51. DES (1985b) *The Curriculum from 5–16, Curriculum Matters 2*, London, HMSO.
52. See, for example, MacDonald, B. (1976), 'Who's afraid of evaluation?' in *Education 3–13*, 4, 2, pp. 87–91.
53. Thomas, N. (1982), 'Testing and assessment', in *Primary Education Review*, 13, p. 4.
54. Garland, R. (1980), 'Department, Inspectorate and the agenda for change', in Golby, M. (Ed.) *The Core Curriculum*, Exeter, University of Exeter.
55. Board of Education, (1931), *Report of the Consultative Committee on the Primary School, The Hadow Report*, London, HMSO.
56. Taylor, P. and Reid, W. (1973), 'Influence and Change in the Primary School', in *Education 3–13*, 1, 1, pp. 29–35.

Towards a Partnership: The Taylor Report, School Government and Parental Involvement

Michael Arkinstall

In historical terms, State Education is not very old. Less than 120 years have elapsed since Forster's Act of 1870 yet, in that short space of time there have been massive changes in society. Sociologists would argue convincingly that the forces of change, be they economic, political, or technological have accelerated to the point where schools and their curricula can no longer keep pace with the demands made upon them by post-industrial society. In the early days following the Act of 1870 when the idea of compulsory education was still new life was pretty grim. Conditions in the schools were harsh and disciplined. The cane was in regular use. Health was poor: children starved and ragged and any attempts to measure success were grounded in evaluation of basic literacy. As one historian put it: 'The state had interfered with the pattern of family life by coming between parent and child, reducing family income and imposing new patterns of behaviour on both parent and child'.[1] In stark contrast, schools of today are clean and airy: curricula are wide ranging and interesting and the teachers rely upon good interpersonal relationships and cooperation rather than fear to maintain order. Far from relying upon conformity and regimentation there is now a general acceptance that schools shall be exciting, open, communities and that children should be treated as individuals, with their school-work being organized around their needs — an attempt to match up the curriculum to each individual pupil. Such a realization, of course, now imposes greater burdens of caring and planning on both teachers and parents. The era of consultation and participation which was heralded in the Plowden Report of 1967 has now arrived.

Plowden had suggested a minimum programme of cooperation with parents.[2] The five point plan of action, which was regarded merely as a starting point for building good attitudes, specified the following: Welcome to the School; Meetings with Teachers; Open Days; Information for Parents and Reports. There was also a firm recommendation that 'special efforts should be made to make contact with parents who do not visit the schools' (I30.f.). Understanding and cooperation between parents and teachers was regarded as crucial to the future of schooling. Moreover, it was stressed, that home, school and neighbourhood 'factors' each had a part to play in child development and achievement. A whole new ideology, a community perspective, was added by Plowden's 500 page report on children and their primary schools. It was concluded that 'community schools' should be developed in all areas but especially in what were termed educational priority areas.

> 'As a matter of national policy, "positive discrimination" should favour schools in neighbourhoods where children are most severely handicapped by home conditions. The programme should be phased to make schools in the most deprived areas as good as the best in the country. For this it may be necessary that their greater claim on resources should be maintained'.[3]

The concept of Educational Priority Areas or EPAs was taken further by the Halsey Report of 1972. In its so-called 'action research' programme, four specific objectives were set out for these EPAs. They were, briefly, to raise children's performance levels, to improve teacher-morale, to increase parental involvement and to build a sense of community responsibility.

Readers who might wish to trace the historical outline of change and development over the last seventy-five years could profitably refer to the special *Times Educational Supplement* summary published in 1985 under the title '75 Years of the TES.' Here, in outline form, is revealed the constant, ongoing, process of analysis, arguing and lobbying which is seen to precede the time when the 'political machine can be geared up to giving it statutory or administrative form'.[4] But there are no such simple short-cuts to understanding 'control' in education and how the balance of power shifts between local and central government, between groups and individuals, creating frustration and dismay in the minds of parents or teachers who feel that 'the system' is definitely against them. It has been argued that there is, in fact, no single system of state education. Instead there is a 'distributed system of educational administration' which is locally administered. Briault describes it as a 'system in which power and responsibility are shared among central government, local government and the teachers themselves and it is hard to identify in many instances single points of decision ... This triangle may be referred to as a triangle of tension'.[5] Briault suggests that the in-built 'checks and balances' involved in consultation within the triangle leads to a kind of consensus between those with responsibility and this 'commands reasonable confidence' among the customers.

Another analysis of participation in education is provided by Weaver[6] and quoted in the Open University Course E222 (The Control of Education in Britain). His analysis describes the Four Estates of Education: First are those authorized to be society's value-setters or goal-determiners — M.P.'s, Councillors, managers and governors. They direct the whole enterprise and are accountable for its validity, effectiveness and efficiency. Generically, called the governors. Next are their servants, central, local and institutional officials. They may be collectively described as administrators. Third come the teachers and academics who control the learning and teaching process — the Professionals. Fourth are the learners themselves, their families, employers and society as a whole — the Consumers. It is becoming clear that the 'education industry' is a very large one and that there can be a considerable distance between the policy makers and the consumers. What is actually happening at a given moment in the life time of six-year-old Joe Soap in his urban classroom might seem to be of little significance in the corridors of County Hall or the conference rooms of Whitehall. Perhaps this realization is behind the inspiration and philosophy of the Taylor Report which seeks a new kind of partnership for the schools.

Councillor Taylor, Leader of Blackburn Council, chaired the thirty-one person committee appointed to make an independent enquiry into the management and government of schools in England and Wales by Mr Reg Prentice in 1975. The terms of reference were clearly stated thus:

> To review the arrangements for the management and
> government of maintained primary and secondary schools in
> England and Wales, including the composition and functions
> of bodies of managers and governors, and their relationships
> with local education authorities, with Head Teachers and

staffs of schools, with parents of pupils and with the local community at large; and to make recommendations.[7]

In July 1975 the Committee invited evidence from interested organizations and individuals and from the general public. Over 400 submissions were received and these, combined with the study produced by the London University Institute of Education[8] were used as the 'starting point' of the investigation. Visits were planned to give the members of the Committee first hand experience of the arrangements that existed and to enable discussions to take place as to the effectiveness of such provision. One year later, in July 1976, the Auld Report on the William Tyndale disaster provided further valuable evidence as to the issues in school management that were of great public concern.[9] But, by that time, states the Report, the Committee which produced its final recommendations and conclusions in 1977, had already focused on the same basic issues which were derived from written evidence and visits.

The Committee based its deliberation upon three assumptions. These were simply that i) the roles of central and local government as laid down in the 1944 Education Act would remain unchanged; ii) arrangements for school government ought to be flexible and capable of adaptation to different and changing circumstances; and iii) proposals should be very realistic, drawing upon existing resources and facilities in such a way that an improved system of school government could be created without any sudden, large increase in public expenditure. There was, therefore, an attempt to provide a 'commonsense', practical evaluation of what was happening around the country and to suggest viable ways and means of improving existing practices.

After describing the existing legal framework for school government as detailed in the 1944 Act and the 'reality' of the research study by Baron and Howell between 1965 and 1969[10] which showed that many local authorities had close control of the composition of managing and governing bodies, where membership might be confined to local councillors or members of the rank and file of political parties, the Report set out a new approach. There was an attempt to 'spell out' the ways in which a positive contribution could be made by parents and others by a careful 'definition of the possible area of debate and discussion and the forum in which it is to be conducted'.[11]

The new 'scheme of things' was analyzed in detail under

separate headings: membership of the new governing bodies, communication and co-operation, the Curriculum, Finance, Appointments, Training the Governors and the ways in which the new approach might be implemented. It was then presented in the established style of Plowden or Bullock[12] with comprehensive lists and summaries of recommendations and conclusions. Interestingly, whereas Plowden had 197 recommendations, Bullock 333, Taylor managed to present a modest eighty-nine as the basis for future growth and improvement.

Limiting the summary of the recommendations to their minimum, for the sake of space, one might present the following as essential to an understanding of how Taylor envisaged a structural shift in the responsibility for governing state schools — an official view of how to make accountability feasible by ensuring that parents, teachers and other interested parties kept an eagle eye on what was happening in their own local schools.

> 3. Section 20 of the Education Act 1944 should be repealed as soon as is possible and from a date to be fixed by the Secretaries of State, every school should have its own separate governing body.
> 5. The membership of governing bodies should consist of equal numbers of local education authority representatives, school staff, parents (with, where appropriate, pupils) and representatives of the local community.
> 11. Those to be appointed as the school's parent governors should be elected by the parents of the children attending that school.
> 32. The governing body should satisfy itself that adequate arrangements are made to inform parents, to involve them in their children's progress and welfare, to enlist their support and to ensure their access to the school and a teacher by reasonable arrangement.
> 37. The governing body should be given by the local education authority the responsibility for setting the aims of the school, for considering the means by which they are pursued, for keeping under review the school's progress towards them and for deciding upon action to facilitate such progress.
> 42. Every local education authority should take steps to ensure that the services of a general adviser are regularly available to each of its schools and that the general adviser

will be available for consultation with, and report to, the governing body on request.

49. Authorities should study the possibilities of making financial arrangements to facilitate initiative and independent action at the school level

54. The selection of deputy heads and other teachers should rest with the governing body...

64. The local education authority should authorise the governing body to have urgent minor repairs carried out up to a limit set by the authority.

69. All local education authorities should be required to ensure that initial and in-service training courses are available for governors.

79. It should be open to the governing body to elect as Chairman any one of its members, except those who are paid members of the staff of the school.

81. Attendance allowance should not be paid to any school governor.

AND, most important in terms of action:

86. A statutory duty should be imposed on all local education authorities to make arrangements for the government of the county schools in their areas conforming to the requirements which we have stipulated as essential to the implementation of the new approach to school government, to publicize the arrangements and to make them known to all concerned.

The Bullock Report on the teaching of reading and the use of English had contained a four-page long written note of dissent. Taylor's Report followed the same pattern with its note of dissent concerning the functions that would be allotted to the new governing bodies. The critic's main concern was that governing bodies were not given sufficient involvement in financial responsibilities and decision-making. There was the promise inherent in the recommendations that 'financial arrangements' and the 'allowances for schools and the ways of distributing them' should be investigated with a view to finding improvements in consultation — ways of making governors more involved in financial matters and, hence, more accountable. But, it was felt, governors should be given more power and more freedom to control internal spending — albeit in consultation with the Head and the staff. Such a comment, of course, presupposes the capacity and the eagerness of the new governors to share in accountability!

Reports usually precede the legislation process and often form the basis for new law. Taylor's recommendations were not completely implemented and the 'formal powers' of the governing bodies were not specifically established. A white paper was issued in December 1978[13] 'The Composition of School Governing Bodies' and in a House of Commons' debate the Secretary of State 'ducked' the decision on formal powers with the claim 'The Bill does not contain any provision relating to the specific powers of governing bodies, partly because I believe that getting the right people on to governing bodies in sufficient numbers will be enough to do the necessary task on its own'.[14]

In 1971 Professor Kogan wrote: 'The purpose of governing bodies is to give the general public a say in the running of the school. Most people would regard this as a pious hope which has never really been fulfilled'.[15] The historical evidence supports this view. Governing bodies were seen to have a predominance of councillors and teachers were specifically excluded from 'governership' The governors had little power in the control of schools since finance and general management devolved on the LEA and the internal organization and curriculum 'belonged' to the Head Teacher and the so-called teaching professionals.

How far then, was the situation changed after Taylor? The 1980 Act which followed Taylor, perpetuated the LEA control over the curriculum but consolidated the influence of teachers and parents in section 2 by the statutory requirement that there should be at least two parent governors and one or two teacher-governors (according to the size of the school). But, the fact that teachers and parents were members of the governing bodies, that there was structural participation, did not mean that there was, necessarily, some shift in the general distribution of power. Head Teachers remained in effective control of the school. The research conducted in Exeter and East Devon in 1983[16] showed that governors took their responsibilities very seriously but that 'the degree of power exercised was largely dependent upon how much power the Head Teacher permitted them to have by allowing access to schools for visits, and upon the level and scope of prior agreement between Head Teachers and governors in setting and managing debates'. Kogan and his fellow researchers from Brunel University spent three years exploring the range of practice found in governing bodies in the South East of England and, in so doing, 'witnessed the gap between the rhetoric of the Taylor Report and the reality of the 1980 Act'. Their research resulted in the creation of explanatory models which would aid understanding of how the governing bodies operated and was dominated by 'political and power-exchange theory'. These 'models' are summarized in *Caught in the Act*[17]:

> The Accountable Model focuses on the school where the purpose is to ensure the satisfactory day-to-day operation and efficency of the institution. Demands upon governors are few.
>
> In the Advisory Model professionalism is the key criterion and leadership is seen as important. Demands upon governors are described as moderate. The Supportive Model has a wider focus on the shcool within the educational system and the purpose is to give the school support along with any other connected interests. Here, it is suggested, the demands on governors are few, except in times of crisis. But there is in this model an almost elitist view of educational government.
>
> In the Mediating Model, focus moves towards the local education system. Consensus is considered to be paramount and demands upon governors are described as considerable.

The Exeter Society researchers doubtless drew upon the finding and the conceptual framework produced by Kogan as they attempted to survey the scene that existed in Devon in 1985. The teacher-governors became the main informants for a study in the secondary school sector of an LEA that had an extraordinary variety and diversity of schools. Although this present chapter is concerned with the primary school in particular, it might be interesting and significant to note what the experienced teacher governors thought of parent-governors.[18]

> Without exception the inclusion of the parent governor is seen by teacher-governors as a positive step forward. They hold a valued place, are a vital commodity! That value seems to take the form of the fact that they are highly supportive of the school.
>
> However, it appears that the actual influence of parent-governors is peculiarly less than the value ascribed to their position. Only in examples where parent-governors were professionally involved in education did their opinions appear to be given standing.

It would appear that the role of the parent-governor is not clearly defined or understood either by themselves or by others. Therefore, they become the 'most isolated' 'most powerless' yet contradictorily 'the most valued' part of the governing body by the teacher-governors.

There is considerable fellow feeling from teacher-governors for parent-governors particularly in regard to the difficulties of representing their constituencies and reporting back.

The Taylor Report, the 1980 Act, the Green Paper 1984 (Parental influence in School), the publication *Better Schools* (DES 1985) and the latest Education Bill (1986) — all support an increasing parental participation in the government of schools. They impose a structural shift that cannot be avoided in primary school management. But, it could be argued, realistically, that the greatest 'operational' changes in the primary schools of the eighties stem from parental involvement that is voluntary and unconstitutional.

Evidence of this could be drawn from projects and experiments that took place in Birmingham primary schools in the last ten years. Writing in 1981, John Rennie described the essential link between Home and School in developmental terms:

In 1970, it was still possible to find notices forbidding parents entry to schools — and many more where the notices had been removed but the attitudes were kept securely in place...

In the decade since 1971, progress has been dramatic. In many areas all over the country, changes have been wrought by small groups of educators sometimes in the face of opposition, but more frequently against a background if not of apathy, then, at best, of mild secpticism. It is to the credit of a minority of teachers that such scepticism has been largely replaced by interest and, increasingly, enthusiasm.[19]

Perhaps the best example of this operational change in primary education is to be gleaned from a study of the Van Leer project in Birmingham and the consequences it created, or precipitated, in many, many, schools.

The Project, to give its correct title, was described as the Birmingham Experiment in Community Education. It had a limited life-span of six years, with two equal time-phases, during which specific aims and objectives were decided and pursued. The original

three 'core' schools — each in areas of the city that were indisput-
ably 'disadvantaged' — were associated with six 'extension' schools
where pre-school workers were appointed to work in the school
community.[20] Whilst it would be true to say that, in the three core
schools there was a specific project objective — 'to improve inter-
ethnic attitudes' since the school populations were heavily weighted
in terms of West Indian or Asian children, in the six extension
schools, scattered throughout the city, the main dynamic came in
the shape of 'pre-school' input. The six schools set out to develop
links with their own communities. What happened is best illustrated
by referring to one particular school.[21]

A pre-school worker was appointed on a part-time basis, working a flexible fifteen hour week. Coming from a nursing background, this worker was experienced in meeting people, helping
them and winning them over by her friendly, approachable, hardworking manner. Going out and about in the school locality and
meeting parents and their friends, the 'pre-school worker's leadership' enabled positive links to be drawn with, first of all, the
parents of young children and later other caring people in the
community. The school population included a very high percentage
of 'one-parent' families and that extra link between school and home
helped to bridge the psychological barrier between the loneliness
and isolation of home and the seemingly implacable fortress of the
school where many of the teachers were perceived as 'different and
distant'.

As the school became more 'open', so the gap between the
teachers and the parents narrowed. Using surplus space, available
because of 'falling rolls', various groups and activities were set up.
Keep-fit sessions, a toy library, play groups, meetings and talks
from experts, get-togethers, a mother and toddler group — all of
these, at different times, helped to break down the reluctance
some parents had for 'going to school' and, brought a new perspective to the work of teachers. It would be hard now to envisage a
return to the 'moat and drawbridge' concept of schooling for the
parents became more and more involved in the general life of the
busy primary school. An added advantage, in terms of efficiency,
was that the pre-school worker was able to build a 'communication
network' within the community to publicize school events and to
represent parental views — pinpointing problems and discussing
needs.

Eight years on from those early initiatives, the same school has
its now, well established, pre-school groups. They are run exclusive-

ly by the mothers — alongside the normal daily work of the school. Accounts are kept, liaison is maintained and the young children are gently prepared by play and experience for the 'life in school' that will follow. The early input of the Van Leer project, supported afterwards by Inner City Partnership funds, certainly changed the climate of the school. In a very practical way, parents became actively involved in the work of the school, helping to create a different ethos. Perhaps it would be true to say that these same parents were far happier working with children than they would ever be as 'governors' or 'agents of accountability'.

Visualizing the concept of 'community school' along a continuum, it might be shown that most schools have parental involvement. Indeed, the economic climate has 'forced' many groups of parents and teachers to devise schemes of working together to try and supplement what are seen as modest and inadequate funds for books and equipment essential to the learning process. The lively primary school provides a hundred and one opportunities for teachers and parents to come closer together as they participate in projects, schemes, visits, expeditions, events and the daily round of school life. One of the greatest values attached to this now cooperative approach in primary schools is that the understanding and mutual sympathy built by teachers and parents working together promotes much better discipline and socialization in the child.

The education industry is guilty of inventing new concepts and phraseology to describe contemporary versions of practices that took place a long time ago. Margaret McMillan was performing valuable social and community work in her Deptford Nursery at the time of the first world war. Her 'outreach' work not only raised consciousness but, in some cases helped survival. Some of the so-called 'outreach' work of today is designed to provide neutral territory, such as shops, libraries or other buildings where the general public and teachers can meet freely and share exhibitions, discussions or group sessions about education. But the evidence of such work is patchy and many different agencies are involved. What happens in Leicester will probably surprise the residents of Weston-Super-Mare or Durham! The whole area of research into parent and teacher relations and involvement in schools gives massive scope for further investigation. This chapter hardly 'scratches the surface' of the debate between the partnership and rivalry of teachers and parents in the control of education.

Calvert carried out a small scale research into parental involvement when he investigated the 'changing patterns of participation' in six primary schools in the Midlands.[22] His intention was to explore the contrasts between the rhetoric and the reality and to establish and then describe what parents were actually doing in and for their school. His analysis evolved around the concept of 'parental partnership', delving into the attitudes and relationships that he found as he saw parents working within the school community. It was one of his conclusions that the 'problems' which prevented parents from 'knowing' their school was not a lack of interest but rather a lack of confidence — brought about by ignorance and a lack of information about the school. Hence, he did stress the importance of 'communication' with parents — something which many schools do badly. When he tried to ascertain what was generally considered to be a 'good School' there were certain recurrent themes: 'The school should be welcoming. There should be standards of behaviour and work. The school should be busy and lively. There must be a willingness to have parents in school and to talk to them. The relationships that existed in a school were seen to be crucial in the creation of 'quality'. Parents wanted the school to be a 'caring' place which had regard for individuals, a place where children could be safe and, above all, happy. Few parents ever mentioned the curriculum of their school. They took it for granted that this area was the province of the teachers — the professional experts who were trained to teach their children.

Calvert found that, although only two schools out of the six he visited had not got parent governors, most schools had some sort of parent or parent-teacher organization which was committed to the well-being of the children. But one of the problems of such associations was the tendency for them to be dominated by small groups. Sometimes, the parents in the groups were the same parents who wore different hats at 'governors' meetings. Other parents sometimes resented the seeming influence of one or two mothers (or fathers) though they were either unwilling or reluctant to become more involved themselves. These cliques, in a sense, contradicted the 'openness' of schools yet, ironically, they provided many parents and teachers with the opportunity to get to know each other better and, presumably, to appreciate the difficulties and the problems involved in educating the children. The research confirmed the fact that teachers accepted the need to encourage parents but teacher-dominance in the classroom was carefully safeguarded. The skills and the specific knowledge of the parents was often completely overlooked. There was a realization that, even when teachers and parents worked together, there should still be 'certain special areas' where the frontiers that bound home or school should remain. But, overall, Calvert considered that there now exists a general willingness amongst teachers and within parents to move closer towards a partnership in education. His investigation revealed 'much potential for further development'.

Perhaps the most important question to be answered in this very brief sketch of change in the primary sector is 'How much power or control do parents have in the schools?' Writing in the *Times Educational Supplement*, Steve Collins argued that parental control was sometimes little more than tokenism.[23] It could be described as a game of snakes and ladders, in which the local education authorities were going through the motions of establishing the parent governors rather than giving them due power as the 'consumers'. Quoting the 'Honeyford' affair, it was then shown, by Collins, that the parents were very much the 'junior partners' when it came to their dealings with the professionals, be they teachers or administrators. The only way they could 'get rid of' the Head Teacher was by making the daily task of running the school an impossible one — not by using their powers that had been bestowed by the 'democratic process'. In fact, using the 'ladder of participation' model borrowed from Shelly Arnstein it was clearly suggested that the parents do not enter the 'citizen power zone'. Their presence on the governing bodies is ineffectual or cosmetic in terms of decision making. But, is this evidence outdated? Only six months later, Headmistress Sue May, was suspended from duty at her Surrey middle school because she was criticized by parents for trying to bring a '19th century school quickly into the 20th century'.[24] In the very same week one local authority issued a policy statement which made it clear that the intention was to strengthen parental involvement in the schools by a variety of strategies.[25]

Greater involvement by parents is seen as an integral part of the wider strategy for getting 'closer to the consumer'. Steps already being taken include:

Pre-school and home-school liaison workers in schools.
Schools have been circulated with examples of good practice.
Application forms for head and deputy head appointments ask for views of parental involvement.
Five elected parents now sit on all governing bodies-making them the largest single group.

£33,000 allocated in 1986/87 for school governor training courses. A video programme is nearing completion.

It could be argued that the greatest single agent of change to
affect primary education has been the growing participation of parents in the everyday life of the schools. So far, this involvement has
been manifested at the social and pastoral level rather than in the
reconstruction and modernization of the curriculum. As the parents
and the teachers have come closer together so, too, has developed, in
many cases, a growing awareness of children's needs and the difficulties which exist both in the home and at school. But, in spite of
legislation, the partnership between parents and teachers will never
be an equal one because the parents and the teachers have different
roles to play: what happens in a compact home situation will never
be the same as what will happen in the institution of school. The
evidence available suggests that although teachers and parents have
moved much closer to each other, in order to promote the well-
being and progress of the children, the barriers which protect both
home and school still exist. Teachers are still keen to protect their
hard sought 'professionalism' and parents seek the 'happiness' of
their children, often putting it in front of any pedagogic or curricular concerns. But, optimistically, the signs are that, at the school
level, there is a greater degree of cooperation between the parents
and the teachers. No longer can a school remain an island kingdom.
Parents have certain rights, as defined by Acts of Parliament, but
their actual impact in the schools is restricted by many practicalities.
School hours very often coincide with work hours. Parents cannot
be in two places at the same time. As children grow up they do not
expect to see their parents in the classroom so, in practice, the
greatest parental input takes place in the nursery and infant years. If
teachers are well paid, surely, argue some parents, it is their job to
provide the motivation for learning and the learning experiences.

So, most primary schools survive by creating a dynamic compromise. Parents are encouraged to take part in certain activities:
teachers protect their classroom privacy and independence. But if
the vision of true partnership is ever to be achieved the social
distance between the parents and the teachers will have to be de-
creased. In a recent book McConkey[26] set out some of the qualities
that are needed to develop real partnership. He wrote:

It is not what you are now that counts but rather what you
are prepared to become:
Are you prepared

To avoid uniformity and welcome diversity
To listen, observe and negotiate
To consult as well as be consulted
To be open about your feelings so that your partners can be
    open about theirs
To ask why and to answer why
Not to go it alone
— if so,
Then you'll find working with parents is a worthwhile
    experience.

Perhaps the same check list could be applied by parents! The conclusion to be derived from all this, is that it is the people in the schools who create the change, or fail to do so, rather than the Acts of Parliament, the reports or the influence of the media.

Notes

1. HURT, J.S. (1979), *Elementary Schooling and the Working Classes* London, Routledge and Kegan Paul.
2. DES (1967), *Children and Their Primary Schools*, Report of the Central Advisory Council for Education. Vol. I. Plowden. London, HMSO.
3. DES (1967), Plowden, *op. cit.*
4. MACLURE, S. (1985), '75 Years of the TES', in *Times Educational Supplement* Special, 27 September, p. 1.
5. BRIAULT, E.W.H. (1976), A distributed system of Educational Administration: an international viewpoint', *International Review of Education*, 22, 4, 429–439.
6. WEAVER, SIR T. (1976), 'What is the good of Higher Education?' *Higher Education Review*, Summer, pp. 4–6
7. DES (1977), *A New Partnership for our Schools*: Tan Jon Report, London, HMSO.
8. BARON, G. and HOWELL D.A. (1974), *The Government and Management of Schools.* London, Athlone Press.
9. AULD, R. (1976), *The William Tyndale Junior and Infants Schools,* London, Inner London Education Authority.
10. See Taylor Report.
11. *Ibid.* p. 11.
12. DES (1967), *Children and their Primary Schools*, Plowden Report, *op. cit.* and DES (1975), *A 'Language For Life*, Bullock Report, London, HMSO.
13. Cmnd 7430, *The Composition of School Governing Bodies.*
14. ROGERS, R. (1980), *Crowther to Warnock: How Fourteen Reports tried to change Children's Lives.* London, Heinemann Books.

15. KOGAN, M. (1971), *The Government of Education*, London, Macmillan.
16. CAMPAIGN FOR THE ADVANCEMENT OF STATE EDUCATION (East Devon Branch) (1983), *The New Governing Bodies*, Devon, CASE.
17. SCHOOL OF EDUCATION, UNIVERSITY OF EXETER (1985), *Caught in The Act Teachers and Governors after 1980, Perspectives 21.* Exeter, University of Exeter.
18. *Ibid.*
19. RENNIE, J. (1981), *Home and School: The Essential Link Coventry*, Coventry Community Education Development Centre.
20. The Bernard Van Leer Foundation supported the Birmingham Local Education Authority by grant aid in this experiment in Community Education. After six years the project was extended and incorporated into the normal schools' arrangements in certain parts of the city.
21. Timberley Primary School, Shard End.
22. CALVERT, J. (1985), *Parental Involvement*, Unpublished research report, University of Nottingham.
23. COLLINS, S. (1986), 'Snakes and ladders to parental control', *Times Educational Supplement*, 28 February.
24. See KEMBLE, B. (1986), The Clash of heads over parent power, *Sunday Times*, 7 September.
25. Birmingham Education Authority
26. McCONKEY, R. (1985), Working With Parents, Brookline Books, Beckenham, Croom Helm.

The Multicultural Primary School

Christine Brown

Introduction

During the last twenty-five years or so primary school provision, as provision in other sectors of the education system, has been affected by substantial cultural changes in the pupil population of certain schools, particularly in inner-city areas which have been the focus of immigrant settlement from the New Commonwealth. Such schools have come to be referred to as 'multicultural' in the sense that pupils attending them represent a variety of cultural affiliations, often distinguished by marked differences in religion, social customs and language. Coupled with this phenomenon have been the growing arguments for the development of a 'multicultural' perspective within the education system as a whole.

This chapter focuses on the educational provision of three multicultural primary schools in the West Midlands, and relates in particular to the nature of their curriculum response to the multicultural population which they served. It is based on the findings of case studies of each school during the period 1980–1984.[1] The three schools in question were similar in size, organization and catchment area. There were similarities and differences in their response, and both similarities and differences appeared to raise some significant issues in considering the whole question of the primary school approach to education in a multicultural society.

Historical Background: The Development of a Multicultural Perspective

The entry into Britain of immigrants from the West Indies in the 1950s, from the Asian subcontinent in the 1960s and subsequently other groups, such as the Ugandan Asians and Vietnamese refugees, served both to foster and to draw attention to the fact that British society was fast becoming multicultural in an obvious sense: entering the community were groups easily identifiable as different — many had no English language, they represented distinct and different cultural values, and the perception of this difference by the general population was often heightened by noticeable physical differences such as skin colour and mode of dress. That British society had long been multicultural is certainly true; for the migration into Britain of a whole range of different cultural groups is not simply a recent phenomenon but one which has occurred throughout the centuries. Nor is cultural diversity necessarily associated purely with periods of migration. One can speak, for example, of diversity in regional or social class culture. Yet it has been since the more recent period of immigration, frequently, though not exclusively, from the ex-colonies, that the notion of Britain as a multicultural society has received extensive official and public verbalization. In the field of education a number of factors have contributed to this emphasis.

1. The Need for Immediate Response Measures

In terms of the population as a whole immigrants from the ex-colonies were indeed minorities, New Commonwealth immigrants representing only about 3.2 per cent of the total population in England and Wales (census figures, 1971), but they concentrated themselves in only 10 per cent of the enumeration districts, having a significant impact on the nature of society in those areas, and making sudden and unexpected demands on the education system. Teachers in some schools found themselves having to cope with classes of children who not only came from very different cultural backgrounds from the teachers, but who often spoke a foreign language or dialect of which the teachers had no knowledge. Teachers had neither the expertise nor the resources to deal with the situation, a situation of which the Department of Education and Science became quickly aware.[2] Immediate curriculum adaption thus became essential to survival.

2.   *Concern for Race Relations*

The concern of successive administrations to avoid the problems of racial discord already experienced in other countries, especially the United States, led to a whole range of legislation, reports, commissions and official and unofficial bodies all concerned to promote racial harmony. They resulted either from a liberal concern to provide equality or simply from a fear that conflict might lead to civil disturbance, a fear born out by hostile attitudes manifest in the indigenous community at large.[3] All in one way or another emphasized the importance and promoted the task of schools as instrumental in creating the basis of a racially harmonious society. Many publications of the Commission for Racial Equality, for example, provide evidence of this emphasis.[4]

3.   *Concern about School Achievement*

Together with the concern to promote racial equality was the rapid and worrying evidence of apparent low achievement by certain groups in the schools, especially those of West Indian origin.[5] Low achievement amongst certain social groups, social class groups particularly, had long been an area of extensive educational research, but the disparity of achievement levels in this context seems to have presented itself to all administrations as an even more serious matter. Perhaps it did not seem so likely at that time that social class division in educational achievement and opportunity would be a major source of civil unrest leading to violent outbreaks, while there was clearly a danger of unrest and discontent amongst black youngsters, for example.[6]

Since this early period, much rapidly accumulating research and education literature has begun to argue for changes in the school curriculum to meet the demands being made as a result of cultural changes in the population, and has drawn attention to the cultural bias and even racism entrenched in the traditional school curriculum and its organization. It has been argued that the curriculum is generally unsuitable for the preparation of children to live in a multicultural society.[7] In this connection the phrase 'multicultural curriculum' has become part of the common parlance of discussion relating to education in a multicultural society, although seldom very specifically defined. Exactly what constitutes a 'multicultural curriculum' or, indeed, any sort of multicultural response, may be a matter of opinion. There is no curriculum which is *the* one. There are lots of them. Generally they can be said to include the notion that British society is comprised of a variety of very different cultural groups and that this should be reflected in the curriculum of the state school. Concern has been voiced, for example, about a curriculum which is biased towards one ethnic culture, an ethnocentric curriculum, and it has been stressed that a greater awareness of the multicultural nature of British society should be reflected in the curriculum as a whole.[8]

So appears to have evolved what Craft[9] describes as a change from 'an assimilationist view' to 'a more pluralist concern' which appears not only in the general literature but in government and associated reports as well.[10] In other words, there has been a movement from policies which have sought to assimilate immigrants into some perception of a mainstream, indigenous culture, with emphasis on teaching English as a second language, towards policies which have sought to open the education system to the representation of cultural diversity.[11] Not suprisingly, given the historical context, much of the discussion so far has related to the representation of cultures associated with some particular groups, especially those resulting from immigration from the ex-colonies. Frequently there is still no serious attempt to consider the need to represent cultural diversity in regional or social class terms, for example, although such a pluralist concern would seem to suggest this. A pluralist concern has much in common with the notion of an 'Open Society' presented by Bergson[12] and Popper[13] which is discussed at some length by Ayer.[14] Essentially it includes the idea of a fluid society, where social institutions are open to question, trial and experiment, combined with equality of opportunity for different social groups, including ethnic groups.[15]

Amongst more recent literature the notion of pluralism is put forward in the Swann Report, 'Education for All'.[16] Here the policy of assimilating minority groups to some idea of a mainstream culture is rejected, and a view of society is advanced in which it is suggested that while members of that society may be committed to certain common values, such as a belief in justice and the right of dissent, different communities should be allowed and encouraged to maintain elements of cultural distinctiveness. Of course it may be suggested that such a position actually raises more questions than it answers. For example, how much and in what ways should cultural distinctiveness be encouraged? What exactly are the common elements to which all members of the society should subscribe and who decides what these shall be? There are no simple answers to these questions, and the dilemma serves to emphasize that the notion of pluralism is not precise: there is room for considerable debate about what such a term may mean.

Three Schools: The Response

In the Swann Report the point is made that very little is actually known about what is happening by way of multicultural education, that there is a need for more extensive research into what is actually going on in schools. It is hoped that the evidence of the case studies referred to in this chapter will go some way towards illuminating the nature of the primary school response and towards raising a number of issues, some of which relate to educational provision as a whole, some of which are peculiar to the primary school context.

The three schools in question were outwardly similar. All were junior-infant schools with nursery provision, divided into departments under the general management of a single Head Teacher. They were similar in size, and housed in Victorian buildings located in inner-city areas. All three catered for similar children: seventy to eighty per cent of Asian origin, ten per cent of West Indian origin and the rest white.[17] In two of the schools the Asian population was largely Sikh, in one Moslem, although all had representatives of a variety of Asian groups. Each school contained one Asian member of staff in a teaching capacity, and one school also had an Asian Head Teacher. All three schools could therefore be described as 'multicultural' in terms of the pupil population and marginally so in terms of the staff. In addition all three schools were attempting to respond to the perceived need to provide education suitable for a multicultural society.

School 1

School 1 was an institution that was attempting to introduce what the Head described as a 'multicultural curriculum' for the first time. In practice this meant that in addition to the existing provision for English as a second language measures were being taken to broaden the cultural perspectives available in the curriculum, to make the curriculum less ethnocentric. Books and materials which depicted different cultures, black and brown people as well as white, were being introduced. Different religions were given some formal recognition through comparative study in Religious Education, in the celebration of some festivals and in reference to these in assemblies.

In particular some topics pursued in an experimental project conducted throughout the school were given a multicultural focus. Thus topic work throughout the school became the basis for a multicultural perspective. This topic work was initially organized centrally by the Head Teacher in the form of a 'whole school project', although it was anticipated that there would be spin-offs in the future for individual topic work as well. During this experimental project each class in the school was engaged in the pursuit of a chosen topic: 'Food', 'Trees', 'Religions', 'Traditional Costumes' constituted junior department topics; 'Food' and 'Ourselves' constituted infant and nursery topics. Prior to the commencement of the project a rationale for multicultural education was formulated and published in pamphlet form by the Head Teacher in conjunction with his staff:

> After discussion with some members of staff, a fair amount of agreement emerged, as far as fundamentals of multicultural education were concerned ... Two basic assumptions were acknowledged — that there are differences (colour, religion, food, dress, homes, natural habitat, climate, languages, writing customs, history etc.). It was generally accepted that due to the presence of people with different cultural backgrounds in this country *differences* are now *real* and *relevant* rather than academic. A creative and imaginative use of these differences is a basic tenet of multicultural education. Secondly, the *interdependence* amongst people of the world (exchanging resources, ideas, technology, concerns for the future and universal problems) is now a viable experimental educational situation, which needs to be exploited.[18]

'Multicultural' was intended to encompass a world view, not just the cultures represented in the school. This was a definite policy and was consistent with the global view inherent in the Head's multicultural approach.

Despite the 'multicultural' inputs the bulk of the curriculum reflected the teachers' interpretation of British culture: emphasis on standard English, the history and geography of Britain in other topic work, western classical music, more time devoted to Christian festivals, hymn singing in assembly, a school uniform which did not take into account cultural variations in modes of dress, literature and story material with a greater focus on European tradition were amongst the most obvious examples. Against this background isolated topic work on 'multicultural themes' and the occasional reference to Divali in assembly appeared as insignificant. Moreover the 'multicultural' elements became inevitably less important because in most cases they did not occur in the areas of the curriculum such as mathematics, science and English, which were given higher status. For example, such areas were often referred to by teachers as the basics; they were given a dominant position on the timetable in so far as most mornings were devoted to them; they were also setted according to ability.

In general educational terms there was emphasis on the deficiency or problematic nature of the children and their world within the catchment area of the school, coupled with a belief in the unquestionable appropriateness of the knowledge presented to them by the teacher. For example, the Head Teacher talked about 'compensating' for experiences that were 'educationally irrelevant', and all teachers held the view that the children were 'educationally deprived' and that it was the duty of the school to compensate for this.[19] Teachers were also regarded as the arbiters of appropriate learning:

> We are prepared to give out professional advice as to the kinds of activities your child may engage in at home.[20]

Most teachers, although there were one or two exceptions, used textbooks and materials they obtained themselves from professional sources for topic work, rather than materials and information provided by the children themselves and the community. Activities out of school tended to take the form of 'enrichment' activities to places further afield, such as London, the seaside, stately homes, and only a few, such as a project on 'Litter', were based in the locality. Although in theory topic work was an important part of the curriculum, knowledge was frequently presented in subject divisions: topics on 'Trees' and 'Food', for example, emphasized geographical perspectives, 'Religions' appeared as an element of comparative religious study in Religious Education, and a number of topics had a specifically historical focus.

School 2

This was a 'community' school by its own designation, and as such this school recognized as a matter of principle the idea that the curriculum should to some extent be negotiable with parents and the community, and should both reflect and cater for the needs and interests of that community. No formal attempt had been made to introduce a 'multicultural' curriculum in the same way as School 1, but the Head and most of his staff regarded the school as providing this as a matter of course, in so far as it followed naturally from the community focus:

> I think to label it or put it on one side is a very artificial division in a school like this ... In this school if we — and I think we do as a school — have a caring attitude and a caring philosophy towards the children, and if staff here are environmentally biased, then you can't but help, because you meet the children and their cultures at every turn ... It's so much a part of being in this school in this area that I cannot now divide it, I cannot say to you, Oh yes, well I do this and I do that and I do the other. If you do a survey of any kind, automatically it becomes multicultural by its pure content, and if you do shops in the area, the library, there are books in Urdu and Punjabi — so you know it flows naturally.[21]

Different religious and cultural festivals were celebrated extensively in assemblies and topic work[22]; there was evidence of a considerable amount of resourcing — books and audio-visual materials — relating to different cultures both in Britain and abroad, and readers reflected a variety of cultures, including an inner-city perspective.[23] In addition to special topics, such as a 'whole school' project on 'Caribbean Carnival', other more general topics undertaken by different classes such as 'Homes and Families', 'People Who Help Us', 'Buildings of Our City' contained a variety of different cultural perspectives.[24] Moreover the need to reflect the contribution of different cultures to work in mathematics and science and the need for cultural variety in the presentation of literature had been accepted by many teachers who consequently tried to make even the more specific subject areas of mathematics, science and English a reflection of the cultural diversity of the pupils.[25] There was no school uniform and children wearing different modes of dress were encouraged to do so and often complimented on their appearance.

Above all the school had initiated classes in Urdu and Punjabi at the request of sections of the local community, and these were recognized as an optional part of the curriculum.

In the curriculum as a whole, knowledge appeared less separated into subject areas than in School 1, for topic work drew on a variety of 'subject' areas: art, English language, mathematics, music, literature and so on. Many teachers seemed genuinely aware of the connections between different lessons, often operating a 'theme' approach to all the work. Everyday or commonsense knowledge appeared even in the more rigidly defined areas of the curriculum such as mathematics, where concepts were related to activities such as shopping, surveying the locality rather than presented as abstract entities. The school was not the one central focus for socialization but became rather one part of a whole range of educational agents and venues, including the people of the community and parents (who were used to extend the experience of children through contribution of materials, talking to children in lessons) and places in the local community (which were used as an alternative venue for learning activities).[26] Control of the curriculum was diffused through a variety of personnel, not all of them teachers.[27] The community and hence the pupils themselves were not regarded as disadvantaged or lacking in educational experience. Rather they were regarded positively as having something to contribute to the educational process within the school.[28]

At the same time some teachers were concerned about preparing children to meet examination requirements in the future and about the demands of the secondary school. More generally teachers combined a positive attitude to the neighbourhood and the contribution of the child to the learning procss with an almost contradictory belief in the need for direction by the teacher and the belief by a few that these children needed compensating in some way.[29] Despite a lowering of the barriers between 'subject' divisions there was a very distinct separation of a large portion[30] of the curriculum by some teachers into English language and mathematics which were taught more formally, with pre-ordained outcomes. Again these were often referred to as 'the basics'.

School 3

School 3 was different yet again. Its response to the multicultural population of the school consisted mainly in the provision of

English as a second language and remedial measures generally. There were very few attemps to accommodate different cultural perspectives within the curriculum, and those which did exist were more confined to the infants. There were a few books and materials which the teachers described as 'multicultural', but these often focused upon religion and in many cases were considerably outweighed by old material with a traditional, European emphasis. In the juniors multicultural perspectives tended to be confined to Religious Education except in the case of a couple of teachers who tried to make other topics more 'multicultural'. 'The Growth of Language', for example, examined different kinds of writing, including some Asian languages, and 'The Locality' examined the changes in population as a result of immigration. The Head Teacher remarked on the celebration of different festivals, but there was no evidence of this in junior assemblies which were almost dogmatic in their Christian content. The school had been asked to respond to a local education authority letter concerning possible measures for a curriculum in a multicultural society, but the Head Teacher tended to confirm an assimilationist standpoint which was inconsistent with the greater representation of different cultural perspectives as a positive feature of school work:

> I very much support the idea of 'when in Rome do as Rome does' ... we have taken due note of our Sikhs and our Hindus, our Moslems and of course our Caribbean children as well. We have introduced many things into school life, shall I put it, the emphasis there, yes, we've assimilated them.[31]

The school had turned down a request from the local authority to make the buildings available for the learning of Asian languages in the evening on the grounds that the premises were unsuitable.

Amongst infant staff, however, there was more of an attempt to include different cultural perspectives in topic work such as 'Ourselves', 'My Home', 'The Street' and in the presentation of different cultures in books and readers.[32] In this respect the kind of provision evidenced in the infants was very similar to the provision evidenced in School 1. In fact the school was an interesting example of the process of development, because in effect there were two levels of response, almost two schools, operating within one building, one with a view of educational provision which was manifestly assimilationist and certainly prior Swann in its ideology, another which was more in step with the notion of providing some kind of multicultural curriculum. The tension between the two perspectives became overt in the relationship between the staff: the one group revealed a thinly disguised disapproval of the other group, and informal contact between them, for example in the staffroom, was limited.

In the curriculum as a whole knowledge was presented in rigid subject divisions which, in the juniors, were timetabled throughout the day. Teaching was often very formal, directed by the teachers and focusing on textbooks and information conveyed from the teacher to the pupil. There was an emphasis on examinations — all children in the juniors sat annual examinations and were allocated positions in class as a result. All children wore school uniform. In the infants teaching was slightly less formal, although there was still a preponderance of direction towards pre-set goals and an emphasis on information provided by the teacher. Some use was made of the locality in topic work, especially in the infants, although there was an overall tendency to regard the locality as deficient in appropriate educational experience and to regard the population of that locality as requiring compensation for 'gaps' in their language, material resources and outlook. Considerable emphasis was placed upon the need to develop mathematics and English, which were again described as 'the basics'. The Head Teacher expressed a firm commitment to 'the 3 Rs' and a policy of:

> providing the best possible education for the very many children who come here with handicaps of one sort or another.[33]

Some Issues Raised by the Responses

In terms of curriculum development the three schools presented an interesting picture. For the movement from policies which have sought to assimilate immigrants into some notion of a mainstream culture towards policies which have sought to open up the curriculum to the representation of cultural diversity was seen in action. School 3 demonstrated a situation which was still essentially a part of the assimilationist/mainstream tradition, although with a few slight moves towards change. School 1 appeared as an institution which had moved further towards the notion of a multicultural curriculum, but which still retained some substantial elements of the traditional perspective. School 2 appeared to have moved the furthest in so far as different cultural perspectives had pervaded a substantial amount of the curriculum, coupled with a more flexible approach to the learning situation exhibited by teachers and a more genuine respect for the multicultural population served by the school. This particular chapter will not, however, focus specifically upon evidence of the developmental process, but upon some general features of the provision which were equally interesting.

The Depoliticization of Educational Provision

Within the three schools there was a wide range of provision both for pupils generally and more specifically for different cultural groups. In the latter case was evidenced everything from remedial provision and emphasis on English as a second language to the participation of different cultures, including the parents, in the curriculum. In addition pupils were viewed as everything from the empty vessel requiring direction to already sophisticated entities capable of autonomous learning. Yet whatever provision was made this was conceptualized by most teachers in educational terms, and justified as representative of sound educational practice. In this way teachers were able to separate in their consciousness educational criteria from a whole range of connected perspectives such as political affiliations, views about the social integration of immigrants, and even personal and idiosyncratic preferences. They were not consciously aware of the process, but such direct appeals to educational justification performed the function of objectifying their various responses as not only theoretically unquestionable, but also therefore as ethically correct. Educational responses to the multicultural society were effectively depoliticized. Although these responses varied considerably, teachers based them on principles that they believed to be educationally sound, and in so doing geuninely believed that they were doing the very best they could for the children in their charge. Whatever else might be said of their activities, in a naive way it was generally magnanimous.

Deficit Views of Inner City Children

It is not uncommon to describe the response of the state education system to the presence of cultural minorities, especially the cultures of black and brown groups, in terms of a dominant, white British culture reacting to the presence of groups which are perceived by that white culture as both threatening and inferior.[34] Yet it must be remembered that such groups have entered a system in which the cultures of certain white groups have already been devalued for decades. Other writers have pointed out, for example, how the culture of the working class has been largely ignored by the state education system except to regard it as somehow deficient and requiring treatment for disadvantage or special needs.[35] It was clear from these three studies that many teachers operated from the perspective of seeing certain experience as educationally appropriate and that other groups were measured in terms of how they were seen to fall short of that experience. Family life was regarded as inadequate, and stress was placed on the lack of material wealth. Children were perceived to have 'problems' of communication, either because their command of the English language was poor generally or because their use of English was different from the standard use prevailing in educational communication. Out of school activities were measured against the kinds of activities the teachers themselves aspired to. For example, reading books, going to the theatre, enjoying serious music, visiting the countryside and places of historical interest were regarded positively; watching the television, listening to 'pop' music, playing in the street were regarded negatively. This phenomenon was particularly noticeable in School 3, and it coincided with very few examples of the representation of different cultures within the curriculum and no attempt to negotiate educational provision with the community. It also occurred in School 1 and provided something of a paradox here because on the one hand the school was attempting to introduce a 'multicultural curriculum' and on other teachers were operating on the belief that substantial elements of the pupils' culture were deficient. This notion of deficiency was negligible in School 2, and it was this School which appeared to have responded most positively to the multicultural nature of the locality. The schools' reponse to particular cultural groups, such as those with Asian and West Indian associations, could not be disconnected from the response to all the children within the school.

The Importance of 'The Basics'

The studies revealed an important feature of primary school provision which had attendant effects upon the nature of the response to different cultural groups. These schools operated within a public framework and that public framework exerted an influence upon their provision however diverse their individual strategies may have been. Crucial to teachers were the perceived requirements of the secondary school, of public examinations, of employers and of the generally competitive nature of the outside world. Although many of them resented these influences, none could ignore them. The teaching of 'basic skills', i.e. literacy in English and numeracy, and the acquisition of high standards in these therefore assumed curriculum proportions that threatened to distort other aspects of school provision. Subject area division was crystallized in these areas, teaching methods were directive and involved the transmission of information from the teacher to the pupil, categorization of pupils by setting and streaming was commonplace. Even School 2, which was generally more flexible in its view of appropriate educational provision, tended to revert to such an approach in these 'basics'. For in this school the emphasis on an integrated presentation of knowledge was superceded by the division of the 'basic' disciplines of mathematics and English, and mixed ability approaches to the organization of learning situations was replaced by informal setting in these areas. So conscious were schools of the importance of 'the basics' that in terms of curriculum time they occupied a far larger proportion of the provision than anything else.[36] Moreover it was in just these areas that the fewest concessions were made to the existence of different cultural groups. Asian languages were of no consequence when compared with the need to acquire competency in standard English, and different cultural perspectives were frequently seen as irrelevant in the teaching of mathematics.

This phenomenon was highly significant for the presentation of multicultural perspectives for it meant that where different cultural perspectives occurred they occurred in areas of the curriculum that were implicitly lower in status and smaller in quantity. Two curricula therefore emerged: high status and non-multicultural (the real curriculum) and lower status and multicultural (the concessionary curriculum). This was entirely consistent with the identification by Stone[37], Rex[38] and Mullard[39] of an ameliorative style of multicultural development. But the stratification of knowledge in this way was something which emerged out of the whole framework of the curriculum, dictated by the priorities teachers felt to be relevant to all of their pupils. At this level it was not a deliberate and conscious modification of the schools' multicultural response; it arose from the positive decision of teachers to concentrate on 'the basics', rather than from the negative decision of teachers to relegate different cultural perspectives to unimportant areas of their work. School 2, for example, made every attempt to give different cultural groups equal status in the presentation of knowledge through books and in topic work, in the direct use of materials and information provided by the community and in dialogue with that community concerning appropriate provision; but the fundamental commitment of teachers to 'the basics', justified in educational terms, had exactly the effect of rendering other features of the curriculum comparatively insignificant.

'Child-targeting' and the Influence of the Progressive Perspective

It was apparent from the studies that the majority of teachers[40] subscribed to a particular view of the learning process which might loosely be described as 'child-centred' or 'progressive'. Amongst the key features of this perspective was the determination to treat children as individuals, to develop individual 'uniqueness', to adhere to 'relevance', i.e. use the immediate experiences of the child, where the child is at, as a basis for development, and in teaching methodology to focus on learning by doing rather than formal transmission teaching. The existence of this kind of perspective was directly significant for the schools' response to their multicultural population. Such perspectives are not incompatible with more negotiable positions concerning appropriate educational provision. They are often accompanied by a more integrated presentation of knowledge in topic work, and everyday experience is given validity; knowledge is related to immediate and everyday living rather than being esoteric or remote. Children are provided with opportunities for self-directed exploration of their environment and wider venues than the classroom are used as learning sources. Where these general principles held good, therefore, it was possible to see 'child-centred' perspectives as accommodating to different views of the world, and it seems more than coincidence that such perspectives were associated with more multicultural representation in the curriculum than, for example, authoritarian and teacher-centred perspectives. It accounted in some measure for the kinds of curriculum input that were found amongst infant departments where the presentation of different cultures tended to be both less remote from the experiences of the children and more open to the direct contribution·of pupils and parents. It also coincided with greater quantity of different cultural representation in books and materials and in the focus of topic work. For child-centred teachers this sort of provision was an inevitable consequence of their general educational perspective and applied equally to junior teachers with similar perspectives.

But this was not a straightforward phenomenon. For often the approach was not, strictly speaking, child-centred, because the child and his experience was not at the centre of the educational process. The children and their world were taken into account, but they exerted a peripheral influence upon the learning activities rather than provided the impetus for the educational process. Teachers described their role as that of a guide who 'coaxes out' the abilities of the children, and very few were able to see their role as part of a two-way dialogue between the teacher and the learner. The applicable metaphor was that of the gardener who nurtures the plant until it reaches fruition. The teaching methodology was frequently management at a distance where children were allowed to direct their own learning and engage in practical, exploratory activities through the use of work-cards or similar materials devised by the teachers. Teachers therefore still remained in the position of director although it was second level direction through their materials. Organization was informal but still the child did not escape the benevolent control of the educator. It was the kind of approach that has already been described as paternal by Paton[41] and Meighan.[42] Categorization of pupils was not overt, but it still existed in the informal grouping that some teachers employed. Curriculum content was designed to relate to the world of the children, and focused upon topics such as 'My Home and Family', 'The Street', 'Going Shopping', which might include some consideration of the different kinds of family life occurring amongst different cultural groups, or the recognition of the multicultural nature of the locality. Other topics were more specifically designed to relate to the presence of different cultures and focused on festivals, on 'Food' and on 'Costume' or different religions. Yet so often the content was filtered through the consciousness of the teacher and the teacher defined the parameters of the study through his or her own visual aids, text books and library books. Different views of the world very easily became remote to the children and stereotyped. Similarly teachers who organized visits to local places of worship, such as the mosque or the gudwara, readily took on the role of guide and were only marginally inclined to step aside and allow Moslem or Sikh children to provide explanations.

It would perhaps be better to describe such approaches as 'child-targeted' rather than 'child-centred', for the educator, as it were, bounced some of the curriculum off the child and his or her experiences without relinquishing his or her own central position in the educational process. Where this occurred the presentation of different cultures became more remote, providing rather the 'children from many lands' view of the world which was more a representation of the teachers' perceptions than representative of the actual experiences of the children.

Professionalism and the Expert Perspective

In addition to the perspective which has been identified as associated with progressive or child-centred views of the educational process, a further perspective was identified. It was an authoritarian perspective because claims to the specialist knowledge encapsulated in the educational paradigm legitimated the existing authority of teachers to make decisions on behalf of the learners, frequently with little or no consultation outside the teaching profession. In the case of Schools 1 and 3 it fostered a paternal approach to the pupils and their parents, who frequently became regarded as extensions of the pupils, lacking the necessary skills, knowledge and experience to make decisions for themselves about what was appropriate for the education of their children. Teachers might be willing to consult parents informally, organize peripheral activities such as special evenings or visits in cooperation with them, or use them as unpaid helpers in the classroom, but they were generally unwilling to allow them to contribute to fundamental decisions concerning curriculum content and teaching method. These were professionally sacrosanct. Even in School 2, where negotiation with the parents and the community had developed far more extensively than in the other two schools, most teachers still maintained the view that curricular decisions were ultimately their unquestionable responsibility as experts, and many teachers at a personal level indicated a measure of resentment over areas where parents and the community were perceived as having encroached upon the professional domain. Thus a barrier between the professional and the client was maintained.

This general phenomenon was significant for the schools' response to the multicultural population. The maintenance of this barrier between the expert and the non-expert, which was not always a conscious activity, was added to the already existing barrier between the culture of the teacher and the culture of the pupils, particularly those of Asian and West Indian descent, and therefore the boundaries between these cultures were even more difficult to cross. Yet at the same time it was a phenomenon which could be related to all the children within the school. The inability of Asian parents to 'understand education' was a common complaint of teachers, but it was a complaint also applied to other groups. If parents of Asian and West Indian descent should feel that the education system was not taking their concerns seriously, many other parents could argue the same.

The Presentation of Multicultural Perspectives

It was evident from the three schools that the notion of a 'multicultural curriculum' in very general terms had been adopted by many teachers, and this included the belief that the curriculum should somehow be responsive to cultural diversity in books and materials, in topic work, in assemblies and so on. In practice attempts to provide a multicultural curriculum were presented in different ways and it became evident that one way of conceptualizing this variation might be in relation to their overall perceptions of the content, emphasis and teaching method appropriate to education as a whole. It was not simply the case that some teachers operated in accordance with their own stereotyped or inadequate perceptions of other cultures, although many of course did so, but they also operated from a view of the educational process generally, which was significant for multicultural approaches at a fundamental level. In this way attempts to introduce multicultural perspectives could not be separated from other aspects of the curriculum.

In School 2 a 'community' approach to the curriculum was adopted. This meant that much of the curriculum content, especially topic work, was focused upon the locality. The resources of the area were used in a positive way and the children frequently extended their learning activities out of the classroom into the local environment. Attempts had been made to foster a more open relationship with parents, and although the division between the professional and the layperson still existed, it was less important. Not only did the school provide a service to the local people in the provision of extra-curricular activities and facilities, but they were encouraged to come into the school, even the classrooms, during the school day. Relationships with the parents and the community were moving towards a situation of dialogue concerning the educational provision which the school was offering and steps had been taken to consult the parents about their curriculum concerns through the establishment of a community committee. This had resulted, for example, in the development of Urdu and Punjabi classes, despite the fact that some teachers were uneasy about them. The population of the area was regarded positively by most teachers, not as comprised of deficient individuals, but of individuals capable of making decisions and having worthwhile knowledge and experience to contribute. Correspondingly pupils were not regarded as lacking in appropriate experiences; for all experience was seen to have an educative function. Outside 'the basics' knowledge was not represented in closed subject divisions, but more integrated and also related to the everyday knowledge of the pupils. Even in mathematics, which was presented more like a traditional subject discipline, concepts were linked to projects in the locality and work in mathematics was seen to inform other aspects of the curriculum. Individual teachers of course varied from these approaches to different degrees, but in general terms the 'community' response was part of the ethos of the whole curriculum.

This kind of framework affected the presentation of multi-cultural perspectives in particular ways. Presentation of different cultures was linked to the immediate locality, at least as a starting point; it was an attempt to reflect life in the area. This meant that multicultural perspectives were not presented through a remote, 'children from many lands' approach, or a presentation of 'Life in India', 'Life in the Caribbean', as divorced from the life of the black and brown children in the area as it was from the experience of the white. Similarly, as teachers were more willing to recognize the possibility that parents and others were capable of making a worthwhile contribution to the education process, teachers were more able to relinquish the presentation of different cultures to others, to involve children and parents in the provision of resources, in the discussion of projects and to encourage their participation in assemblies and festival celebrations. It was less a case of different views of the world being filtered through the consciousness of the teacher or presented secondhand through textbooks and materials devised by the teachers alone. The mixed community was regarded as an asset, as a source of interest and variety. Consequently many teachers had become able to relate to the notion of difference without feeling threatened; they were less concerned to emphasize 'brotherhood of man' images (i.e. that people may be superficially different, but fundamentally the same) and more able to accept the notion of difference at its face value. In this way the distortion of cultures through overemphasis of similarity and presentation of difference as somehow exotic was avoided. Staff consciously recognized that their commitment to multicultural education was an inevitable part of their whole educational approach and strongly resisted the idea of considering it as a separate issue. In so far as it was not a feature which had been tacked on to the curriculum, but emanated from its central philosophy, multicultural perspectives pervaded a much greater portion of the curriculum than in the other two schools. This was further assisted by the recognition of the interrelationship between kinds of knowledge; there was less likelihood of multicultural perspectives being confined to a few specific subject areas such as geography, history or Religious Education. There were indeed some limitations on the development of multicultural perspectives in areas of basic skills, but even here there was an element of permeation which did not exist in Schools 1 and 3.

In School 1 the Head had attempted to promote a 'multicultural curriculum' against a background of the existing curriculum which was not fundamentally changed. He had initiated an experiment in multicultural education which had consisted of a series of projects in topic work throughout the school on what he described as 'multicultural themes'; he had encouraged the use of books and resources depicting black and brown children as well as white, books on India, Pakistan and the Caribbean, on different religions and so on. He had attempted to include some festival celebrations in assembly and was looking for more representation of different cultures in music and art. Against this was a background of provision which was concerned to emphasize not only the basic skills of English and mathematics, but a kind of mainstream knowledge which would equip pupils for competing in the secondary school and in the struggle for jobs, coupled with a view of the locality, the parents and the pupils as deficient.

Children were regarded as having 'gaps' in experience, or experiences which were educationally inappropriate. Activities outside the classroom were perceived as exercises designed to enrich the children's inadequate experience and the home environment was regarded as limited and requiring compensation. Parents were welcome in the school, but liaison with them was kept to peripheral activities such as Open Evenings, fund raising activities or occasionally they were employed in menial activities[43] in the classrooms of some staff. So far from being regarded as capable of making fundamental decisions concerning the education of their children, they were seen to require guidelines as to appropriate ways of assisting in their educational development. Outside mathematics, English and science, knowledge was not presented in subject disciplines but presented in topic format; yet there were many teachers whose topic work amounted to a focus on subject disciplines — it had a clear historical, geographical or religious focus, for example.

Against this general background the presentation of multicultural perspectives assumed particular forms. As the curriculum was focused away from the locality towards a view of the world which was regarded as educationally appropriate (a 'universal' view actually corresponding to a mainstream view of reality) so the experiment in multicultural education presented a world perspective which was often remote from the experiences of the children. Life in India, the geography of third world countries bore little relationship to the life of children of Asian and West Indian descent who had spent all their lives in a British inner-city. The mismatch between the realities of the children's life in Britain and the presentation of multicultural perspectives is a phenomenon which has been referred to elsewhere by Dhondy.[44] Acutely conscious of their special role as professionals, and at the same time regarding parents and children as deficient in appropriate experience, teachers controlled the presentation of other cultures themselves; it was filtered through their own consciousness and subject to the stereotyping and distortions of their own limited experience. It was made further remote by being presented by them secondhand through text books and similar materials. Emphasizing a world view also encouraged teachers to stress commonality rather than difference, a denial of the relativity of experience in favour of a more 'objective' standpoint. 'Brotherhood of Man' images became preponderant. This was further fostered by child-centred or child-targeted teachers who paradoxically believed that treating all children as individuals meant regarding all children as fundamentally the same. Finally, although at a superficial level knowledge was presented as integrated in topic work, there were many teachers who were either unable or unwilling to dissociate their material from subject discipline forms. Different cultural perspectives were rapidly converted into the more traditional material of history and geography, or became associated with specific subject areas such as Religious Education instead of the whole curriculum. As the experiment in multicultural education had been tacked on to the existing curriculum, multicultural perspectives did not make substantial inroads into the rest of the school's provision.

In School 3 the infant department and the few junior teachers who were akin to the infant department in their approach followed a similar pattern to School 1 in the presentation of multicultural perspectives, and this was consistent with a similar approach to the curriculum as a whole. Elsewhere in School 3 there was an even greater emphasis on basic skills, on the presentation of subjects in discipline form, on the demands of the secondary school and competition in examinations, coupled with staff emphasis on a mainstream reality which coincided with a view of 'British' culture and the academic tradition of the British education system. Views of the children and the locality as deficient were maintained. At this level 'multicultural' had become a term for limited, peripheral activities such as the occasional celebration of a festival in assembly or an 'Asian evening', or at best confined to a few subject areas such as Religious Education.

Implications of the Responses

The simple connection between notions of a suitable pattern of immigrant adaption to the host community and educational provision generally has already been pointed out by many writers. Strategies of heavy concentration upon English as a second language and remedial provision, accompanied by the adaption of immigrant cultures to the existing curriculum can be linked to notions of assimilation, and increased multicultural perspectives can be linked to the idea of promoting a plurality of cultures existing side by side. Indeed it is not uncommon to label strategies as being either assimilationist or pluralist, assimilationist being consistent with the maintenance of dominant, white power groups.[45] There is a sense in which this simple notion held good in the evidence from the three schools and there is a general and loose connection between their educational provision and their view of a suitable pattern of immigrant adaption. This was demonstrated particularly in School 3 where the Head Teacher's commitment to assimilation was accompanied by an emphasis on English as a second language and negligible representation of different cultural perspectives. However the relationship was not a straightforward one, for not all the teachers in School 3 supported assimilationist strategies, and the Head Teachers and their staff in Schools 1 and 2 certainly did not.[46] It was not simply the case of advocates of pluralism needing to persuade teachers that this was the appropriate response to the multicultural population of their schools; they were already convinced. Yet their perceptions of the whole curriculum gravitated against strategies which would have encouraged such a notion in practice.

It has already been pointed out how these teachers were able to view education as a process distinct from other activities and thereby release themselves from the connection between education and the political realities of society at large. It may be suggested that their view of education and the curriculum was influenced by an unconscious adherence to the perspectives of dominant groups in society[47], not just in relation to the cultures associated with recent immigration, but also in relation to more established cultures, which they had internalized long before the question of responding to the presence of immigrant cultures had become an issue. This connects entirely with the feature consistently illustrated in the evidence from the three schools: the transaction of their responses to the multicultural population of their schools, justified in terms of 'pure' educational theories, could not be dissociated from their view of the whole curriculum and of all children.

If the notion of multicultural education is to be taken at all seriously teachers and policy makers will need to be involved in some radical rethinking of educational provision for all children, not only in relation to its content, but in relation to teaching and learning methods, use of resources, and the organization of learning situations. Moreover, as professionals, teachers will be required to examine their attitudes towards the people whom they serve, especially the parents and the children themselves, not only in relation to their perception of different cultures, but in relation to their perception of themselves as members of an independent and often unchallengeable profession, capable of making decisions about appropriate educational provision on behalf of others.

Notes

1. BROWN, C. (1984), *Multi-ethnic curricula: A sociological analysis of the response of the state school system in England.* Unpublished PhD thesis, the University of Birmingham.
2. DES (1963), *English for Immigrants*, Ministry of Education Pamphlet 43, London, HMSO; DES (1965), Circular 7/65; DES (1971), *Survey 13: The Education of Immigrants*, London, HMSO; DES (1972), *Survey 14: The Continuing Needs of Immigrants*, London, HMSO.
3. For example, SMITH, D.J. (1977), *Racial Disadvantage in Britain*, Harmondsworth, Pelican; REX, J., and TOMLINSON, S., (1979), *Colonial Immigrants in a British City*, London, Routledge and Kegan Paul; RATCLIFFE, P., (1981), *Racism and Reaction*, London, Routledge and Kegan Paul.
4. For example, CRE (1974), *The Educational Needs of Children from Minority Groups*, London, CRE, March; CRE (1974), *Teacher Education for a Multicultural Society*, London, CRE, June; CRE (1974), *In-service Education of Teachers in Multiracial Areas*, London, CRE, October; CRE (1977), *The Education of Ethnic Minority Children*, London, CRE, June, and the CRE Education Journal, *passim*.
5. For example, COARD, B. (1971), *How the West Indian Child is Made Educationally Subnormal in the British Education System*, London, New Beacon Books; LITTLE, A.N. (1975), 'The performance of children from ethnic minority backgrounds in primary schools', in RUSHTON, J. *et al.* (Eds.) *Education and Deprivation*, Manchester, Manchester University Press; SELECT COMMITTEE ON RACE RELATIONS AND IMMIGRATION (1978), *The West Indian Community*, London, HMSO; NUT (1980), *The Achievement of West Indian Pupils*, London, NUT, May; DES (1981), *West Indian Children in Our Schools: Rampton Report*, London, HMSO; TAYLOR, M.J. (1981), *Caught Between: A Review of Research into the Education of Pupils of West Indian Origin*, Windsor, NFER/Nelson.
6. NUT (1980), *After the Fire*, Bristol, NUT. Generally there is no evidence to link the inner-city disturbances during the 1980s with black discontent about the education system specifically, nor indeed to associate all these disturbances with the disaffection of black groups. What is important, however, is the fact that such disturbances have caused alarm sufficient enough to stimulate the consideration of black disadvantage and high unemployment levels in relation to a variety of factors, including education.
7. Early examples of this argument include: KUYA, D. (1971), 'School books attacked for warped outlook on race', in *The Guardian*, 17 April; MILNER, D. (1974), *Children and Race*, Harmondsworth,

Penguin; GILES, R. (1977), *The West Indian Experience in British Schools*, London, Heinemann. NUT (1978), *All Our Children*, London, NUT; NUT (1979), *In Black and White*, London, NUT; EDWARDS, V. (1979), *The West Indian Language Issue in British Schools*, London, Routledge and Kegan Paul; JEFFCOATE, R. (1979), *Positive Image: Towards a Multiracial Curriculum*, London, Chameleon Books in association with Writers and Readers; LITTLE, A.W. and WILLEY, R. (1981), *Multi-ethnic Education: The Way Forward*, London, The Schools Council.

8. There is a problem of terminology. 'Ethnic' is a term which has tended to supercede the term 'race', probably because of the unfortunate and inaccurate connotations of substantial genetic difference inherent in the term 'race'. Yet ethnicity is broader than culture, because there may be several cultures associated with one ethnic group. Moreover, physically inherited features such as hair, facial structure and skin colour may still be associated with ethnicity in so far as commonality of appearance can be a unifying factor in the cultures of particular groups. Although the term 'multicultural' is now commonly used, in practice it frequently refers broadly to the cultures associated with different ethnic groups, and there is little attempt to consider the representation of cultural diversity in regional or social class terms.

9. CRAFT, M. (1981), *Teaching in a Multicultural Society: The Task for Teacher Education*, Lewes, Falmer Press.

10. For example, BULLOCK, A. (1975), *A Language for Life: The Bullock Report*, London, HMSO; DES (1978), *Primary Education in England*, London, HMSO; DES (1979), *Aspects of Secondary Education in England*, London, HMSO.

11. For example, MATTHEWS, A. (1981), *Advisory Approaches to Multicultural Education*, London, Runnymede Trust; and, more recently, SWANN, LORD (1985) *Education for All: Report of the Committee of Enquiry into the Education of Children from Ethnic Minority Groups*, London, HMSO.

12. BERGSON, H. (1977), *The Two Sources of Morality and Religion*, ASHLEY AUDRA, R. *et al.* (Trans), Notre Dame Indiana, University of Notre Dame Press.

13. POPPER, K.R. (1966), *The Open Society and Its Enemies*, London, Routledge and Kegan Paul.

14. AYER, A.J. (1971), 'The character of an open society', in BRITISH HUMANIST ASSOCIATION, *Towards an Open Society*, London, Pemberton Books.

15. NANDY, D. (1971), 'Race as politics', in BRITISH HUMANIST ASSOCIATION, *op. cit.*

16. SWANN, LORD, (1985), *op. cit.*

17. Based on an approximate estimate by the Head Teachers.

18. Extract from the pamphlet produced by School 1. Italics are the pamphlet's.

19. Data from questionnaires to staff and comments of staff when interviewed.

20. Extract from the Handbook for Parents, School 1.

21. Verbatim comments of Head Teacher, School 2.
22. Almost every week there was an assembly related to a particular festival or some special aspect of the pupils' culture, and this was frequently extended in topic work.
23. Ginn reading scheme and 'The Terraced House Books' published by Methuen. The school had set aside one classroom as a special 'multicultural' resources room. It contained not only a variety of professionally prepared books and visual aids, but also a great deal of material provided by the parents.
24. Because they focused on the immediate locality they were inevitably multicultural. In 'Homes and Families' children described their own family life and compared it with that of other children; in 'People Who Help Us' children considered all the people who worked within their community who inevitably came from a variety of cultural backgrounds; in 'Buildings of Our City' a consideration of the local mosque, gudwara and church were included.
25. For example, in mathematics surveys of the locality were used to develop all kinds of number work, including elementary statistics and measurement; in science the children examined the nutritional composition of different foods which resulted in a visit to a local market to investigate the great variety of produce available; in English children considered the creative use of dialect and developed this in drama.
26. For example, some children had 'story-time' sessions in the local library conducted by an assistant librarian; many lessons were conducted in the street, in local shops, places of worship, the park. These were not occasional activities, but were part of the school week of every child within the school.
27. As part of its community programme the school had set up a consultative committee with representatives of teachers, parents, community residents, the LEA and the social services. Although the committee had no power to implement curriculum policies its concerns were taken very seriously, as evidenced by the institution of Punjabi and Urdu classes within the school day.
28. Views expressed by staff during interview.
29. Data from questionnaires to staff.
30. Ranging from two thirds to a whole morning of the school day.
31. Vebatim comments of Head Teacher, School 3.
32. Some reading books for older infants containing traditional tales of Asian and Caribbean origin.
33. Verbatim comments of Head Teacher, School 3.
34. For example, MULLARD, C. (1980), *Racism in Society and Schools: History, Policy and Practice, Occasional Paper 1*, Centre for Multicultural Education, London, University of London; REX, J. (1981), 'Aims and objectives', in CRAFT, M. (Ed.) *Teaching in a Multicultural Society*, Lewes, The Falmer Press; STONE, M. (1981), *The Education of the Black Child in Britain: The Myth of Multiracial Education*, London, Fontana; MULLARD, C. (1982), 'Multiracial education in Britain: From assimilation to cultural pluralism', in

TIERNEY, J. (Ed.) *Race, Immigration and Schooling*, London, Holt Education.

35. For example, BERNSTEIN, B. (1970), 'Education cannot compensate for society', in *New Society*, 26 February; VULLIAMY, G. (1978), 'Culture clash and school music', in BARTON, L. *et al.* (Eds.) *Sociological Interpretations of Schooling and Classrooms: A Reappraisal*, Driffield, Nafferton.
36. On average, most of the morning every day of the school week.
37. STONE, M. (1981), *op. cit.*
38. REX, J. (1981), *op. cit.*
39. MULLARD, C. (1982), *op. cit.*
40. Data from questionnaires to teachers indicated approximately 85 per cent.
41. PATON, K. (1977), 'The great brain robbery', in SMITH, M. (Ed.) *The Underground and Education*, London, Methuen.
42. MEIGHAN, R. (1974), 'Concepts of authoritarian and democratic regimes and classroom discipline', in *Dudley Education Journal*, Spring.
43. For example, cutting up paper for topic work, pinning work to classroom walls, tidying up book cupboards, hearing children read under the teacher's supervision.
44. DHONDY, F. (1978), 'Teaching young blacks', in *Race Today*, May/June.
45. For example, REX, J. (1981), *op. cit.*; MULLARD, C. (1982), *op. cit.*
46. Evidence from interview and questionnaires.
47. 'Dominant' in the sense of having the power to make their particular perspectives appear to be the appropriate ones.

Passions and Purposes: Curriculum Design and the Creation of Meaning

David Winkley

To those outside the maelstrom of schools, designing a curriculum looks a bland enough proposition, little more, perhaps, than a kind of policy statementing based upon common sense. Indeed, 'curriculum', is often confused with 'written intention' or syllabus. The first task, then, for anyone seriously wishing to grapple with curriculum is to undermine the mythology that planning a curriculum is comparable with planning, say, for the development of a new industrial product, or planning a house. Curriculum is a complicated story, in which statements of intent pass through a stage of development and transmission, and lead to a classroom delivery. The test of curriculum is not in the elegance of the design, but in the success of the outcome. It is in this tension between the fixed elements, the written, defined features, and the delivery, that the story of curriculum properly lies. For curriculum without the test of experiences is mere dancing on pinheads. It is, then, the story of this more complex, fuller, meaning of curriculum that I shall now pursue.

The Significance of Values

The first fly-in-the-ointment for curriculum planners whether for a primary school, or a university, is the impossibility of avoiding questions of value.[1] Indeed some commentators have argued graphically that curriculum is by definition *about* the transmission of values. Moreover curriculum is value-laden in different ways. The modern primary school curriculum expresses in its shape and design the consummation of our present contemporary view of 'what matters' in our social and national perspectives on teaching children. There are tremendous and passionate conflicts about what matters in curriculum which can most obviously be divided into political and cultural perspectives on learning. These express a social view of what children are and what we wish them to become in the 1980s.

Different political views will give priority to different features on the curriculum landscape. On a broad front politicians will disagree about such matters as locus of control allowed in curriculum planning, about formality and informality in teaching, about types of curriculum for children of different ability. On a narrower front there will be differences of view about detail, the political left putting special value on (say) peace studies, the political right on traditional national history. Then there are less controversial political issues, which reflect social concern or national interest. Currently, for example, we might argue that health is moving up as a priority with (say) computer science. Anti-smoking and anti-drug information is perceived as important to health, and computers are important for the future technical prosppects of the nation.

Then there are, at a deeper level, *cultural* perspectives. There is, for instance, the powerful tradition of minority elitist values embraced by a line of writers from Matthew Arnold through T.S. Eliot, D.H. Lawrence and G.H. Bantock.[2] In opposition to this are writers such as Williams[3] who express concern for the culture of the large majorities of working people. The powerful impetus behind these is egalitarianism, the idea that everything should be available to all, or (as a compromise) that we should all at least have some knowledge of the differences between our cultural experiences, which effectively requires some knowledge for all of us of each other's experiences. The current concern with a 'multicultural ethic' is arguably a development within this tradition. Hence in the most recent versions of the egalitarian model we move away from 'English culture and history' in the Great Tradition, to concern with much wider cultural traditions. The Christian touches respectfully upon the experience of the Muslim; the English white on the historical experience of blacks.

Another approach to cultural values in curriculum might look at attitudes towards children *vis á vis* authority, and note that these are constantly changing. Attitudes to authority express a general cultural consensus which has a considerable effect, in the long run, on how we teach. The liberal evolution of curriculum design for young children has a long history, with roots in 19th-century thinking about children which reaches its philosophical climax with De-wey, its most radical practical expression in Susan Isaacs and its official acknowledgement in the Hadow Report, 1931 and the Plow-den Report, 1967. The shift, over the years, has been broadly away from the confident notion that the teacher transmits the authority of knowledge, to the Deweyan perception of teacher-as-colearner.

The culmination of such 'general' or national cultural attitudes is the argument for a core or centralized curriculum which some would argue acts as a binding agent on society as a whole, giving coherence to social life. Indeed commentators such as Reynolds and Skilbeck have argued that all curriculum is in essence an expression of cultural values, a kind of cultural mapping:

> enabling all schools to provide a common core curriculum; one which is based on the different funds of experience available in our culture...[4]

Such a notion of 'core' could equally be described as 'consensus' curriculum, and it is, in effect, consensus about the broad outlines of curriculum that has emerged in our current practice. It is at this level that we might read *Curriculum 5–16*[5] — an immaculate statement of a consensus view of curriculum: aims and objectives in curriculum design 'for all our children'. The consensus is, broadly speaking, one between a liberal and a pragmatic view of what children should learn. Our growing querulousness towards received authority, our post-Plowden view of children has been modified by parental and political pressures to develop the kind of competences that get children through examinations, or, in the language of be-haviourism, 'promote skills'. Teachers have to a considerable extent run an uneasy line between these prevailing winds. It is no surprise that some commentators find classrooms too formal, others too informal, whilst others note that most schools operate similar curriculum compromises on a broad front.[6]

Conventions and Constraints

Values provide, then, the complex base for curriculum choice; but this is, as it were, only the material from which the product will be made. The next problem for the curriculum designer is one of *transmission*. Curriculum in design is a peculiar amalgamation of elements that pass through many hands. There is a pedagogical, political, managerial and parental interest in outcome; each may have different values and views about what should be transmitted and how. It is as though a great series of committees were writing the outline for a piece of music, some visible with dripping pens, others *eminences grises* in the background, others with loud voices and obvious influence.

In this crowded environment there are various ways in which the curriculum can be shaped. We might, for instance, design a curriculum according to weight of status, the music, as it were, being written by managers, or politicians, with the Secretary of State (perhaps) acting as the *prima mobile*; in that case the transmission would be down-the-line with the teachers playing the role of mere performers. Alternatively the music might be the product of commercial forces, a conglomerate of the tunes that most people would prefer to hear. Or then again, the teacher-practitioner might design a curriculum as Mozart wrote an opera — aware of an audience, one eye on the patron, inheriting a particular under-standing of conventions, traditions and values, but in the end stamping them with his or her distinctive originality.

The truth is that curriculum design in practice is far more *constrained* than most of us are prepared to admit and the greatest constraint is 'accepted practice', a compromise between cultures and transmissional influences. Few people have managed to make much intellectual sense of the primary school curriculum, 'a real fragmentation and incoherence of qualitative inconsistency' as Alexander rather brutally calls it.[7] Wickstead[8] come nearest with his interesting distinctions between the skills of 'surviving' (the basic curriculum), of 'relating' (concern with emotional development) and 'celebrating' (valuing the arts). This schema has the particular and unusual satisfaction of pleasing all-comers and cleverly giving sense to disparate elements. Given the difficulties it is not surprising that we tend to develop our curriculum planning in a piecemeal fashion and many schools adopt a similar format which uneasily combines commercially designed text-book work on the 'basics', liberal management practices, and a measure of activity work which tends to diminish as the child grows older. They are occasionally encouraged to shift one way or the other by inspectors and the like, and are all supremely constrained by resources. (At my school we can still manage to afford art paper and brushes, but little in the way of musical instruments. At the school up the road the parents can all afford to *buy* their children instruments. Both schools include elements of music in the curriculum, but ours is tailored to the threadbare cloth.)

It is easy, then, to get the impression that teachers in this constraining world have little influence over events. The English primary school, as Taylor observed it,[9] already seems tightly bound by procedure, tradition, managerial forces and parent expectation. None the less, my argument will now consider a new feature, transmission of curriculum in action, on the ground floor, and it is here that the teacher has considerable influence. It is in delicate matters of interpretation, exploration, experiment, and attitude that teachers can bring the dead material of formal curriculum design alive. There is, as it were, an internal and external element to curriculum. Any Head will know the difference between the elegant statement of intent enshrouded in the 'syllabus' kept by teachers in their desk, and the sharp reality of what actually happens in the classroom. And in a great many schools teachers shrug off constraints through the vigour, eccentricity, (or sometimes causalness and thoughtlessness) of classroom practice.

It is useful here, it seems to me, to think of the constraints of curriculum expectation as similar to the constraints of stylist style for a composer. A stylistic convention may be described as a way of focusing a language which becomes a language in its own right; it is this focus which makes possible the personal style or manner of the artist.[10] All curriculum decisions are inevitably embedded in a ground of expectation. But constraints of convention do not necessarily prevent the writing of great music. The constraints on Mozart, the pressures of stylistic precedent, were enormous. He also had patrons with definite expectations. None of this prevented the creation of music of the highest quality. Similarly on matters of curriculum, primary schools are not yet prevented from doing astonishingly imaginative and impressive things with the conventions they have to work with.

It is certainly possible that we need to say no more about curriculum than is said in *Curriculum 5–16*[11], presenting the bland and general outline of curriculum expectation, and leaving the detailed interpretation to the theatre of classroom exploration. But it is equally possible that a clear knowledge of the conventions, and even some further self-imposed constraints may actually facilitate the production of greater music (as it were) by the teacher of genius. I shall continue the argument, therefore, into more detailed questions of the transmissional stage of curriculum planning by the teachers themselves, and here I shall begin to draw on my own experience of trying to develop a curriculum over a number of years.

Transmission in Detail: The Composer at Work

The designing of primary curriculum has suffered from the illusion that 'teacher autonomy' requires a process of decision-making in schools that discourages any sustained commitment by individual teachers to group decisions. There are still schools, perhaps many of them, where the planning of curriculum at an institutional level rarely goes beyond generalities, restatements of the expected conventions exhorted by HMI, governments and the like. As a result there is often an unconvincing relation between intention and delivery in the classroom. The most recent work of Bennett et al.[12] is powerful evidence of this.

The essence of detailed planning — i.e. what is initially planned to 'go on' in classrooms — needs to begin at an institutional level with the participation of all the teaching staff. Meetings need to resolve a variety of crucial issues, at the heart of which is the question of how the 'conventions' can be used to express valuable meanings: what are the priorities and why?

There need to be well articulated starting points. In recent years these have been labelled by LEAs, in the spirit of business enterprise, as 'Aims and Objectives', and schools have often been under pressure to provide them in a crisp, business-like form. This is, I think, in a sense what is required. But the problem with the presentation of aims-and-objectives models has been their managerial and behaviourist origins. The outcomes of many schemes of aims and objectives have either been so derivative that they scarcely go beyond the generalities of what I have called 'conventions'; or else they have been of the checklist kind, designed as though the school is producing an industrial product, and largely presentational, failing to grapple with the messy problems of designing a curriculum that truly relates to what actually happens in classrooms.

My attempt to provide a structure for thinking about purpose, therefore, is deliberately intended to allow for a kind of flexibility and depth which links up with the experience of the classroom and the children's experience of learning.

There are five sections which are best thought of as points of focus, beginning with attention to children as individuals.

1. Focusing on Children

Children, and beyond them their families and communities, provide a necessary beginning, and curriculum needs to be appropriate to their special needs. One general aim of schools, for example, according to HMI, should be 'To help pupils understand the world in which they live...'[13] This will mean something very different depending on whether you live in Handsworth or Solihull. Children are not empty vessels. They bring to school views, experiences, personal worlds which substantially shape their minds; and in this shaping the school plays an important part and must respond to *what matters* to individuals. In making this response I have my own (value-laden) commitment here to a view of learning that not everyone will share, that emotional and social growth are as important a feature of school purpose as intellectual development; that there is a profound, active link between emotional maturity, balance and motivation, and intellectual performance. And in consequence 'teaching' is more than about the teaching of formal skills. As Smith puts it:

> Our feelings, attitudes and so on, then — our qualities as a person in depth — are a part of the context in which we teach and cannot be regarded as an irrelevance.[14]

This is a value-laden proposition of great complexity. It means more than the oft misused notion of 'child-centredness'. It acknowledges the role of child-as-client, certainly. But it also implies a philosophical perception of learning which makes quite precise claims about what schools ought to be up to. And there are certainly critics of this view, from behaviourists, politicians, researchers and others, who would argue for, or implicitly value, a much more perfectly *definable*, measurable, or academic view.[15]

All this has considerable consequences for the planning of a curriculum. At my own school it takes the form of three principles:

a) To respond to the children's emotional needs, placing emphasis on attitudes, personal maturity, motivation. To offer a counselling service to individual children. To encourage teachers to give value to children's feelings. To allow children a voice, to attend to their views and criticisms.

b) To assess the progress of the children individually in a way that is (i) easy to operate (ii) useful, (iii) reasonably comprehensive, (iv) gives valuable information about what they have learned.

This has led in practice to the development of a 'pupil profile' book for recording the development of each child, for teachers, parents and the children themselves to read and to contribute to.

c) To be as flexible as possible in timetabling in order to respond to the more striking needs of the children. This involves careful timetabling of staff, and placing of children in a variety of appropriate groupings.

In practice this means we ought to be able (or to try to be able) to take account of the intelligent, the slow-learner, the disturbed and unhappy, the ten-year old who reads Shakespeare, the precocious mathematician, the special talent, the second language speaker, the eccentric.

2. Focusing on Knowledge

The next question is how we 'break down' and analyze the components of the content of the work we intend to engage in. This draws us at once into the debate about subject-orientation and integration of subjects into topics or projects. It is at this stage that the relative worthlessness of a syllabus of General Intentions becomes clear. There is a huge gap between elegant statements of general intent and the transmission of these into meaningfully useful detail. Schools can easily be blown, like boats, off course. Common sense seems to me to dictate some rules to the game.

The first is that clarity of thinking is an essential prerequisite of any planning. This requires, of necessity, some 'breaking down' of curriculum into 'units' of some kind. It is not possible to amalgamate all experience under one experiential umbrella. The Plowden arguments for 'integration' underrated the sheer complexity of the task — as do most non–teaching commentators.

In practice 'integration' often becomes a superficial trifling with bits and pieces of content with little overall coherence apart from the 'theme' of the moment or the interests of the teacher. A primary project drawing together a touch of history here, a touch of maths there, suffers from the flaw of the juggler attempting to gyrate too many balls at the same time. The general overview looks interesting but the detailed experience of activities is random, often superficial and disconnected. Often there is no connection between one project and the next. One HMI once told me that his son had 'done' canals in three different years at his primary school without the school even realizing. The project finally meanders to a conclusion that is attractively presented but fails to move on the learning of individual children. Its claims to be child-centred, the expression of 'the way children naturally look at the world'[16] is fraudulent, because despite the abundance of 'free-activity' the theme is very much the choice and interest of the teachers.[17]

In 1978 HMI,[17] having similar perceptions, shifted the ground fairly dramatically back to more conventional subject analysis. But somewhere in between the extremes of the watertight demarcated 'subject' and the free-for-all of the patchwork quilt project lies the kind of clear, flexible and subtle analysis of 'content' I am looking for. The 'process' analysis also espoused by HMI (which labels it 'elements of learning') has its usefulness, but identifying such qualities as 'observation', 'communication', 'study', 'problem solving', does not obviate the problem of choosing content *to* observe, study, solve and so on. Part of the problem is the confusion between 'knowledge' and 'content'. It has been presumed[18] that when 'content' is ordered into subjects (or sometimes it is argued in any way at all) it must produce mechanistic forms and structures of thinking, which do nothing but make us 'well-informed'. But this is not necessarily the case; knowledge *without* content is meaningless. 'Content' requires some kind of analysis, some kind of attention as a phenomenon. So wide a concept requires some kind of 'discipline' and 'discipline' immediately invokes the notion of a language, a mode of argument, a 'shaping', an ordering and limitation.

The resolution my staff has moved towards over the years has been subject-orientated *at first*, focusing on the following objectives, which gradually draw us into deeper waters.

a) To look at curriculum *content* in a way that (i) tackles a 'body of knowledge' in some key subject areas, (ii) is incremental from one year to the next and (iii) makes sense to the children.

b) To structure some areas of the curriculum more precisely in order (i) to provide support for teachers, (ii) to make the teaching more interesting, (iii) to make the work more appropriate to children of different abilities.

c) To go beyond a 'body of knowledge' to look at underlying factors which cut across content/specialist areas. Here we are concerned with the development of children's skills.

Some skills will need precise attention, and here behaviourist principles of analysis may be invaluable; others will be hard to define and overbearing to implement. There is great skill in choosing which is which, and it has to be said that in general the analysis of skills by checklist in classroom practice is much more difficult than even Alexander, with his most subtle analysis of curriculum issues[19] appreciates. On this issue, Smith's argument[20] that much of the problem with the 'skills approach' 'is precisely that it ignores so much of the context in which teaching takes place' seems to me immaculate. On the other hand there is evidence that some close focuses on skills for specific purposes may be useful.[21] At Grove, for instance, we are currently finding the American behavioural DISTAR programme useful for small numbers of slow learners.

It is clear that some 'skills' need to be mastered in order to make any kind of progress in learning.

d) To enact the 'content design' in the classroom context in as flexible and imaginative way as possible, expressing meanings across the different subject barriers and languages. A history project, for example, would be concerned certainly with planned choices in history content, themselves based on value judgments about what seems worthwhile, and would be concerned with building up skills in helping the understanding of history, but would also be expressed in part in the languages of other 'areas' — science, say, or art; and would be concerned too with the general development of the child's ability to master fundamental learning bases — observation, critical thinking, clear communicating and the like.

3. Focusing on Pedagogy

A pragmatic and deeper view of curriculum appreciates in the process of transmission the importance of the individual class-teacher's interpretation of events. Managerial presentations of curriculum tend to overlook this. But anyone who has worked in schools will appreciate the importance of teacher-style. A good deal of research on classroom technique confirms the variety of teaching methodology — and its significance. Study of classroom behaviours and performances will show subtle and striking differences in the enaction of curriculum in the theatre of the classroom; some of these differences will be invisible to first impressions. But differences will be noticed even in visible evidence.

We might, for example, examine the art work presented in any primary classroom, and then work back to the procedures that led to the types of production in evidence. The work on display will reflect the knowledge, skill, sensitivity and attitudes of the teacher. It will tell a good deal about how controlling the teacher is in use of materials and in handling the children; it will express, in different proportions, teacher values or individual child values. There will be different views expressed about art, and about presentation. In one classroom the art will show a high teacher profile (maybe *done* by the teacher); in another it will show group work, in another the individual imaginative and varied expressions of lots of different children. It will show how well the teacher sees the possibilities of different art media. It will show the importance to the teacher of displaying and valuing art-work. It will reveal the depth of the teachers' view of what 'art' really is. It will express the degree of the teacher's obsessionalism and subject interests, his/her valuing of realism versus fantasy or surrealism (for instance). It will show the standards the teacher attains to — high or low. It will show the proportion of time the teacher has apportioned to art, and so on.

Whilst group-planning tends to reduce qualitative differences between teachers, there will always be some significant differences of skill, mind and character between classroom performances — and in some degree rightly so. For the act of teaching is a personal act of mind and imagination.

The long-term development of a successfully practising school requires some resolution of what might be perceived as a key conflict, between the need of the school to harmonize practice as an institution and the need for individual teachers to develop their own techniques and perceptions.

In the stated aims of the school, therefore, there are, it seems to me, at least six points which ought to be taken into consideration.

a) To acknowledge in content and pedagogy the existence and virtues of a multicultural society. To discuss and openly inhibit racism.

b) To create an awareness by the teachers of the need for a balance between teacher-direction and the need to create space for the children to think for themselves.

c) To accept that formal statements of intent ('aims and objectives', syllabuses, etc.) are brutal and inadequate, no more than guidelines in an unpredictable world. It's (i) what goes on inside people's heads and (ii) what actually happens in the theatre of the classroom, that matters.

d) To allow for eccentricity, unpredictability and the formidable influence of teacher-style and personality in teaching achievements.

e) To programme for both routine and variety.

f) To give high-value to both convergent and divergent activity, in both the arts and the sciences.

4. Focusing on Organization

Curriculum design requires an organizational setting, indeed, curriculum doesn't begin as an institutional proposition without attending in some degree to the way people come together to plan it. That the school needs to find the time for staff to meet together goes without saying. The key to organization is the principle of cooperation — and cooperation has to be seen as double edged. On the one hand the 'leader', whether managerial or curriculum, needs to defer to the feelings and experience of the group; on the other teachers need to acknowledge (i) special expertise amongst colleagues and (ii) to be prepared to commit themselves to the principle of group decisions. There's no point in having a curriculum intention to which individual teachers only pay lip service.

There is a place, too, for consultation *outside* the group — using external advice when it seems appropriate and considering consulting with parents and children about what they feel ought to be happening in school, and how their experience meets up to expectations.

Finally, 'organization' needs to build in a feature of evaluation; no plan should be conceived as a finality, and it requires honest assessment, continuous updating and radical reappraisal where necessary.

There are, therefore, seven major principles in this section to attend to.

a) To encourage teachers to become more reflective about their own practice via INSET, group discussion and a good information flow.

b) To set up a structure of teacher-meetings which allows (i)
    for a sense of cooperative design and (ii) decision-making
    of a kind which uses the special talents of different
    teachers, (iii) allows teachers to feel in control of their own
    working conditions, (iv) allows for continual reappraisal.
c) To use external and internal advice of the highest quality.
d) To formally evaluate through external assessment.
e) To hold a balance between commitment to routine and
    openness to change.
f) To make the most efficient use possible of diminishing
    resources, particularly staffing resources.
g) To create a high quality school-parent link, which is both
    consultative and informative.

5   Focusing on Outcomes

There is yet more controversy about the value of achievement. The
presumption, by some commentators, is that attention to the
objectives of identifiable achievements is everything or nothing. If
it is everything, then teachers are exposed to the naivety of the
officious assessor, the metricating examiner, the methodical
behaviourist, all damaging the notion of 'education in its own right'.
If nothing, then children can be liberated to explore 'experiences' or
(to the opposite perspective of the hard-line utilitarian) to lose all
sense of purpose. That the truth might lie on that great ocean of
possibilities between and might confuse the rhetoric, is thus
avoided. The principle, however, that curriculum is in some sense
profoundly linked to the notion of achievement seems to be
inescapable, firstly because it is, as we have said, grounded in *values*
and secondly because it is concerned above all with the transmission
of purposes. However stylish a golfer's swing the outcome of his
game — the score — is of some relevance to the success of his enterprise. Or to use our regular analogy, what the music sounds like is
the purpose of the composition.

'Success', of course, may not be everything. The music may in
fact be rather fine, but perhaps beyond the present sensibility of the
listeners. And certainly a part of the virtue of teaching is the
excitement of the journey, the sheer brilliance of the performance.
But success matters too, and whilst it is in teaching, a highly
complex proposition, it is not impossible to make some moves
towards assessing it. There are problems, of course, not least of

which is 'who decides what success means?' The conductor? The composers? The audience? The players? The orchestra managers? The critics? The wider public? But such questions are pedagogical hazards. No-one should come into teaching these days who cannot tolerate some insecurity and conflict. Schools invoke passionate responses, and rightly so. But as schools determine in detail the 'meanings' of the languages of curriculum, so they must have an ear for the quality of the world they are creating for their audiences. Audience awareness thus has a role, and it is arguable that this is a particularly weak area in the present highly managerially orientated modern state school. How many schools live with their eye on the bureaucracies that manage them rather than on the children and parents themselves?[22]

Definitions of values of outcomes are worth discussion at great length, and distinctions can clearly be made between the different kinds of evidence available, principally between the visible and invisible, those elements which can be seen or assessed with relative ease, and those which are inter-personal, to do with behaviour and ethos. It will suffice, here, to put nine of the key determinants of the success of curriculum planning. The principle is to determine 'success' in many different ways, namely —

a) happiness, self-confidence and self-valuing of the children.
b) maturity of the children, reflected in common sense, self-criticism, balance, openmindedness and sense of humour.
c) an ability to cope with immaturity.
d) flexibility of staff (and the school as a whole) in responding to children's needs.
e) ability of people (teacher-teacher, teacher-child, child-teacher and child-child) to listen and communicate with each other.
f) quality of 'final products' which come from the children.
g) balance, self-criticism, openness, job satisfaction and enthusiasm of teachers.
h) progress and assessed by data of three kinds (i) general observation (ii) statistical, if necessary using testing (iii) external assessment/opinion.
i) views of the children, parents and community about the school.

This view of curriculum design, sketchy though it still is, will not escape criticism from some quarters. For some might still see in it an unnecessary kind of prescription. It begins, after all, with intentions and ends with outcomes — both fixed propositions, some of which can be written down in detail. Intentions can be expressed as policies; and outcomes can in some sense be presented as (say) photographs of the art on the wall, examination or test results, solid evidence of 'achievements'. There is a sense here, in which curriculum can be seen as single frame polaroid photographs. And this is precisely the view that management, LEAs, and advisers often take. Similarly researchers, caught up as they are in the onus of 'proof', put particular value on the kinds of visible evidence that can be expressed, one way or another, in numerical terms. It will, however, not have escaped attention that the nature of the curriculum I have been discussing changes as the definitions unwind. The fact is that the further down the line we go in the examination of the dimensions of curriculum the more dynamic and elusive our sense of it becomes.

The visible elements, I should insist, and as the design above I think bears out, are only the outer shell. The broad sweep of the analysis, of course, argues for *purposes* but then I do not see how education can proceed at all without a sense of purpose. But the complicating elements emphasize matters that are harder to pin down in detail, and even in transmission are curiously elusive. This is because curriculum in action is dynamic, it expresses movement, events pass quickly, and are often of multiple complexity. This curriculum, expressed as purpose, experience and achievement, is moving constantly like a river. It is precisely because of this that the experiences of those inside and outside the classroom tend to diverge. It is all too easy for an observer to try to assess a school like a tourist taking snapshots. At a superficial level these may seem to catch reality. It is hard to appreciate that the teacher, often be-leaguered by the sheer pressure of events, has a feeling which is much more like being inside a movie, writing, acting in, producing and watching the film, all at once. Teachers, rightly, are unimpress-ed by researchers and managers who generalize from the lofty heights of the polaroid photograph.

Curriculum design, then, must try to allow for these multiple experiences, and acknowledge at its heart that transmission is a part of the objective planning function. The plan above does, I think, inherently avoid some of the more obvious pitfalls, the main one of which is conceiving curriculum as purely a content based formation, something to do with statement of fact rather than dynamic purpose. It allows, above all, a recognition of the sheer complexity of the exercise. It shows, too, I think, if in a somewhat truncated and anecdotal way, the potential richness of the teachers' and schools' contribution to curriculum planning within accepted conventions.

Which leads to the final irony: that the achievement of schools, unlike the achievements of musicians, is strangely *silent*, which makes teachers, however good, peculiarly vulnerable to the Salieris of the educational world. Despite my claims for various techniques and indicators in 'focusing on outcomes', in the end, the final justification is in the hearts and minds of people — silent indicators. And it is a profound problem for teachers, unlike the experience of businessmen, architects, golfers or musicians that at the very heart of his or her intentions is the mystery of whether or not and in what degree his or her objectives have been achieved. Much of life, for the teacher (despite the fact that it is ostensibly a very noisy job) is a deafening silence. We suspect, we have indicators, ups and downs, intuitions and partial evidence, but there is, too, a great deal of the unknown. Was it all worth it, teachers might ask? In the end we have to fall back on an act of faith that the values we attempted to express in our curriculum design, and then to enact in the classroom, prove over the years to be truly valuable to those who experience them.

Notes

1. *cf* Speech by Prof. John Ashworth at the British Association, 4th September 1986, in which he argued that the issue for Universities at present is less the content of the curriculum than the values it embues.
2. Bantock gives a good exposition of this tradition. *cf* BANTOCK, G.H. (1984), *Studies in the History of Educational Theory, Vol. 2. 'The Minds and the Masses'.* London, George Allen and Unwin.
3. WILLIAMS, R., (1961), *The Long Revolution*, Harmondsworth, Penguin.
4. REYNOLDS, R. and SKILBECK, M., (1976), *Culture and the Classroom*, London, Open Books.
5. DES (1985), *The Curriculum from 5–16, Curriculum Matters 2, An HMI Series.* London, HMSO.
6. RICHARDS, C. (1982), 'Curriculum consistency', in RICHARDS, C. (Ed.) *New Directions in Primary Education*, Lewes, Falmer Press.
7. ALEXANDER, R.J. (1984), *Primary Teaching*, London, Holt Rinehart and Winston.
8. WICKSTEAD, D., (1982), 'Surviving, relating and celebrating: Towards a new definition of the basics'. Unpublished mimeo.
9. TAYLOR, P.H., *et al.*, (1974), *Purpose, Power and Constraint in the Primary School Curriculum*, London, Macmillan Education.

10. For a discussion of this notion of convention and style, *cf* Rosen, C., (1971), *The Classical Style*, London, Faber and Faber.
11. *The Curriculum from 5–16, op. cit.*
12. Bennett, N., *et al.*, (1984), *The Quality of Pupil Learning Experiences*, London, Lawrence Erlbaum Associates.
13. *Ibid.*, p. 3
14. Smith, R., (1985), *Freedom and Discipline*, London, George Allen and Unwin.
15. *cf* for example an interesting criticism of the child-centred approach in Stone, M., (1981), *The Education of the Black Child in Britain*, London, Fontana.
16. For a detailed presentation of this view, *cf* Blenkin, G.M. and Kelly, A.V. (Eds.) (1983), *The Primary Curriculum in Action*, London, Harper and Row.
17. DES (1978), *Primary Education in England and Wales: A Survey by HMI*, London, HMSO.
18. *cf* Blenkin, G.M. and Kelly, A.V. *op. cit.* pp. 16–23.
19. Alexander, R. *op. cit. cf* especially his discussion of curriculum, p. 69.
20. Smith, *op. cit.* pp. 19–20.
21. For recent research on direct teaching techniques in the USA *cf* (1986), 'A multifaceted study of change in seven inner city schools', in *The Elementary School Journal*, 86, 3.
22. For a detailed recent discussion of the relation of schools to bureaucracies, *cf* Winkley, D.R., (1986), *Diplomats and Detectives*, London, Robert Royce.

Gender in Primary Schooling

Nanette Whitbread

In the early days of elementary schooling the National and the British and Foreign School Societies preferred to segregate the sexes and recommended using a curtain or partition where numbers did not warrant separate, adjoining schoolrooms or single sex schools. As the monitorial system gradually gave way to class teaching, the grant-awarding Committee of the Privy Council on Education favoured 'coeducational teaching on the Scottish model, with boys and girls sitting on alternate benches in four separate classes, according to their proficiency in the 3 Rs.'[1] This pressure for attainment grouping was reinforced by the Revised Code with its system of Standards. Infants, however, were always taught in mixed schools or schoolrooms.

The most overt and enduring curricular differentiation by gender occurred in the late nineteenth-century Elementary Codes requiring girls to do plain needlework and allowing time for this to be taken from arithmetic. This led the Cross Commission in 1888 to recommend compensating for 'this disadvantage ... by modifying the arithmetical requirements of the Code in the case of girls'. The option of a wider curriculum by adding two 'specific' subjects was restricted for girls by requiring them to make domestic economy their first choice in Standards IV to VI. As a contemporary commented: 'it is comforting to know that some thousands of girls annually leave the Board Schools who are expert practitioners in all kinds of useful domestic arts.'[2]

Further differentiation came in the 1890s when drawing became compulsory for boys and manual instruction was recognized for grant. The consolidated Day School Code of 1902 firmly established drawing for boys and needlework for girls within the compulsory curriculum of elementary schools administered by the new local

210

education authorities. These disparate foci endured into the second half of this century. The social function of state schooling involves socialization to conform with cultural mores including ascribed gender roles. These were not yet seriously challenged, though they were becoming increasingly disfunctional to women's employment patterns.

Although it outlined a distinctively elementary curriculum for working class children, the greater flexibility of the 1904 Code opened the way for developmental and child-centred educational theory. This matched the challenge of postwar reconstruction after 1918 and the growth of a democratic philosophy of education. Moreover, the problem posed by increased numbers of older pupils led LEAs to begin transferring them to senior schools even before the 1926 Hadow Report accelerated this process. This reorganization brought 'a new freedom to junior and infant schools to develop along their appropriate lines' with a more child-centred curriculum[3], and made coeducation the norm throughout the primary stage.

Debate was already under way on sex differentiation and single sex or coeducation in the new maintained secondary schools and led to considerable research into observed sex differences in behaviour, and whether or not these might be innate. Much of this was reviewed by the Consultative Committee which reported in 1923. As early as 1903 an American study had concluded that 'the psychological differences of sex seem to be largely due, not to differences of average capacity, nor to difference in type of mental activity, but to differences in the social influences brought to bear on the developing individual from early infancy'. E.L. Thorndike argued in 1914 that 'differences within one sex so enormously outweigh the differences between the sexes in these intellectual and semi-intellectual traits that for practical purposes the sex differences may be disregarded'. Despite his belief that 'the fighting instinct in the male and of the nursing instinct in the female' are inborn, he had observed that they were accentuated by training and same sex companionship for play. A key psychological witness before the Committee was Cyril Burt. He told them that sex differences in reasoning were almost imperceptible in infant school, and that girls were somewhat in advance of boys at six or seven because of their slight precocity in ability to read and use words, but that boys outstripped girls around ten years of age. Junior school teachers observed that boys were more methodical, critical, logical, independent in thought, readier to work with their hands and more interested in mechanical matters; that girls were capable of more sustained effort, produced neater, more painstaking work with greater attention to detail, and excelled at writing expressively. The Committee concluded:

> Our witnesses were agreed that there was probably no necessity for any very explicit differentiation in the curriculum as between boys and girls up to 12 years of age except in manual work... In Physical Training, several expert witnesses thought that girls and boys might do the same physical exercises up to 10 or 11 years of age.[4]

A shift in official opinion can be detected in successive editions of *The Handbook of Suggestions for Teachers*, reflecting mounting research evidence on the absence of innate, cognitive sex differences. The 1937 edition advocated no differentiation in any subjects. By then the availability of cheap machine-made clothes meant that 'Needlework in school has lost what association it may ever have had with domestic drudgery, and is free to flourish as a fine constructive and decorative craft on its own merits'.

In 1931 the Hadow Report on *The Primary School* endorsed and further encouraged the developmental and child-centred approaches to primary education that had been slowly gaining ground over the past decade. It devoted considerable attention to the physical and mental development of children between the ages of seven and eleven, but noted that there had been much less research on this age range than on younger children and adolescents.

Cyril Burt was again a key witness and much attention was paid to educational retardation among children from poor districts and to the wide range of individual differences in intelligence as measured by tests. Again it was noted that 'sex differences in educable capacity up to the age of eleven appear negligible', despite girls' earlier facility in reading and use of words. 'On the emotional side, however, the interests of the boy and the girl are moving further and further apart between the ages of seven and eleven', which was attributed to inherited instincts 'much increased by the effects of tradition and convention'. While there was no sex difference in dexterity, there was in 'muscular endurance' which suggested that sex differentiation was necessary for games and physical exercises. Significantly, 'the heavy domestic duties, especially those carried out by young girls in the home, often make for listlessness and fatigue'. The New Educational Fellowship argued against any noticeable curricular differentiation. Teacher witnesses repeated the same sort of observations on sex-typical behaviour as their colleagues in the previous decade.[5]

The child-centred primary school, where teachers were urged to start from the child's own interests, may have inadvertently reinforced gender stereotyping. Indeed, an extended passage of exemplary advice in the Committee's introduction to their report supports this likelihood:

> A boy is interested in steam engines; let him start from his interests, make a rough model..., discover something about the historical process of its invention..., make a map of the transport system..., learn something about the lives of famous engineers,... A girl has heard her parents discuss the price of food: let her learn something about the countries from which it comes, the processes..., the crafts concerned in its production and preparation,...

The recommendation of the two Hadow Committees in 1931 and 1933[6] became the received wisdom guiding the development of primary education until further amplified by the Plowden Committee in 1967. Gender was not viewed as a problematic issue in the intervening period. Endorsing the Hadow blueprint in 1959 HMI disregarded gender, except to note: 'At five, boys and girls already move differently, and seem to have different interests and aptitudes in physical activities'. They favoured total coeducation, specifically including art, crafts and games, though they accepted that sex preferences were shown. A guiding principle was to allow as much individual freedom and choice as children can manage without disrupting each other.[7]

Equality of educational opportunity was not a function of primary schools until after the Second World War. It was first enunciated as an objective in the 1943 White Paper on Educational Reconstruction[8] which foreshadowed the 1944 Education Act. For the next twenty years the focus was on eradicating inequalities associated with social class. Research therefore centred on social class differences, sometimes including gender alongside. For instance, J.W.B. Douglas found that lower working class boys performed worse than lower working class girls on arithmetic and sentence completion tests at eight and eleven, whereas middle class boys surpassed middle class girls in arithmetic at eleven but were inferior in sentence completion. He suggested that girls' overall superiority in primary school subjects at eight and eleven might relate to their interests and their better relations with mainly female teachers, and that teachers' lack of sympathy and understanding of boys might be having an undesirable effect on their behaviour and progress.[9]

W.A.C. Blyth observed that 'sex-typing ... is reinforced by the school as the two sexes draw apart', but noted that there was little research evidence on social attitude formation. He argued that the developmental primary school should aim to combat any form of stereotyping. 'This involves maintaining ... a wide range of roles and ensuring, if necessary through active intervention, that all the children sample many of them'.[10] Commenting on the 'persistent sex-traits' in child behaviour, he concluded 'that the monosexual structure of the peer group reinforces this type of cultural difference' and that 'the cross-sex deviant has a hard time of it'.[11]

Insofar as there was any interest in gender in the primary school it was expressed as concern about poor achievement of boys, especially those from the lower working class. This was tentatively attributed to teachers' intolerance towards boys' unruly behaviour, which was seen as even more characteristic of such boys. As intelligence tests revealed no consistent or significant sex differences among primary school children, boys must have been under-achieving and the responsibility had to be laid on the schools.

The National Child Development Study of the age cohort born during one week in March 1958 provided a mass of data that has been variously analyzed and classified. The first report on seven-year-olds expressed concern at 'boys being more backward in reading' but none at girls' inferiority in arithmetic problems and number; here the same percentage of both sexes was assessed as 'below average' in contrast with the much smaller percentage of girls for reading.[12] These sex differences occurred in tests and teachers' ratings, and tended to persist or even accentuate through junior school; but not for another decade was there comparable concern about girls' mathematical underachievement. This was perceived as acceptable sex-role behaviour. Moreover, women primary teachers, often lacking confidence in their own mathematical competence, may have expected less of girls.

The Plowden Report itself largely ignored gender, subsuming both sexes as 'children' and being more concerned with social class and environmental deprivation especially in inner cities, and language problems of immigrants. Sex differentiation was accepted for games and, to a limited extent, top juniors' crafts; but sex stereotyping was not seen as problematic. Such stereotyped remarks as 'Boys will be boys' were repeated without comment and the assertion made that 'boys need an element of adventure'. An analysis of the thirty-six photographs of children in contemporary primary schools reveals eight depicting sex-typed activities, three of individual or small same-sex groups engaged on stereo-atypical activities, sixteen of boys and girls working together or in parallel (including one where a lone boy is reading among a group of girls with whom the teacher is talking), and nine of individuals or same-sex small groups in neutral activities. The implicit comment was that all were equally commended. Moreover, the various sex differences recorded in the research included in appendices to the report were not even discussed: they were not mentioned. The simple message was to commend those schools where teachers were alert to foster 'children's own interests'.[13] That this might itself reinforce sex stereotyping unless guarded against was not considered in a major report twenty years ago. The Plowden Report gave a powerful boost to the general thrust of the earlier Hadow Reports, with a new emphasis on individualization and in the context of equal opportunity as 'the touchstone' and further research on child development.

Equal opportunity is one context in which to view sex differentiation and role stereotyping to assess whether detrimental discrimination results. Another is the developmental philosophy of education which presumes the desirability of all-round cultivation of individual potential and must, therefore, deplore enforcement of certain attributes or stultification of others except when necessary for the protection of other individuals' freedom.

The Department of Health and Social Security commissioned Dr Kellmer Pringle, Director of the National Child Development Study, to write a source document about children's developmental needs. Published in 1974, this effectively demolished previous theories that sex roles are innately determined and provided authoritative information on how these are learned from birth. She showed how sex-appropriate behaviour becomes well established during the pre-school years:

Clothes, toys, subtle differences in words, play, hugs, rewards, punishments and parental example, surround the child with a world which clearly distinguishes behaviour expected from boys and girls.

Those psychological characteristics considered appropriate will be developed by about the third year of life; and throughout childhood the 'assigned' sex role will be practised in social relations, in play and in fantasy, and be continually reinforced by the responses and expectations of others.

On sex differences in primary school achievement she supported observations that 'girls are ahead of boys in language development — until the age of eight, if not later', and brought together a variety of information that might help to explain boys' problems in adjusting to school, especially in the early years. More boys exhibit emotional and behavioural problems such as enuresis, stammer, school phobia. Their skeletal and nervous systems are less mature than girls' and they are more accident prone. They are subject to greater peer pressures, much of it competitive, and experience more conflicting and inconsistent expectations from adults. Dr Pringle made no value judgments about gender role socialization, merely commenting that 'expectations may now be changing, or at least becoming modified'.[14]

It is significant that John and Elizabeth Newson paid no particular attention to gender in their 1965, 1968, 1976 and 1977 studies of child-rearing, but reworked their research data to discover what it revealed about sex typing for a symposium published in 1978. They found that children aged seven to eleven play mostly with others of the same sex and identify strongly with their own sex, whether peers or parents. By seven, and still more by eleven, their interests have drawn apart and even polarized. Far more parents share an interest with a child of the same sex. Yet mothers see their own children primarily as individuals and do not discourage but even support atypical interests when these are expressed. Even so, they tend not to perceive a daughter's expertise with a sewing machine as displaying 'mechanical skill' such as they readily recognize in a son's mechanical activities. The Newsons concluded that there are powerful cultural constraints on children to conform to sex-associated attitudes and behaviour at home.[15] Maccoby and Jacklin also stressed that parents treat their children as individuals, responding to their temperament, abilities and interests and supporting cross-sex hobbies and activities when evident. They found no conclusive evidence of consistent sex stereotyping by parents and, despite some indication that fathers may punish cross-sex play, were inclined to refute earlier contrary assumptions.[16]

Post-sputnik anxiety in America about low standards in schools led to research in the 1960s which sought to explain how elementary schools disadvantaged boys by alienating them so that they under-achieved. This was countered by the emergent feminist movement inspired by the publication of Betty Friedan's *The Feminine Mystique* in 1963. New research in the 1970s sought to expose the damaging effects of sexism at school on girls.[17] However, as Alison Kelly remarked, some feminist accounts adopt a crudely behaviourist approach on child rearing, stressing differences in how boys and girls are treated but ignoring similarities.[18] It is impossible to isolate the influences at work within a primary school from the many cultural influences operating outside school, such as media, toys, playmates, adults other than parents. Nevertheless, it is worthwhile trying to identify and analyze school factors because it should be possible to control them, at least to some extent.

In Britain the government asked the Inspectorate to examine whether curricular differences in schools contributed to inequality of opportunity between boys and girls. Their report was published in the year of the Sex Discrimination Act and the creation of the Equal Opportunities Commission with a remit that included education and training. Next year the Assessment of Performance Unit began work and James Callaghan launched the Great Debate on education and whether schools were adequately serving the needs of a modern industrial society. The 1977 Green Paper firmly stated that all the aims of schools must 'apply to boys and girls' and continued:

> Equal opportunity does not necessarily mean identical class-room provision for boys and girls but it is essential that, in translating their aims into day-to-day practice, schools should not by their assumptions, decisions, or choice of teaching materials, limit the educational opportunities offered to girls.[19]

Here was the first official inclusion of gender as a factor in securing equality of educational opportunity since that became an objective in 1943, and it significantly identified girls as those at risk of discrimination.

A mass of data was available on gender in the primary and preschool years from major studies, sociologists investigating social class had often correlated for sex and ethnographic studies, such as *Classrooms Observed*[20], mentioned sex differential treatment and expectations of primary pupils. Teacher expectation, pupil self-concept, the self-fulfilling prophecy and the hidden curriculum were now recognized as important. Initially, the new focus on sex inequality was directed at secondary schools and, in particular, at mathematics and science for girls. However, it was reasonable to look for the roots of differential secondary performance in primary school experiences.

The Equal Opportunities Commission and the Schools Council embarked in 1979 on a joint venture to pool expertise which resulted in the latter's project on *Reducing Sex Differentiation in Schools* and four publications under its Programme 3 on *Developing the Curriculum for a Changing World*: all focused on girls, two entirely on the primary school. These projects exemplified stereotypical differentiation and offered suggestions for its elimination.[21] This was also the thrust of feminist writing on education which became increasingly concerned with nursery and primary as the formative years for learnt sex-typing and with teachers as the dominant influence. Some of this was subjective and polemical, exemplified by the title *Learning to Lose*.[22]

The Inspectorate adopted a cautious stance. They found that although there was no timetabling differentiation at the nursery and infant phase, 'boys and girls do behave differently ... and are expected to behave differently'. Separation by sex occurred at junior level for games, often for craft where girls did needlework and boys a wider range involving a variety of practical skills, and for some extra-curricular activities for which sex stereotyped choice occurred. The Inspectors concluded:

> All in all, the different treatment of boys and girls in primary schools is a subtle process, in step with the social attitudes of the time, and more likely to be modified by changes in those than by any other means. The subtlety of the process does not diminish its power: attitudes learnt early often persist.
>
> Schools and colleges must respond also to some extent to the expectations which parents on the one hand and employers on the other have about life styles and career patterns...
>
> Subject to a proper recognition of these realities however, the schools ought to be satisfied that differences in the curriculum as between the sexes do not unfairly and unnecessarily militate against the personal development or the career prospects of girls. There is evidence in the survey that some differences do have this effect.

Their specific advice was merely 'that separation of boys and girls for craft work at the junior stage is to no-one's advantage', though they were critical of infant teachers' failure to encourage girls to take an interest in mechanical things and constructional activities.[23]

The spate of studies of sexist stereotyping in primary schools through the late 1970s and early 1980s tend to be corroborative, sometimes plagiarist and often repetitive. Where there are inconsistencies these may reflect the changing state of social attitudes making for less consistent behaviour by teachers and pupils between schools studied during this period. Given that primary schools are coeducational with an overtly common curriculum, except for some crafts and games with upper juniors, studies have looked for sex differentiation in the hidden curriculum, interaction within classrooms, teachers' attitudes and behaviour and teaching materials; and there has been particular interest in girls' experience in mathematics and science.

Nursery and infant classrooms have generally been perceived as reinforcing traditional sex roles through the socialization process of play and structured activities such as sex-typed adult role playing, use of available toys and same sex grouping for many activities. However, Lisa Serbin has shown from observational and experimental studies that the teacher can effectively intervene to promote cross-sex selection of toys, such as girls using construction blocks, and mixed sex cooperation, either by positive comment or by positioning herself invitingly in the vicinity of a particular activity.[24] Rosie Walden and Valerie Walkerdine, in a study of four nursery classes in outer London, found not only that sex differences in the type of spontaneous play was not statistically significant, but that, contrary to the teacher's expectation, girls will take up types of play normally ascribed to boys if they are not discouraged from doing so.[25] Serbin noticed that little girls tend to stay nearer the teacher, thereby receiving more verbal stimulation, while more boys spend more time in independent play with blocks and trucks and in problem-solving activities with peers. Both Serbin and Walden and Walkerdine concluded that the problem lies in teachers allowing children to perpetuate already learnt sex-typing, reinforcing stereotyping in many subtle ways of which they are unaware, and failing to encourage alternatives to sex stereotyped activities. Hence they argue for more interventionist strategies to free children from the rigidity of traditional behaviour patterns in early childhood schooling.

Gender is overtly used for many internal organizational and

administrative purposes within primary schools and classrooms, as for listing on the register, for lining children up, for competition in class tests and quizzes as well as for some mixed games. Even though there is little sex difference in strength and weight at this age, girls tending to be taller and more physically mature, teachers persistently ask boys to do the strength-related tasks and girls the errands and courtesy and tidiness tasks. These procedures emphasize gender as a normative classification and reinforce ascribed social behaviour. Moreover, the most authoritative positions among teaching and non-teaching staff are usually held by men, thereby providing valuation models within the micro community which are negative for a girl's self-image. That the vast majority of teachers and ancillary workers are women provides a social context that may make it easier for girls to conform as good, hardworking, cooperative pupils while provoking boys' propensity for independence and defiance.

Teachers have long recognized these and other differential characteristics, just as they have consistently rated girls as better at reading and writing, boys at mathematics and mechanical ability. Insofar as these perceptions inform teachers' expectations, they are likely to contribute to self-fulfilling prophecies. Ironically, this seems to have been so over time in teachers' reactions to boys' expected disruptive behaviour: Douglas noticed that they criticized boys twice as much as girls for indiscipline and, twenty years later, Judith Whyte[26] and Katherine Clarricoates[27] allege that they discriminate against boys by reprimanding and punishing them more severely for similar misdemeanours, thereby both rewarding naughty, attention-seeking behaviour by boys and alienating them through unfairness. Indiscipline as male stereotypical is thus continually reinforced in the minds of teachers and pupils.

Other patterns of differential teacher-pupil interaction seem less consistent. This may reflect bias by some observers or the variety of observational schedules used rather than real variations. Reviewing the literature in 1981 Alison Kelly claimed that 'most researches seem to concur in finding that boys get more attention from teachers in primary schools', but noted that the ORACLE studies 'are an exception here'.[28] These found that 'the teacher's attention was generally equally divided between the two sexes, though there was a slight (but statistically non significant) tendency for boys to receive more attention than girls individually, in a small group and in whole class teaching. Low achievers also got slightly more attention.[29] The greater attention that other studies find teachers paying to boys often relates to controlling disruption and helping underachievers. Douglas found teachers assessing far more girls and far fewer boys as deserving grammar school places than were allocated them under 11+ procedures even when more girls than boys were successful.[30] Recent feminist researchers, on the other hand, persistently claim that teachers not only overestimate boys' and underestimate girls' abilities, but also pay boys more attention with both praise and blame and compliment girls on their appearance, boys on their work. They suggest, too, that teachers disparage girls' intellectual achievements, describing them as 'only good at computation' but lacking real understanding of concepts, whereas boys' poor work is attributed to carelessness or laziness masking their real potential.[31] Perhaps teachers are now more tolerant of carelessness and laziness, having come to accept it from boys; or perhaps they have become so influenced by Piaget's mathematical model of thinking that they now assume mathematical performance indicates a child's level of overall cognitive development, as Walden and Walkerdine suggest. Conceivably, many observers do not notice sexism[32] whereas feminists selectively perceive teachers' responses as negative for girls.

The inconsistency of findings on interaction points to a need for more sophisticated analyses that take account of teacher types and teaching styles. Unfortunately, the ORACLE analysis of teaching styles and pupil behaviour did not pursue this to distinguish gender for pupil responses. However, the NFER investigation into the effects of streaming nine and ten year olds found that the strictest 'obsessional' teachers, who strongly disapproved of 'bad manners', rated more boys as difficult and had more boy isolates in their classes; and that the ablest girls experienced the highest anxiety levels when taught by pro-streaming teachers.[33] Joan Barker Lunn's full report showed that teachers allocated an unwarranted number of lower working class boys to low streams and of middle class girls to top streams; and the curious phenomenon that boys of below average ability related best with anti-streaming teachers in nonstreamed classes, while more of them had 'a good academic self-image' in streamed schools.[34] Douglas' finding that a school's academic record had least influence on lower working class boys' generally poor achievement is also relevant. Social class is a factor that has been ignored by feminists investigating gender.

In today's primary classrooms the usual practice of grouping children is intended to serve a socialization as well as a work function. In the ORACLE study most groups of three or more are, indeed, mixed sex, though nearly a third may be single sex. Children spend most of their time working on the task in hand, but about a fifth on interacting with each other. Most of this is between several of the same sex, whatever the grouping; and same sex pairs interact together about twice as much as mixed sex pairs, where the individuals manage to interact more with another of the same sex sitting elsewhere. 'The "typical" pupil interacts very largely only with pupils of the same sex' during lessons in junior schools.[35] The kinds of successful intervention strategies advocated by Serbin for nursery and infant teachers would clearly be far more difficult and complex. Children learn and sustain social roles at junior school, a few acquiring individual roles as star, wit, clown, know-all; but sex-role is crucial among peers, and deviance spurned. Blyth's sociometric studies showed the sexes 'beginning to concentrate their choices within their own ranks' so that between eight and nine 'this tendency has already become marked, and thereafter it continues to intensify'. Parallel single sex social groupings form, with leadership and popularity structures more marked among boys while close-knit pairs and trios are more marked among girls, social class affinity operating for both; and there was some evidence that home neighbourhood peer grouping was more enduring for girls.[36] Gender identity is a powerful force in classroom dynamics.

Junior school teachers, trained in the precepts of the developmental, child-centred tradition since the mid 1920s[37], have sought to harness this force to motivate children through their perceived inherent interests, apparently applying sound pedagogic principles. In this they were encouraged by the Hadow and Plowden reports and by HMI. Tackling classroom management problems posed by potentially disruptive boys, who are stereotypically less inclined to conform to the work ethos of school, they either gear their lesson content to boys' interests or offer sex stereotyped choices for group and individual work. 'I do tend to try and make the topics as interesting as possible for the boys so that they won't lose their concentration', Katherine Clarricoates quotes a teacher as saying in this context.[38] Educational publishers responded to the postwar vogue for topic and project work by producing series of relatively cheap, slim and profusely illustrated booklets on such themes as Transport, Weapons, Homes and Clothes. Only in this decade did a new message begin to be received that such practices constitute sex role stereotyping and, as such, conflict with the principle of equal opportunities. This has been the message of the Schools Council projects mentioned earlier.

Sex bias in primary reading schemes had already begun to attract attention, following on the criticism made of them for their white middle class image. Work on sexism in children's books began in Scandinavia in the 1960s but was not taken up in Britain until the next decade. In 1972 the Northern Women's Education Study Group examined 200 books in nine reading schemes and found that all contained more male than female characters, with central figures presenting rigidly stereotyped sex roles for adults and children.[39] Probably the best known study is Glenys Lobban's analysis of 225 stories in six reading schemes, two of which were newly published. She demonstrated that all 'rigidly divided the sphere of people's activity into two compartments, "masculine" and "feminine" with very few common characteristics', the former exceeding the latter and being more active, instrumental and related to the outside world whereas the latter 'revolved almost entirely around domestic roles'. She concluded: 'The world they depicted was not only sexist, it was more sexist than present reality'.[40] Seven years later, David Whiting replicated her analysis to compare the revised 1980 version of Ladybird's *Things We Do* with the original 1964 text and concluded: 'there is no evidence that the book ... has moved any faster ahead in relation to the society it serves than when Lobban asserted the reading schemes were more sexist than reality'.[41] When Lobban reviewed investigations of primary readers to date in 1978 they were all reporting similar findings, as did Valerie Hannon's summary of research for the Equal Opportunities Commission in 1980.[42] Indeed, there is evidence that sex bias in children's books of all kinds was greater in the 1960s and 1970s than in the 1940s, when it declined in comparison with prewar, and is persisting in the 1980s.[43] A recent study of the *Breakthrough to Literacy* scheme found eighteen girls but thirty-four boys as central characters, both usually stereotyped for activities, and only two instances of a working mother.[44] The Leeds Literature Collective's examination of the representation of girls in primary science books found most pictures and pronouns were male[45], and Byrne found boys depicted as actively engaged but girls looking on.[46]

Some publishers and authors have tried to respond, and there is guidance available to help teachers and librarians. A parents' group recently published a list of nonsexist children's books[47] and a Schools Council project compiled a checklist of questions and advice.[48] However, if the Electricity Council's current publications are typical, it seems that the message has been only partly understood: these show less sex role stereotyping of domestic activities, but all adult occupations are stereotyped and the drawings demonstrating how to do simple experiments with batteries, wires and bulbs all show male hands with straight-cut nails.

The significance of the extensive stereotyping and bias in children's books is that children are introduced to the written word through primary reading schemes and that these and other textbooks are encountered in the authoritative context of classrooms. Primary readers and stories invite children to identify with the central characters as models and, except in fantasy tales, purport to depict a realistic adult world. In fact they encourage and reinforce stereotyped self-concepts for both girls and boys while offering the former far fewer models, and very few achievement models. Experiments have been conducted that show how children who had listened to a story about an achieving girl were more inclined to see a girl as an achiever in another story where she was less central; and how seven and eight year olds who had heard stories featuring working mothers increased their belief that boys and girls could succeed at a wide range of activities.[49] As the Bullock Report stated: 'It is never too soon to start thinking about the ways in which attitudes may be influenced by reading'.[50] Even sexist books can be used by teachers to promote discussion of stereotyping.

Despite the unexciting representation of females in so many children's books, girls continue to read avidly. It is possible that the increased sex bias from the 1960s, involving more active, adventurous roles for boys, was a deliberate attempt to attract boys to reading: if so, it has not proved successful. The latest APU survey finds that 'by the age of 11, boys have begun to develop more negative attitudes towards reading than girls, and that this negativism is correlated with poorer performance'.[51] More boys both do and do not prefer reading about their hobbies to reading stories, but girls decisively prefer stories.[52] As a group girls also write better and positively enjoy all kinds of writing, whereas boys find it difficult and tiresome but are more positive about writing as part of project work.[53] However, they perform equally well in oracy where 'no significant overall gender difference has so far emerged in the surveys, though there have been differences on one or two specific tasks'.[54] The long recognized sex differences in reading and writing ability may derive from girls' faster physiological maturity related to the cortical structures relevant to speech, which explains their earlier talking and so their forging ahead with language structures; this gives them an advantage over boys when reading and writing are first tackled. These relatively passive occupations then continue to attract girls as matching their sex role while boys are readily distracted towards more active pursuits.[55] The maturation explanation allied with girls' greater, voluntary exposure to the written word could account for girls' superiority in spelling and syntax.

Discrete areas of mathematics in which girls outshine boys at the age of eleven have recently been identified by the APU. These are in computation with whole numbers and decimals in money contexts and when 'context free' and in providing explanations or rules for number pattern sequences.[56] The former is an aspect of their superiority at computation that has been generally noticed before and has sometimes been attributed to their greater experience of handling money and change through shopping for their mothers; they are now shown to be less adept than boys at applying this skill to contexts perceived as male spheres of interest. Linguistic skills may be a factor in the other area. Boys' general superiority in mathematics has often been attributed to more developed spatial and perceptual-analytic ability, and this in turn to greater exploratory and manipulative experiences with masculine toys and tinkering activities with their fathers. This tends to be substantiated by Serbin's reports of two experimental studies in which American elementary school girls were found to benefit more than the boys from brief, ten to twenty minute training and practice on a visual-spatial task: this suggests that girls 'have a practice-deficit in visual-spatial problem-solving' which specific training can eliminate.[57] If this is true, there are implications for nursery and infant teaching strategies to go beyond intervention merely to counter sex stereotyping in play.

So far HMI has eschewed the contemporary debate on gender in primary school. As in the more remote past, it has continued to report differences in performance on tests for mathematics and reading and to comment on segregated differentiation for crafts and games. In 1978 it at last totally condemned these practices; but in an in-depth survey conducted in 542 primary schools between autumn 1975 and spring 1977 there is no indication of any probing across the rest of the curriculum into how this served the two sexes or how they fared by gender, though match and mismatch by three arbitrary ability levels was a prominent theme.[58] This was again a preoccupation in the 1982 survey of new teachers which also ignored gender. Whether the Inspectorate is oblivious or has deliberately distanced itself is not known.

The feminist movement, operating as a pressure group, has

raised consciousness and put sex role stereotyping on the educational agenda in the context of equalizing opportunity. That sex-typed
curricular options at secondary level have their origins in primary
school experiences is now widely recognized. In some respects
many primary schools have not kept pace with changes in social
attitudes and so are still preparing girls and boys for social roles that
are not those of present reality, still less those of the adult world
they will enter; but much of this is inadvertent on the part of
teachers who unconsciously reinforce sex stereotyping learned outside school. They need to be more critically aware of the messages
conveyed through their teaching materials and methods, casual remarks, expectations of individuals categorized by gender, and school
organization. As an agent of socialization the primary school has the
potential for widening all children's perceptions of social roles so
that both girls and boys become less constrained by traditions that
are no longer appropriate; and in its academic function to take steps
designed to eliminate sex differential achievement in specific areas.

Further research is required both on this and on interaction in
the classroom. It has not yet addressed 'the general ineffectiveness of
schooling in preparing males to cope with domestic tasks efficiently
or to assume the full responsibilities of parenthood'.[59] There has
been less consideration of how pressures to assume a tough, macho
image and repress gentle, nurturant qualities is as damaging to boys
and for society as those on girls to be passive and docile: both
distort the true developmental tradition of primary education.
According to Maccoby's hypothesis, these social demands 'play a
role in producing some of the sex differences ... in intellectual
performance'.[60] Further research is needed on this too. How intran-
sigent the strongly conformist peer pressures may be among junior
children themselves remains to be seen.

There is a subtle but important distinction to be made between
the psychologically necessary development of gender identity during
the nursery-infant years and socially learnt stereotyping of all kinds.
Alison Kelly has warned that cognitive theory indicates that
attempts to eliminate sex differentiation may cause anxiety and
confusion regarding gender identity in very young children.[61] Kohlberg's application of Piagetian theory to psychosexual development
suggests that:

> The child's basic sex-role identity is largely the result of a
> self-categorization as a male or female made early in de-
> velopment. While dependent on social labelling, this categor-

ization is basically a cognitive reality judgment. . . The stabi-
lization of judgments of sex-role constancy and of physical
constancy closely parallel one another in terms of individual
development as well as age group norms.[62]

Consequently, sex-role identity is not firmly established until a
child is six or seven years old, though being linked with cognitive
growth it may be secure younger for some children. However, boys
and girls also acquire self-identity as 'children', a category which
subsumes gender as does 'grown ups'. Children are now living in a
social world where many adult sex-roles are interchangeable in
domestic and work contexts: school learning should now reflect this
reality. Nursery and infant teachers need to distinguish between
sex-identity and sex-role stereotyping in encouraging young children to engage in cross-sex and mixed activities so as to maximize
equal and all-round development from an early age: they will thereby be truly interpreting the developmental tradition of early childhood education for today.

   Our schools are always being urged to take on new challenges
— to tap the pool of ability, to compensate for social or environmental disadvantage, to inculcate flexibility for adapting to future
change — while continuing to teach the essential instrumental skills
of literacy and numeracy to all. They rarely lack criticism. Now
feminists have joined with social reproductionists in arguing that
schooling perpetuates social and economic inequality. In meeting
the new challenge to incorporate gender within their objective of
equality in educational opportunity, primary schools can simultaneously accept the other challenges to the benefit of all pupils.
Perceptive recognition of individual differences as a precept of child-
centred education implies rejection of categorization by class, race
or gender. Used as a tool for research and monitoring such classification can serve a useful function by revealing prejudicial practices and processes which should change. Above all, teachers and
ancillary workers need to be critically aware of what they do and
say when dealing with children throughout the nursery, infant and
junior phases of primary education so as to guard against inadvertent stereotyping restricting balanced development for both girls and
boys: at this stage it is a mainstream educational issue, not a feminist
preserve.

Notes

1. SEABORNE, M. (1971), *The English School: Its Architecture and Organization 1371–1870*, London, Routledge and Kegan Paul.
2. GORDON, P. and LAWTON, D. (1978), *Curriculum Change in the Nineteenth and Twentieth Centuries*, London, Hodder and Stoughton.
3. LOWNDES, G.A.N. (1969), *The Silent Social Revolution*, 2nd ed., London, Oxford University Press.
4. CONSULTATIVE COMMITTEE TO THE BOARD OF EDUCATION (1923), *Differentiation of the Curriculum for Boys and Girls respectively in Secondary Schools*, London, HMSO.
5. CONSULTATIVE COMMITTEE TO THE BOARD OF EDUCATION (1931), *The Primary School*, London, HMSO.
6. CONSULTATIVE COMMITTEE TO THE BOARD OF EDUCATION (1933), *Infant and Nursery Schools*, London, HMSO.
7. BOARD OF EDUCATION (1959), *Primary Education: Suggestions for the consideration of teachers and others concerned with the work of Primary Schools*, London, HMSO.
8. MACLURE, J.S. (1965), *Educational Documents: England and Wales 1816–1963*, London, Chapman and Hall.
9. DOUGLAS, J.W.B. (1964), *The Home and The School*, London, MacGibbon and Kee.
10. BLYTH, W.A.C. (1965), *English Primary Education, Vol. I: The Schools*, London, Routledge and Kegan Paul.
11. BLYTH, W.A.C. (1965), *English Primary Education, Vol. II: Background*, London, Routledge and Kegan Paul.
12. CENTRAL ADVISORY COUNCIL FOR EDUCATION (1967), *Children and their Primary Schools, Vol. 2: Research and Surveys*, Appendix 10, London, HMSO.
13. CENTRAL ADVISORY COUNCIL FOR EDUCATION (1967), *Children and their Primary Schools, Vol. 1.*, London, HMSO.
14. PRINGLE, M.K. (1974), *The Needs of Children*, London, Hutchinson.
15. NEWSON, J. and E. (1978), in CHETWYND, J. and HARTNETT, O. (Eds.) *The Sex-Role System: Psychological and Sociological Perspectives*, London, Routledge and Kegan Paul.
16. MACCOBY, E.E. and JACKLIN, C.N. (1974), cited in KELLY, A. (1981) *The Missing Half*, Manchester, Manchester University Press.
17. FRAZIER, N. and SADKER, M. (1973), *Sexism in School and Society*, New York, Harper and Row.
18. KELLY, A. (1981), *The Missing Half*, Manchester, Manchester University Press.
19. *Education in Schools: A Consultative Document* (1977), London, HMSO.
20. NASH, R. (1973), *Classrooms Observed*, London, Routledge and Kegan Paul.
21. MILLMAN, V. and WEINER, G. edited four *Newsletters: Reducing Sex Differentiation in School* and a Final Report (1985), *Sex Differentiation in Schooling: Is there really a problem?* London, Longman; EDDOWES, M. (1983), *Humble Pi: The Mathematics Education of Girls*; HARDING,

J. (1983), *Switched Off: The Science Education of Girls*; STONES, R. (1983), *'Pour out the Cocoa, Janet': Sexism in Children's Books*; WHYTE, J. (1983), *Beyond the Wendy House: Sex Role Stereotyping in Primary Schools*, London, Longman for Schools Council.

22. SPENDER, D. and SARAH, E. (1980), *Learning to Lose: Sexism and Education*, London, The Women's Press.
23. DES (1975), *Curricular Differences for Boys and Girls*, Education Survey 21, London, HMSO.
24. SERBIN, L.A. (1978), 'Teachers, peers and play preferences: An environmental approach to sex typing in the preschool', reprinted in DELAMONT, S. (Ed.) (1984), *Readings on Interaction in the Classroom*, London, Methuen, and 'The Hidden Curriculum: Academic consequences of teacher expectations', in MARLAND, M. (Ed.) (1983) *Sex Differentiation and Schooling*, London, Heinemann.
25. WALDEN, R. and WALKERDINE, V. (1982), *Girls and Mathematics: The Early Years*, Bedford Way Papers 8, University of London Institute of Education.
26. WHYTE, J. (1983), 'How girls learn to be losers', in *Primary Education Review* 17, pp. 5–7, London, National Union of Teachers.
27. CLARRICOATES, K. (1983), 'Some aspects of the "hidden" curriculum and interaction in the classroom', in *Primary Education Review* 17, pp. 10–11, London, National Union of Teachers.
28. KELLY, A. (1981), UK National Report for the Council of Europe Educational Workshop on Sex Stereotyping in Schools: *Research on Sex Differences in Schools in the UK*, unpublished typescript.
29. GALTON, M. and SIMON, B. (1980), *Progress and Performance in the Primary Classroom*, London, Routledge and Kegan Paul.
30. DOUGLAS, J.W.B. (1964), *ibid.*
31. WHYTE, J. (1983), and CLARRICOATES, K. (1983) in *Primary Education Review op. cit.*
32. DELAMONT, S. (1980), *Sex Roles and the School*, London, Methuen.
33. CENTRAL ADVISORY COUNCIL FOR EDUCATION (1967), *Children and their Primary Schools, Vol. 2: Research and Surveys, Appendix 11*, London, HMSO.
34. BARKER LUNN, J.C. (1970), *Streaming in the Primary School*, London, National Foundation for Educational Research in England and Wales.
35. GALTON, M., SIMON, B. and CROLL, P. (1980), *Inside the Primary Classroom*, London, Routledge and Kegan Paul.
36. BLYTH, W.A.C. (1965), Vol. I., *ibid.*
37. SELLECK, R.J. (1972), *English Primary Education and the Progressives, 1914–1939*, London, Routledge and Regan Paul.
38. CLARRICOATES, K. (1983), *op. cit.*
39. LOBBAN, G. (1978), 'The influence of the school on sex-role stereotyping' in CHETWYND, J. and HARTNETT, O. (Eds.) *The Sex-Role System*, London, Routledge and Kegan Paul.
40. LOBBAN, G. (1974), 'Presentation of sex-roles in British reading schemes' in *FORUM for the Discussion of New Trends in Education*, 16, 2, pp. 57–60.
41. WHITING, D. (1981), 'Sex role stereotyping and Ladybird books', in

FORUM for the Discussion of New Trends in Education, 23, 3, pp. 84–5.

42. HANNAN, V. (1980), *Ending Sex-Stereotyping in Schools*, London, Equal Opportunities Commission.
43. STONES, R. (1983), *ibid.*
44. MILLMAN, V. and WEINER, G. (1985), *ibid.*
45. KELLY, E. (1981), 'Socialization in patriarchal society', in KELLY, A. (Ed.) *op. cit.*
46. MILLMAN, V. and WEINER, G. (1985), *ibid.*
47. BYRNE, E.M. (1978), *Women and Education*, London, Tavistock Publications.
48. STONES, R. (1983), *ibid.*
49. McARTHUR, L.Z. and EISEN, S.V. (1976), and JENKINS, S. (1977), cited in STONES, R. *op. cit.*
50. BULLOCK A. (1975), *A Language for Life*, London, HMSO.
51. THORNTON, G. (1986), *APU Language Testing 1979–1983: An Independent Appraisal of the Findings*, London, HMSO.
52. GORMAN, T. (1986), *The Framework for the Assessment of Language*, Windsor, NFER-Nelson.
53. WHITE. J. (1986), *The Assessment of Writing: Pupils Aged 11 and 15*, Windsor, NFER-Nelson.
54. MACLURE, M. and HARGREAVES, M. (1986), *Speaking and Listening: Assessment at Age 11*, Windsor, NFER-Nelson.
55. This is an extension of the proposition by MACCOBY, E.E. (1966), 'Sex differences in intellectual functioning' reprinted in LEE, P.C. and STEWART, R.S. (Eds.) (1976) *Sex Differences: Cultural and Developmental Dimensions* New York, Urizen Books. It tends to be supported by DAVIE, R., BUTLER, N. and GOLDSTEIN, H. (1972), *From Birth to Seven*, London, Longman.
56. MASON, K. (1986) 'Areas of mathematics in which girls are ahead', in *APU Newsletter*, 8, pp. 1–2.
57. SERBIN, L.A. (1983), *op. cit.*
58. DES (1978), *Primary Education in England: A Survey by HM Inspectors of Schools* London, HMSO.
59. HANNAN, V. (1980), *ibid.*
60. MACCOBY, E.E. (1966), *op. cit.*
61. KELLY, A. (1981), *ibid.*
62. KOHLBERG, A. and ZIGLER, E. (1967), 'Physiological development, cognitive development, and socialization antecedents of children's sex-role attitudes' reprinted in LEE, P.C. and STEWART, R.S. (Eds.) *op. cit.*

Notes on Contributors

Michael Arkinstall is headteacher of an urban primary school. He has long and varied experience as a primary school teacher, and has published on various aspects of education and local history.

Christine Brown is a Principal Lecturer in Education in the Department of Educational Studies, the Faculty of Arts, Design and Education at Wolverhampton Polytechnic. She is currently the Course Leader for the MEd Degree Course within that institution.

Joan Browne, CBE MA, was formerly Principal of Coventry College of Education, and Honorary Professor in Education, University of Warwick. She is the author of *Teacher of Teachers — A History of the ATCDE*, (1979), and 'The Transformation of the Education of Teachers in the Nineteen-Sixties', in *Education in the Sixties*, (History of Education Society).

Peter Cunningham lectures at Westminster College, Oxford. He studied history of art and architecture, and recently spent a year teaching in an Oxfordshire primary school. His forthcoming book *Tradition and Innovation: Progressivism in Primary Education since 1944* will be published by Falmer Press in 1988.

Robert Dearden is Professor of Education at the University of Birmingham, Faculty of Education. Prior to that he was Lecturer and then Reader at the University of London Institute of Education. His publications include *The Philosophy of Primary Education* and *Problems in Primary Education*.

Donald Jones is a Lecturer in Education at the University of Leicester. His research interests were initially concerned with nineteenth-century education. He is currently completing a biographical study of Stuart Mason, Director of Education for Leicestershire, 1947–71.

Roy Lowe is a Senior Lecturer in Education at the University of Birmingham and taught previously in a variety of schools. He has published widely on aspects of English education and is currently editor of *History of Education.*

Frank Musgrove was formerly Professor of Education in the University of Manchester (now Emeritus). His books include: *Youth and the Social Order* (1964), *The Family, Education and Society* (1966), *School and the Social Order* (1979) and *Education and Anthropology* (1982).

Malcolm Seaborne taught in schools in Northamptonshire and worked on school planning for Nottinghamshire County Council before becoming a Senior Lecturer in Education at the University of Leicester. He is now Principal of Chester College of Higher Education. He has written a number of books on the history of education and on school architecture.

Nanette Whitbread is Joint-Editor of the educational journal *Forum* and was Principal Lecturer in teacher education at Leicester Polytechnic until the recent course closure. She is presently chairperson of the Standing Committee for the Education and Training of Teachers in the public sector. She is author of *The Evolution of the Nursery-Infant School.*

David Winkley has worked at the Universities of Cambridge and Birmingham, and has a Doctorate in Philosophy of the University of Oxford, and has written and lectured widely on education. His book on advisers and educational management, *Diplomats and Detectives* was published recently. He is Head of Grove School, Handsworth.

Jayne Woodhouse is Lecturer in History at La Sainte Union College of Higher Education, Southampton. Formerly, she was a primary school deputy head teacher, and taught for eleven years in rural and inner-city schools.

Index